PIONEER DAYS IN THE BLACK HILLS

Accurate History and Facts
Related by One of the Early Day Pioneers

by
JOHN S. McCLINTOCK

EDITED BY
EDWARD L. SENN

Foreword by
WAYNE R. KIME

UNIVERSITY OF OKLAHOMA PRESS

NORMAN

Library of Congress Cataloging-in-Publication Data
McClintock, John S., 1847-1942
  Pioneer days in the Black Hills : accurate history and facts related by
  one of the early day pioneers / by John S. McClintock ; edited by
  Edward L. Senn ; foreword by Wayne R. Kime.
    p. cm.
  Originally published: Deadwood, S.D. : J.S. McClintock, 1939.
  Includes bibliographical references.
  ISBN 0-8061-3191-8
  1. McClintock, John S., 1847–1942. 2. Pioneers—South Dakota—
  Deadwood Region—Biography. 3. Frontier and pioneer life—South
  Dakota—Deadwood Region. 4. Frontier and pioneer life—Black Hills
  (S.D.and Wyo.) 5. Deadwood Region (S.D.)—Biography. 6. Black Hills
  (S.D. and Wyo.)—Biography. 7. Deadwood Region (S.D.)—Social life
  and customs. 8. Black Hills (S.D. and Wyo.)—Social life and customs.
  I. Senn, Edward L. II. Title.

F659.D2 M37 2000
978.3´91—dc21
[B]
                                                         99-055842

The paper in this book meets the guidelines for permanence and durability of the Committee on Production Guidelines for Book Longevity of the Council on Library Resources, Inc. ∞

Oklahoma Paperbacks edition published by the University of Oklahoma Press, Norman, Publishing Division of the University. Manufactured in the U.S.A. First edition, 1939. First printing of the University of Oklahoma Press edition, 2000.

      2   3   4   5   6   7   8   9   10

DEDICATED TO

my fellow plainsmen and pioneers of the sixties and seventies, living or dead, who dared to leave their homes and enter upon a crusade in defiance of the protests of hostile savages and the mandates of the Federal Government, to brave the dangers, endure the privations and sufferings even unto death, in their determination to enter into and to open to civilization vast areas of rich and unexplored regions of the Great Northwest.

CONTENTS

CONTENTS

FOREWORD

IN August 1874 Brevet Major General George A. Custer captured national attention with the announcement that members of a reconnaissance expedition under his command had discovered gold "among the roots of the grass" in the Black Hills of Dakota Territory. Within weeks, scores of adventurers had reached frontier cities like Cheyenne, Sioux Falls, and Bismarck, prepared to search out for themselves the new gold bonanza. Reaching the Black Hills, however, posed severe challenges. Routes for travel to the little-known region had not yet been established, and would-be miners who attempted the trek across the country ran a grave risk of violence. By a treaty ratified in 1868, the Black Hills formed part of a reservation established for sole occupancy and use by the Sioux Indians. American citizens had no legal right to the mineral wealth of that country, and the Sioux naturally would contest any attempt to assert it. Moreover, the good faith of the United States government was at stake. Trespassers in Sioux territory who managed to avoid Indian attack faced arrest, confiscation of their goods, and even imprisonment by army commands sent out to enforce federal law. The golden fruits of the Black Hills were forbidden, and the effort to obtain them would be fraught with peril.

Such considerations, along with the added assurance of severe weather in the coming winter, kept all but the hardiest citizens away from the Black Hills for a time. Nevertheless, the potential for future conflict with the Indians was not lost on federal authorities. The Department of the Interior organized a scientific survey, under Walter P. Jenney of Columbia College, New York, to investigate the mineral resources of the Hills and help estimate the region's value in trade with the Sioux. Between May and October

1875 the scientific party, dwarfed in number by an eight-company army escort under Lieutenant Colonel Richard I. Dodge, Twenty-third Infantry, conducted its examination. Owing in part to the elaborate security measures he adopted, Colonel Dodge encountered no hostile Indians during the entire summer, but he soon came upon groups of miners who had established working claims. These men reported encouraging but not fabulous results. Dodge and Jenney both concluded that while placer mining might indeed be pursued with profit on the eastern slope of the Hills, the greater value of the area was as grazing country. Whatever the source of its allure to U.S. citizens, to the Sioux the Black Hills remained a sacred birthright that was not for sale. Acting in cooperation with Brigadier General George Crook, Colonel Dodge managed to induce most of the trespassing miners to depart the Hills temporarily, it being understood that they could make good their original claims once the region had been opened to settlement. But no date for future occupation by American citizens could be predicted yet with confidence. In fact, the United States and the Indian tribes of the northern plains evidently were verging toward armed conflict.

Early in 1876 the Great Sioux War broke out, a series of sometimes desperate engagements that occupied the available U.S. army troops through the nation's centennial year and well into 1877. During this period disaffected Indians continued to reside at agencies within easy reach of the Black Hills, but the primary sphere of military activity was further west. Because the army lacked sufficient manpower to continue enforcing the 1868 treaty, the provision forbidding trespass in Sioux country became in effect a dead letter. Citizens willing to brave the known dangers were free to enter the Hills, and miners, merchants, supply trains, and fortune-hunters of all descriptions began crossing the plains, usually in small groups for mutual protection. They established settlements first in the eastern part, and then in the more productive northern parts of the gold-bearing region. Discovery of rich placer yields and accessible underground veins in the latter section caused new towns like Deadwood and Central City to spring into existence virtually overnight. American enterprise had established a beachhead in the disputed northern wilderness.

John S. McClintock, the author of the present volume, arrived at Deadwood with a group of friends in April 1876. Like his companions, this twenty-eight-year-old native of Missouri had contracted gold fever several years before. Relying on a fund of mining experience and on his versatile intelligence, he at once entered upon a series of employments, associations, and speculations that won him moderate prosperity in the years that followed. Unlike most of his chronically footloose fellow adventurers, McClintock made Deadwood his permanent home, residing there until his death in 1942. Thus he participated in the splendidly chaotic first years and helped rebuild the town after a fire in 1879 had consumed some of its claims to reputation as a Gomorrah of the mountains. He took part in the adoption of bylaws, election of city officers, and establishment of public services that conferred on Deadwood a degree of civic respectability. He observed how the original mining operations by individuals and small corporations were swept aside by great underground mines like the Homestake and the De Smet.

Marrying in 1880, McClintock set aside mining and took up other occupations, all of which kept him in regular contact with residents of Deadwood and the communities nearby. He purchased a livery stable, and as a side business he began carrying passengers in a hack between Deadwood and Central City, subsequently extending the route as far as Spearfish. He invested in transit companies that ferried supplies from the still distant railheads. During the 1890s he owned and operated the Deadwood Opera House, continuing a tradition of entertainment by traveling performers that dated back to the town's first months of existence. Eventually he witnessed the emergence of the Black Hills as a tourist attraction, justly renowned for its scenic beauty and colorful history. As years passed he grew interested in preserving an accurate record of the region's rich heritage. As an alert spectator and also a participant, he was in an ideal position to record the history of the Black Hills. *Pioneer Days in the Black Hills,* issued in 1939, was the fruit both of his own recollections and of inquiries he and others had pursued over many years.

Pioneer Days is not a comprehensive account but rather a gathering of glimpses that together comprise a varied sketch of the place and time its author had come to know so well. It describes mining methods and devices in use during the 1870s and afterward—for example, sluice boxes constructed in modular form to permit easy dismantling and reassembly at a new claim. It offers information about early modes of wagon transportation, some of it painful to read, such as the brutal means adopted by "bullwhackers" to extract the whole strength from their oxen teams. It conveys admirably the "feel" of early mining towns, their inhabitants subject to no code of laws yet on the whole congenial and good natured, at least when sober. The daily existence of early Deadwood residents seems to have combined at random the comic, the deadly, and the surreal. As McClintock observes, "a state of expectancy and wondering what would happen next" was normal. His book sets forth real-life exploits by a gallery of characters, with names like "Black Dan," "Madame Mustache," "Buckskin Johnny," and "Big Thumb Jake," who were to become the stuff of frontier legend.

In fact, by the time he began writing the series of newspaper articles that form the core of *Pioneer Days*, several persons whom he had known or encountered in the 1870s had already become legendary. Among these were Martha Canary (better known as "Calamity Jane"), Wild Bill Hickok, and the protean Deadwood Dick. In his accounts of the celebrated figures, McClintock is at pains to distinguish "fanciful fiction" from the personalities and events he had known. Yet by describing the actual circumstances of their sojourns around Deadwood he dispels none of their strange glamour. The book manifests his belief that early scenes in the Black Hills were worthy of permanent record, because they provide in part the historical context for later legends.

Recalling the period when the Hills were wrested from the Sioux, in particular passages McClintock regards events from either of two opposed viewpoints. On one hand, he portrays the westward emigration of American citizens in a positive light, as an errand into the wilderness by representatives of a higher civilization destined to supplant Indian savagery. From this perspective, the miners and those who accompanied them were opening up a remote land to future use by a citizenry entitled to its occupation by the inexorable laws of progress. On the other hand, he sometimes represents the American invaders as rapacious, defiant of law, and no less savage than the Indians they feared. The motif of severed Indian heads dragged into town and placed on display as curiosities, "pickled," or offered for sale as souvenirs marks the expression of this critical attitude. On balance, the tone of national and civic pride prevails. At some points McClintock even indulges in boosterism on behalf of

the Black Hills, the "Switzerland of America." His book concludes
with a standard feature of self-congratulatory local histories, a
series of capsule biographies identifying early civic leaders and
famous sons and daughters of various communities. Contributed by
Edward L. Senn, editor of the Deadwood *Telegram,* this final chapter is one of several by authors other than McClintock himself, making the work in an almost literal sense a community history.

Without gainsaying the greed, treachery, and indifference to
native rights that actuated some early settlers, *Pioneer Days in the
Black Hills* conveys a measure of the optimism, vitality, and—to use
an expressive contemporary term, the "go-aheadativeness" of the
period it portrays. Flavorful and full of variety, the work reprinted
here should have lasting appeal. To specialists in the early history of
Western mining towns its value as a first-person reminiscence is
self-evident. To readers with more general interests it offers a liberal sprinkling of unanticipated delights, passages that linger in the
memory. One of my favorites is the laconic account of a scene following an altercation between "Tricksie," a prostitute, and a man
who had been beating her. The author happened along the street
just after the enraged Tricksie had leveled a pistol at her antagonist
and shot him behind the eyes. "A doctor came and ran a probe
through his head," he recalls. "However, there were no brains, at
least in that section of his skull." Humbling though this emergency
examination must have been to the gunshot victim, it seems to have
led to a successful course of treatment, for McClintock concludes
his account by observing next that "I met the same man on the
street" a few weeks afterward. Little wonder that in later years he
was moved to record these moments and others equally bizarre "for
posterity."

WAYNE R. KIME
June 1999

EDITOR'S PREFACE

JOHN S. McCLINTOCK was born in Lawrence County, in the southwestern part of Missouri, on January 15, 1847, of Scotch and English ancestry. His father had migrated to that section from Tennessee in 1842, and had obtained government land. At the outbreak of the Civil War the family was prosperous with four hundred acres of fine land. Most of their possessions were swept away early in the war by the contending military forces, making it necessary to move to St. Francis County, Mo., when John was sixteen years old. Here he resided with the family until 1869.

He then went to western Montana. He prospected and mined in German Gulch, Deer Lodge, Helena, Blackfoot, Cave Gulch and El Dorado Bar. While in Montana, in 1872, he planned to go with a party of "sooners" to the Black Hills, lured by the rumors of gold. It was then Indian reservation and parties invading would have to contend both with the Indians and the government. The project was abandoned and he returned to Missouri in 1872.

Early in 1876 he came to the Black Hills and engaged in placer mining and various business enterprises. He purchased and operated the Deadwood-Central City toll road and established a livery and express business. He later became owner of extensive real estate holdings, including surface title to the site of the present Franklin Hotel in Deadwood. For more than thirty years he operated a stage line between Deadwood and Spearfish.

Until past the age of ninety he was able to be about the city. At the time of this writing, though confined to his home by physical infirmities, his mind is still vigorous and active.

This writer became acquainted with him on coming to Deadwood in 1909 to take possession of the *Deadwood Daily Telegram.* Ascertaining that he had a wonderful memory and vivid recollections of early-day occurrences, he was induced to prepare a number of historical articles for publication in the *Telegram*. From this experience, with encouragement and assistance, came the aspiration to leave to posterity in permanent form his knowledge of early-day history of the Black Hills. This volume is the fruition of his efforts.

In writing this record of early-day conditions and events in the Black Hills, Mr. McClintock has confined his stories largely to matters of which he has personal knowledge, or information direct from reliable persons who had such knowledge. Doubtless there were many other momentous and tragic events, of which he has made only casual mention, if any, because of lack of personal knowledge or dependable information. This volume does not purport to be a complete history of important occurrences in early days in the Black Hills; it does purport to be accurate in all matters presented.

Mr. McClintock's reputation for veracity is unimpeachable. Because of this, and his remarkable memory, the writer has reached the conclusion that his stories are accurate, except possibly in some minor details; and that in case of conflict with other writers, his recollections are most likely to be correct. The *Deadwood Daily Pioneer Times*, on January 16, 1937, in a biographical sketch of Mr. McClintock, taking note of his ninetieth birthday, said in part:

"Possessing a remarkably clear and accurate memory, Mr. McClintock has written an account of the history of Deadwood and the Black Hills. He is regarded as an authentic historian and his word is accepted as final on many controversial points of Deadwood history."

The *Black Hills Weekly*, published in Deadwood, in an article commenting on his ninety-first birthday, said:

"He came to the Black Hills in 1876 and has recorded his experiences in manuscript form which he hopes to have published ere long. An authentic historian, his records have proved more than one point in Black Hills history."

Mr. McClintock's wife and two daughters are yet living. His only son was killed in an auto accident in 1921.

Deadwood, S. D., May, 1939.

AUTHOR'S PREFACE

In presenting this volume for consideration it is hoped that it will be accepted as a contribution of merit in the annals of the Black Hills.

All of the occurrences herein related have been told as correctly as it was possible for the author to do when writing chiefly from memory. They came to the knowledge of the writer under such conditions as to indelibly fix them upon his mind. It is a privilege and a duty to record these recollections ere the writer is called hence.

The writer was well along in his eighties when he undertook the task of putting this historical material into book form. However, much of it was in manuscript form earlier, having been prepared for newspaper publication and other purposes.

With little encouragement or assistance, and limited resources, the work has been slow. However, it now appears to be assured that publication will be made in the near future.

The author desires to make grateful acknowledgment of the assistance he received in preparing this volume for publication from Mr. E. L. Senn and Mr. D. M. McGahey, curator of the Adams Memorial Museum in Deadwood. Without such assistance, publication would not have been possible.

JOHN S. McCLINTOCK.

I

INTRODUCTORY

IN presenting personal recollections as well as general knowledge of early days in this narrative, I shall, so far as is practicable, refrain from drifting into my own life history, and from injecting my own personality too freely into the story, though I have, during more than threescore years in the western mountains, shared in many of the dangers, hardships, troubles, and disappointments incident to life in the western wilds. While my life has not been wholly devoid of dangers and thrills, I shall endeavor to find other and more appropriate material than personal exploits and self-laudatory "bunk" such as too frequently finds its way into print. While it is regrettable that varying versions of many events which transpired in the Black Hills during its pioneer days have already passed into history, it should not be expected that, after the lapse of so many years, all accounts written from memory should harmonize in all particulars. Each writer should transmit his version of those events as they were impressed upon his individual memory. This rule I will adhere to in whatever I have to say or write, regardless of what others may have said or written, although they may have been equally honest in their statements as I have been in mine.

To give the following stories of the Black Hills a proper staging, I will revert to the time when I first became interested in their history. This was back in the later sixties while traveling west from Omaha, and during a conversation with an elderly gentleman who claimed to be a westerner. He pointed to a dark streak far to the north of us which I believed to be a cloud on the horizon.

"That dark streak that you now see," said he, "is not a cloud as it appears to be. It is the Black Hills of Dakota and is a part of an Indian Reservation. It belongs to the Indians. White men are not permitted to explore it. But there are legends to the effect that small parties of white men have long ago attempted to do so, and were never heard of again. It is generally believed that these mountains, like the Rockies, are rich in gold and other precious metals."

This choice bit of information impressed and interested me deeply, inasmuch as I was then on my way to the Rockies in quest of gold. His story had such weight that it resulted in a resolution to hold myself in readiness to be among the first white men to explore the dark and mysterious region should an opportunity to do so ever present itself, although I had no thought at the time that such an opportunity was so near at hand as it proved to be.

Nothing further concerning the Black Hills was heard until the winter of '71 and '72, at which time it was freely discussed with such enthusiasm among the miners throughout Montana territory that it left no doubt in the minds of many of them that the Black Hills country was wondrously rich in gold and other precious metals.

None of these enthusiasts had any knowledge whatever of the resources of the Black Hills. However, the agitation resulted in a determination of many of them to prepare themselves for a rush for the Hills, should one be inaugurated. The *Helena Gazette* and other Montana newspapers contained favorable comments concerning the possible resources of the Black Hills. In one instance an article was copied from a Sioux City paper, wherein it was stated that a small party of Nebraskans were making preparations to go from Cheyenne, Wyoming, to the Black Hills. However, nothing further was heard of that enterprise. From facts brought to light in recent years, I am inclined to believe that the late Captain Thomas H. Russell, whose party (the Gordon) was the first to reach the Hills, two years later, was the chief factor in that movement.

This writer was one of the most anxious of the Montana enthusiasts to take the risk in entering the Black Hills in 1872. The Indian situation was not fully comprehended, and was but lightly considered at the time. It is not known just how many small parties prepared to take the initiative, and would have done so had not wiser counsel prevailed. There was one party of whom three did finally reach the Hills at later dates. These were William Smith, George Bosworth, and myself. I went East in the winter of '72-'73 and after a futile attempt to do so in '75 finally reached the Black Hills in the spring of 1876.

General Custer's expedition through Dakota in 1874 and the reported discoveries of gold made in the Black Hills by members of that expedition, stirred the people throughout the country to a high pitch of excitement. It caused many in the nearby states and Indian Agencies to make a start for the newly discovered gold region, and many thousands of others to make hasty preparation to leave their all behind and take immediate flight to that wonderland which was supposed to be bulging with wealth and opportunities.

This hasty movement on the part of such would-be sooners resulted in promulgation by the Secretary of War at Washington of a drastic restraining order forbidding any and all persons from going upon or in any manner trespassing upon the domains of the Great Sioux Indian Reservation of which, at that time, the Black Hills were a portion. While this most decidedly unpopular order was generally, though reluctantly, obeyed by a very great majority of those anxious would-be sooners, it was ignored by many others who were hurriedly striking the trails for the Black Hills region. One group of such impatient intruders known as the "Gordon-Russell Party" consisting of twenty-six men, one woman, and one boy came through from Sioux City without molestation late in the fall of '74. They arrived near Custer on December 23, 1874. This party constructed a stockade on French Creek near the site of the present city of Custer.

After the failure of two attempts by the military to locate and arrest this party, they were finally located, promptly arrested and escorted from the reservation by a detachment of soldiers under the command of Captain Mix.

In the month of June, 1875, Professors Jenney and Newton were sent to the Black Hills under military escort by the Federal Government for the purpose of making a thorough scientific investigation into their mineral resources. These mining engineers established a camp and a stockade in the southern part of the Black Hills and spent several months in prospecting in various sections of the region. Their report on the mineral resources as submitted to the

Federal Government, and later given out to the world, was not only favorable, but was simply astounding. Whether or not Professor Jenney made the statement, it was broadcasted throughout the country that he had given it out as his opinion that a certain gravel bar, which was afterwards known as "Jenney's Bar" on Rapid Creek, contained a sufficient amount of placer gold to liquidate the national debt, which at that time was something near two billions of dollars.

At the same time that these discoveries and scientific reports were being made under governmental authority and protection, the principal newspapers throughout the country were broadcasting the ironclad restraining order and advising the people to keep cool and to keep away from the Black Hills. They were also at the same time trumpeting to the world news of the wonderful and unparalleled gold discoveries that were being made in the same forbidden territory, thereby arousing and keeping the people worked up to a high state of excitement. The situation in 1875 became so tense that, notwithstanding the treaty rights of the Indians, the governmental restraining order, and the strict surveillance kept up by military guards, many tried to reach the Hills. Even though many of the intruders were intercepted and placed under guard and several wagon trains of commodities were captured and destroyed, there were a number of small parties who eluded the military patrols and succeeded in entering and secreting themselves and their animals in the southern part of the Black Hills late in the fall of '75. They spent the winter in that section, prospecting, and locating mining claims and townsites.

A score or two of these sooners who had eluded the military watchers reached and entered the northern hills in September and October, 1875. They made discoveries of gold and located a number of claims in Whitewood and Deadwood gulches that year. All this time the news of great discoveries of gold in the Black Hills region was being heralded throughout the country and to the world. The people everywhere were worked up to a high pitch of excitement and impatiently waited the opening of the spring of '76.

That almost unparalleled gold mining excitement was unabated during the winter following the issuance of the restraining order, but increased in intensity. Notwithstanding that the restraining order had not been rescinded, for some reason it was not being

[4]

effectively enforced. Uncle Sam apparently adopted a hands-off policy, as it was generally known that small parties of intruders were drifting into the Hills without molestation. The reason for this forbearance was not known to the public until December, 1876, when President Grant in his last annual message to Congress made the statement that, had he attempted to enforce the order, it would have resulted in loss, by desertion, of the bulk of the troops sent to enforce it.

That view was unknown to the people. However, the inactivity of the War Department was so apparent that it gave rise to inferences which added new impetus to the gold fever. It could no longer be restrained, and precipitated one of the most stupendous stampedes of fortune seekers to a new Eldorado that has ever occurred.

All barriers had given away and the big rush to the forbidden territory was on. Before the first of April, '76, all trails leading in to the Black Hills were literally lined with people of all classes of frenzied humanity, coming apparently from all parts of the country and from all walks of life, including preachers of the gospel, educators, bankers, lawyers, farmers, laborers, and tradesmen of every description, apparently all inspired by the hope of being among the first to set foot in the new gold region.

Such was the tumultuous condition of affairs at the time I arrived here in the spring of 1876.

II

THE BLACK HILLS

THRUST upward out of the undulating prairie stand the Black Hills, a distinct group of mountains. North, south, east, and west are the plains, drinking thirstily of the crystal clear streams that find their sources in the shaded slopes of the guardian peaks.

Although in reality mountains, they have retained the name given them by the Indians as translated from the musical "Pa-ha-Sa-pa" of the Dakotahs. Blue spruce and Ponderosa pine in eternal struggle to conquer the rugged, rock-topped peaks give the mountains the color of midnight blue, so they remain the Black Hills, though undervalued by the name.

Up to fifty-three years ago they remained uninhabited except for the occasional visits of Indians. Then came the gold rush of '76, the final and greatest battle of the red men against further encroachment of the white men, and the Black Hills passed forever from the dominion of the Indians.

The mystery and magic with which the red men imbued these mountains still remains, and the gold fever abating has brought their scenic splendors again into prominence. Friendly, inviting and of rare charm, the Black Hills are becoming known each year in wider circles for their unique beauty.

The Black Hills are the highest mountains east of the Rockies on the North American continent and cover an area of about one hundred miles north and south and fifty miles wide. To the north is a great government irrigation project fed by the streams of the mountains spreading out into the vast range country beyond. To the south are the mineral springs with their health restoring waters centering in the town of Hot Springs. Between these outer points are the mining and lumbering interests, and scenic attractions, typical of their location—all happily interspersed with pretty mountain farms.

Nature gave these Hills foundations of gold and studded them with forests of pine and spruce, and vari-colored trees and shrubs; she reared them into the purest of dry, invigorating airs, laden with the fragrance of the pines and possessed of qualities both pleasant and beneficial; she warmed them with the brightest of sunshine; she gave to them a salubrious climate; she pierced their sides and brought forth murmuring brooks and streams, which she filled with trout of various species.

In fact, the Black Hills are a natural playground and sanitarium. It is the land of balm to the sleepless; of strength to feeble; of rest to the weary; and of joy to all. It is in reality the land of pure delight to the pleasure seekers, the health seekers, the home-seekers—for all humanity.

III

THE THOEN STONE—FIRST DISCOVERY OF GOLD

Among the many discoveries of material importance made in the Black Hills of South Dakota since their occupation by white people, two at least are of national historic value. One, owing to its seemingly miraculous discovery, naturally created doubt. This was dispelled from the minds of a great majority, if not all, of those who entertained it, when all the facts relating to the discovery and the reputation of those who made the find were fully known. This find was made by two reputable citizens of Spearfish, South Dakota, namely the Thoen brothers, Norwegian men, whose reputation for integrity and veracity was above question or suspicion.

Generally, discovery of the Thoen stone has been credited solely to Louis, the elder, who in reality did make the discovery while his younger brother, Ivan, stood nearby and saw him make it, being therefore a party to the find. The writer learned the story from each of them, with whom he was intimately acquainted. Both of them are now deceased. This is the story as related by them:

Louis obtained a small tract of land east of and adjacent to the city of Spearfish, fifteen miles from Deadwood, at the western base of Lookout Mountain. Seeing exposed a few hundred feet above the level ground, on the mountain side, a ledge of usable building stone, which skirted the entire western slope of the mountain, he conceived a plan of building a stone residence, which he subsequently put into effect.

In March, 1887, with his brother Ivan he went up one of the several ravines which jut down along the mountain side, for the purpose of quarrying stone. While thus engaged he found many loose stones which had become detached from the ledge and had slid down into the crevice at the bottom of the draw, and were partially covered by sand and vegetation.

[8]

While removing a large flat stone which lay upon a small one of about 12 inches square, and 2½ inches thick, Louis picked up the small stone. He noticed some scratches upon its smooth surface which he showed to his brother who was working close by. Together they examined the stone, and found distinct marks on both sides. They immediately returned to their home and washed the dirt from the stone. They found, plainly inscribed with some steel pointed instrument, presumably a pocket knife, the following tragic story, on one side:

"Came to these Hills in 1833, seven of us, De Lacompt—Ezra Kind —G. W. Wood—T. Brown—R. Kent—Wm. King—Indian Crow— all dead but me, Ezra Kind, killed by Indians beyond the high hill, got our gold June 1834."

On the reverse side was inscribed:

"Got all the gold we could carry, our ponies all got by the Indians I have lost my gun and nothing to eat, and Indians hunting me."

Here plainly inscribed upon that cold, mute tablet of stone was a pathetic story, a sorrowful farewell message to the world; a message brimming with pathos, one to touch the soul and awaken tender emotions in the heart of any mortal, save that of a savage; a message which was penned while its despairing author was laboring under the strain of his impending doom, while the darkening shadows of death were closing around him, after all hope of escape and life had been abandoned. Even with this heavy weight of woe pressing upon his tortured mind and body, he decided to attempt with what must have seemed fruitless endeavor, to acquaint coming generations with the horrible fate of himself and his associates.

Strange as it is, his last forlorn hope was realized in one decade after the advent of civilization in these Hills. Whether by accident or a decree of fate is immaterial in this recital. After reposing for more than a half a century in its cryptic abode at the bottom of a deep ravine, in an unexplored region, this momentous chapter of early Black Hills history was revealed to a civilized people; a chapter which tells of ambition, of hope, of adventure, of hardships, of weary months of strenuous toil and final success. Then all was changed to darkness and death struggles, the brandishing of tomahawks and scalping knives, ending with the savage extermination of the first party of adventurous argonauts known to have entered the Black Hills of South Dakota in search of gold.

Mr. Cashner, with many other citizens of Spearfish, became deeply interested in this mysterious discovery and sought to trace these unfortunate men back to their original starting points, if it were possible to do so. He wrote letters to a number of eastern newspapers and one to the *St. Louis Republic,* giving a full description of the very short titles. Several answers came, one from a man named T. Brown, stating that an uncle of his, T. Brown, left Troy, Missouri, for the West in 1832, accompanied by a man named R. Kent, and that neither of them was ever heard of again.

Another came from a man whose address is lost, stating that a relative of his, Ezra Kind, started for the west in 1832 and had never been heard of by his people.

Another letter received by Mr. Cashner made the statement that one R. Kent left his home in an eastern state about 1832, and had never again been heard of by his people or friends. No further information concerning this sad story was obtained through the researches of Mr. Cashner.

Conceding the statements in this chapter of early Black Hills history to be true in all essential points, the question arises as to where these first comers obtained so large a quantity of placer gold as related in the story. There is but one gulch known, where it might have been possible for them, with their crudely improvised facilities for mining, to have succeeded in obtaining such results. This is Gold Run Gulch, at the head of which the Homestake mine is located, which was found to be exceedingly rich in gold placers in 1876. What disposition of their treasure was made by the Indians is another question that has not been, nor is likely to be, satisfactorily answered. However, there is an Indian legend that gold amounting to $18,000 was sold or bartered to the Hudson Bay Trading Company. There is, connected with this story, a tale as to how it was obtained, so disconnected that little credence could be given it.

Some years subsequent to the failure of Mr. Cashner in his efforts to trace more of these first comers definitely to their original starting points, the writer, impelled by a knowledge of circumstances acquired largely through traditional sources, took up the research. Several letters of inquiry were sent out, some of which were published in the newspapers. While no documentary evidence bearing directly upon the matter was obtained, sufficient was learned to lead to definite conclusion that these men, or some of them at least crossed the Missouri River, not later than the spring of 1832 came together at that time at Keytesville, Chariton County, Missouri, and were employed as teamsters by Fredrick Hicks, a wealthy citizen of that town, who outfitted and sent out a large train loaded with commodities, principally bacon, as part of a great caravan of several hundreds of wagons and men, which went out from Independence, Missouri, in the spring of 1832, for the purpose of opening the trail to Santa Fe, New Mexico, under protection of a regiment of United States soldiers, with two cannon, commanded by a General Walker. While the rest of this story is conjecture, it is reasonable to assume that the white men named on the Thoen stone, while on the trip to Santa Fe, met with the one designated as Indian Crow, who probably, was in reality a Crow Indian, a tribe residing in this vicinity, who had knowledge of the existence of gold in the Black Hills, and led them to it the following spring of 1833.

IV

EARLY-DAY GOLD SEEKERS

THE tragic story of a party of gold seekers in 1832-33, as related on the Thoen stone, is told in the preceding chapter. It is well established that Father De Smet, a Catholic missionary who worked ·many years among the Sioux Indians, was in the Black Hills at an early date and received from the Indians gold nuggets. It is related that he kept this a close secret and cautioned the Indians to do so lest the white men come and take away their "hunting grounds."

Judge Horatio N. Maguire, in his book, "The Coming Empire," published in 1878, tells of an ill-fated expedition of nineteen gold seekers into the Hills in 1852. While the story is not otherwise authenticated, except possibly by later discoveries of long abandoned shafts and other indications of early day gold seekers, the story has been credited by many subsequent writers and is here reproduced in part as follows:

"The foregoing facts seem sufficiently well authenticated. I think there is no reasonable doubt that the signs of old mining operations so numerously found in the Black Hills, are evidences left behind by the unfortunate little party of adventurers who went thither from Fort Laramie in 1852. It is equally certain that they were all, save the three who went through to California, and probably one other, massacred by the Indians. The reader will be given what the author knows of one having escaped of the sixteen who remained in the Hills.

"Hearing that information could be had at Salt Lake City of a man having escaped from an Indian massacre, somewhere north of the North Platte, in the fall of 1852, I wrote to an old mountain friend at that place to make inquiries in regard to the matter. My correspondent has furnished me with some apparently conclusive facts. He found a man, named Hale, reported to be veracious, and an old settler of Utah, who made a statement that seems to solve the mystery of the fate of fifteen of the sixteen missing prospectors. I will give the substantial facts, as thus reported:

"About the 10th of October, 1852, a pitiable wreck of a man, with deep-sullen, wild-bleering eyes, skin seemingly clinging to the very bones of his skeleton frame, his scanty raiment in tatters, with the legs of a pair of old boots wrought into a sort of sandal-protection for his otherwise exposed feet, came hobbling, just after nightfall, into a camp of Mormon hunters on the Green River. He was in the last stage of starvation, and could not have lived many hours longer. He said he had been since noon of the previous day, when he first caught sight of the smoke, trying to reach their camp; and that, had it been moved during that time a single mile, he would have despaired of ever again seeing the face of a human being. Fortunately, the hunters were engaged 'jerking' buffalo meat, and had no occasion to change their location.

"The rough but kind frontiersmen, knowing it would be certain death to allow him to eat to satiety, fed him a small quantity of strengthening broth, and furnished him with a comfortable bed of robes.

"In the morning, though the unfortunate man was scarcely able to turn over, he looked with fiercely greedy eyes upon the long strings of savory buffalo-meat suspended around the great log camp-fire.

"Again he was given some nourishing broth, and in more liberal quantity than the evening before. Notwithstanding his frantic appeals for a more generous supply, the hunters, whose knowledge, gained from painful experience, had made them skillful physicians in such cases—resolutely gauged his capacity; and continued this wise dietetic discipline until the sufferer was carried out of danger, and became comparatively comfortable. Then, his mind restored from its delirium, he told the story of his terrible sufferings.

"He gave his name as Thomas Renshaw, formerly of Cincinnati, Ohio. Said he was one of a party of prospectors who had turned north from the North Platte emigrant road, at Fort Laramie, to hunt for gold mines which 'friendly' Indians had told them existed in the Black Hills.

[13]

"Entering the Hills on the south, with two ox-teams and several saddle-horses, they sank shafts and found gold; but not in satisfying quantities.

"They then 'cached' their wagons, packed their oxen and horses with supplies, and penetrated into the interior, finding a little gold everywhere, and very good prospects on a clear, swift river about four days' travel from where they first struck the mountains (undoubtedly Rapid creek); but they could not open ground there, owing to the great quantity of water flowing into the shafts.

"They then went on farther north, traveling four days over rough, high ridges, and through dense forests and network of fallen timber—unable to make over seven or eight miles a day—when they descended from a high mountain into a deep gorge, through which flowed a little stream. (This description applies to Whitewood creek, near the mouth of Deadwood.)

"They got down to bed-rock on this little stream, without difficulty, and found prospects ranging from ten to twenty cents to the pan.

"At this juncture, three or four weeks having elapsed since they turned off from the emigrant road, three of the party started back, to report the discovery to friends on their way to California, who had agreed to tarry awhile in Salt Lake City, and wait for them three weeks at the Humboldt River.

"The party then hewed out sluicing lumber, and had one string of sluices in operation, yielding from an ounce to an ounce and a half a day to the hand, and were busily engaged getting out timbers for more, when Indians came upon them, murdering all but the narrator.

"Continuing his narration, Renshaw said he went out one morning to kill a deer, and did not return until late in the afternoon. Approaching the camp, he noticed unusually large volumes of smoke rising from the gulch, which excited his apprehension, and caused him to approach covertly; and these first fears were soon confirmed by his hearing a medley of piercing, wild yells.

"Throwing aside the meat he was carrying, he crept up to the brink of the mountain over the camp, and, looking down, beheld a blood-curdling scene. The prospectors' 'shacks,' or brush-covered tents, were ablaze, and around the bonfire a hundred savages were engaged in a fiendish dance, his companions' reeking scalps—fastened to the ends of poles, and passed from hand to hand in the demoniacal demonstrations, being the leading features in the horrible orgies.

"Renshaw then hid until nightfall, when he forced his way through the forests, as best he could, in a southwesterly direction, hoping to reach the emigrant road a distance west of Fort Laramie, and intercept an emigrant train.

"He had a few matches, his rifle and a small supply of ammunition, and, as he passed through a country abounding with game, he did not suffer from hunger, to any great extent, the first three or four weeks; but he dared not make a fire to cook with, except in the most secluded places, and suffered extremely from the chilling night air.

"He also had a pocket compass, and knew the general direction he should take—knew if he could continuously bear to the southwest he would emerge upon the North Platte road, if he lived long enough to reach it; but to follow a general direction, in such a country, was not so easy. He soon found his way blocked with savage cliffs, which could not be scaled, necessitating long and tortuous efforts to pass them by circuitous routes; and he frequently suffered from thirst, when lost and bewildered among the savage crags of the divides.

"Finally, he succeeded in reaching the plateau country between the head of the South Fork of the Cheyenne and the North Fork of the Platte. But his last match was gone, his last bullet fired, and his greatest sufferings were yet to be endured. Hunger began to gnaw, and his tongue was often parched with thirst. The soles of his boots were gone, and his clothing had been literally torn from his person by the thorns of the innumerable thickets he had passed through. His strength was rapidly failing, and his gun and accoutrements, all save his knife, were cast aside as useless incumbrances.

"Thenceforth his main dependence for subsistence were chokecherries, which he occasionally found in the ravines, and the pulpy part of the prickly-pear leaf, juicy and somewhat nourishing, from which he stripped the outside skin with his knife. This succulent plant, which abounds in those regions, was to him both food and drink; he would have perished of thirst in some of the long stretches between water had it not been for the moisture it afforded. Roots, too, when procured, were eagerly devoured.

"At last the emigrant road was reached; but the last train, for that year, had passed, and the unfortunate man, his strength nearly exhausted, and suffering intensely from excruciating pains of various kinds, especially internal gripings caused by the unnatural food he was forced to eat, felt that he had only reached it to leave his skeleton there as a mute and ghastly witness of his horrible fate. But 'as long as there is life there is hope' is a sentiment that animates to the last, and he wearily pushed on to the westward, traveling, for the most part, after dark, and sleeping through the warm hours of the day, until he joyfully saw the smoke curling up from the camp-fire of his rescuers."

V

EXPLORING EXPEDITIONS

So far as history definitely records, the first exploring party to reach the Black Hills, less than a dozen men, headed by Jeddediah Smith, came in 1823. James Clayman, secretary of the party, kept a diary which was left to posterity. The party came from the Missouri River, up the valley of the White River, crossed the southern part of the Hills and went on to the Rocky Mountains.

In 1855, General Harney led a military exploring expedition from Fort Laramie, Wyoming. This was accompanied by Lieutenant G. K. Warren, Dr. F. V. Hayden, and other scientists, who made careful examination of the topography, geology, and flora of the greater part of the Hills. This expedition terminated at Fort Pierre, South Dakota, in 1856.

In 1857, Lieutenant Warren and Dr. Hayden led another scientific exploring expedition from Fort Laramie into the southern Black Hills. Extended reports of the findings of these four expeditions are given in United States government reports.

In 1875, Professor W. P. Jenney led another scientific exploring expedition into the Hills.

As a result of these expeditions, the topography, geology, and flora of the Black Hills and adjacent areas became well known. These parties made no efforts to discover gold deposits, though its probable existence was reported. Dr. Hayden in an address delivered to the Dakota Historical Society in 1866, said:

"In the formation of these Hills, as in all mountain ranges, the unstratified rocks are heaved up in a broken and confused mass from below, and are destitute of all traces of animal life. Intermingled with these rocks and in the layers above, are found the gold bearing formations which are developed in the Black Hills.

Little particles of gold can be found in almost any little stream in the vicinity of the Hills. But gold is not always found in paying quantities where 'color' is raised. While there is every indication of rich, gold deposits in the Black Hills, my explorations have been for the purpose of collecting old fossil remains rather than glittering dust."

It was this and other similar reports which caused general belief of rich gold deposits in the Black Hills many years before the discovery which led to the big gold rush in 1875-1876.

VI

THE CUSTER EXPEDITION—DISCOVERY OF GOLD

THE activities of the Sioux Indians were largely responsible for an expedition of about one thousand men, comprised of ten companies of cavalry, two of infantry, together with the usual number of scouts, teamsters, guides, interpreters, etc., under General George A. Custer. This expedition left Fort Abraham Lincoln, near Bismarck, in the present state of North Dakota, on July 2, 1874, with orders to proceed to the northern hills, exploring the country to the west and south, and penetrating the interior as far as practicable.

The expedition entered the Black Hills proper at Inyan Kara, near the present Sundance, Wyoming, and traveled south and east to a point about ten miles south of Harney's Peak, in the southern Black Hills. Here a "permanent camp was established on French Creek." From this point exploring trips were made covering a considerable area to the southwest, south and southeast, to the South Fork of the Cheyenne River. Returning, the trail was followed back to a point about thirty miles south of Custer Peak; thence north skirting the Hills, and northwest along the Dakota-Montana boundary to a point west of Fort Abraham Lincoln, thence east to the Fort, arriving on August 30th.

It was on this expedition that the first thoroughly authenticated discovery of gold, in commercial quantities, was made in the Black Hills. There is such conflict in the reports of various members of the expedition that it probably can never be determined to a certainty, the time, place and discoverer. Dr. Cleophas O'Harra, for many years president of the State School of Mines at Rapid City, made painstaking geological and historical researches over a long period, which entitle him to be considered high authority on matters which he investigated. He presents concisely the conflict of reports and records of members of the expedition, concerning the discovery of gold, in an article in *The Black Hills Engineer*, November, 1929, published by the School of Mines. From the evidence he presents it appears:

"That two practical miners, Horatio N. Ross and William T. McKay, accompanied the expedition; that on arrival in the vicinity of Custer, on July 27th, they began 'panning' the creek gravels for gold; that one of them, or both together, obtained 'color' on that date, along Castle Creek; and that such discovery may have been at any time between July 27th and August 2d; and that it may have been on French Creek where permanent camp was made."

From a careful study of the records and reports of several official and other members of the expedition, it appears that this discovery of gold was of minor importance to them, hence lack of concordance in reports as to the exact time and place. The discordance of evidence entitled to be given credence is such that Dr. O'Harra does not venture to determine the facts any more closely than is above stated. General Custer first reported the discovery on August 2nd, but does not fix the date or place.

Captain Ludlow, chief engineer, in his report under date of July 27th, says, "The gold hunters were very busy all day with shovel and pan exploring the streams," but does not state that they then discovered gold. In a report dated July 31, he states that, "The gold hunters redoubled their efforts." In a report dated August 2d, he states that he saw in General Custer's tent particles of gold, which "the miner said he had obtained during the day."

N. H. Winchell, geologist of the expedition, in his report dated July 30th, says: "The gold seekers who accompany the expedition report the finding of gold in the gravel and sand along the valley," but does not state whether it was found on that day, or prior thereto.

Charley Reynolds, the scout sent out by General Custer from his permanent camp on French Creek, on August 3d, to carry messages to Fort Laramie, said on reaching that point, "For several days the miners have been successful in obtaining gold colors."

William E. Curtis, correspondent for the *Chicago Inter Ocean*, a member of the Custer expedition, in a letter to that paper written at Castle Creek on July 27th, said:

"Yesterday, July 26th, for the first time were found indications of gold and today we remained in camp while parties have gone out prospecting in every direction." In a subsequent dispatch, sent with Reynolds when he left for Fort Laramie on August 3d, he says:

"The discovery was made on the 2d of August in the bed of a creek we suppose is French Creek on the maps, and the yield was about thirty-five cents in dust to three pans." Continuing he tells of brief prospecting by Ross and McKay enroute to French Creek, and says, "It wasn't very satisfactory prospecting to leave a lead as soon as they got 'the color' and they got it frequently."

Ross himself is quoted by Frank W. Bower in an article in the *South Dakota and Western Advocate,* October 15, 1901, as saying:

"On the morning of July 30th, 1874, my partner McKay and I took our miner's pans and went down to the bank of French Creek and discovered gold in the gravel of the stream."

Harper's Weekly of September 12th, 1874, had an article stating that, "On the 31st day of July, gold was discovered along the bank of a (French) Creek."

Professor W. P. Jenney, of the Jenney-Newton Black Hills Survey in 1875, says in his report of the Custer expedition:

"Gold was discovered in gravel bars on French Creek early in August, 1874, by Ross and McKay." Further on he states that he had been informed by McKay "that Ross and himself failed to find gold in prospecting on Castle Creek; but on a small branch in the northern part of Elkhorn Prairie, they obtained the first 'color' of gold from the Black Hills, July 28, 1879."

Captain North, a member of the Custer expedition, in a letter in 1924 to Dr. G. B. Grimwell, paleontologist of the expedition, said:

"Ross was the man that washed out the first gold. I remember it as if it were yesterday. You and I stood right behind him when he did it." But Captain North fails to definitely fix the place and date.

Mr. Ross returned to Custer in 1875, and made it his home until his death in 1904. A monument has been erected there in his honor, as the "discoverer" of gold in the Black Hills. Custer has its annual "Gold Discovery" celebration on July 26-27. Apparently the people of that city have settled upon Horatio N. Ross as the discoverer, the date, July 27th, and the place Castle Creek, as French Creek was not reached until July 30th. Those who dispute these claims can find much evidence to sustain other contentions. The differences possibly may be reconciled by supposition that Ross and McKay first found "colors," minute particles, of gold on July 27th, and that it was not until several days thereafter that sufficient quantity was found in the pans to justify collecting it.

VII

THE GORDON EXPEDITION OF 1874

FOR several years prior to the General Custer military expedition in 1874, rumors of gold discoveries in the Black Hills led to efforts to organize parties of gold seekers to invade that region, then Sioux Indian reservation. Prominent in promoting such efforts was Charles Collins, then editor of the *Sioux City (Iowa) Times.* Such activities came to the attention of General Hancock, commander of the Department of Dakota, at Ft. Snelling, Minnesota, and he issued the following order:

"That any expedition organized for the purpose of penetrating the Black Hills be immediately dispersed, the leaders arrested and placed in the nearest military prison."

Collins' articles attracted many to Sioux City, including Thomas H. Russell, an experienced frontiersman. He joined with Collins and they organized a party to invade the Hills. This came to the attention of General Hancock. Following this, Collins and Russell closed their Chicago recruiting office and as a blind to the military authorities wired their associates in Sioux City as follows:

"In view of the recent order of General Sheridan, the Collins and Russell expedition has been abandoned for the present."

Secretly, plans were perfected for a party to make the trip. In a short time they were ready to leave Sioux City defying the military authorities. Mr. Russell accompanied the party. Mr. Collins did not, but came to the Black Hills subsequently, and became the first postmaster at Central City, two miles from Deadwood, in 1877.

In 1878, Mr. Collins published the first directory of Deadwood and adjacent mining camps. In a preface to this he relates in detail his efforts which culminated in the Collins-Russell expedition in

1874, later known as the Gordon party. Mr. Collins states that in 1871 he had an interview with Father De Smet on his arrival by steamboat at Sioux City, in which this noted pioneer missionary to the Sioux Indians admitted that he knew of the existence of gold in the Black Hills.

That in 1872 he organized the "Black Hills Exploring and Mining Association" at Sioux City, and prepared for general circulation a pamphlet setting forth the known and presumed facts concerning the Hills, with plans for organizing parties to go there, and advising as to routes, equipment, etc. The cost of a list of "indispensible" articles for a party of five persons to make the trip, with supplies for four months, totaled over $600.

That he obtained from the government land in Brule County, and in 1873 laid out at a point opposite the mouth of the White River, "Brule City," near the present city of Chamberlain, South Dakota. The route for projected parties was to be along the Missouri River to Brule City, thence along the White River to the Hills. He then planned to make Brule City the capital of Dakota Territory, which was then at Yankton.

In this account, Mr. Collins relates in detail events preceding the Gordon expedition, the names of members of the party, and the events following.

A detailed account of what occurred to the Gordon-Russell party in 1874, enroute to the Hills, and subsequent to arrival until expulsion by the military, is given by Mrs. Annie D. Tallent, a member of the party, first white woman to enter the Black Hills, in her book, "The Black Hills or Last Hunting Grounds of the Dakotas."

This first historic party of gold seekers to the Black Hills has been known variously as the Gordon party, named after the leader of the expedition, John Gordon; also as the Collins party and the Russell party, to honor the organizers of the expedition.

On the afternoon of October 6, 1874, the expedition set out from Sioux City, Iowa. It was composed of twenty-six men, one woman, and a six-year-old boy. For equipment there were six canvas-covered wagons, twenty-four head of cattle used as draft animals, five saddle ponies, and two greyhounds.

After traveling a few miles, the party halted for the night and the question of leadership came up. A long discussion finally resulted in the election of John Gordon as the leader of the train, largely because he claimed to have traveled the country as far as the foothills several years before.

The train was composed of five groups. Prior to starting these groups had assembled in small parties and camped together, so this division was the result of the previous camp arrangements. The first group was composed of Captain Tom Russell, Lyman Lamb, Eaf. Witcher, and Angus McDonald. Members of the second group were B. B. Logan, Dan McDonald, or "Red Dan," Dan McDonald, or "Black Dan" (both men having the same name, they were thus described because of colors of the shirts they always wore), James Dempster, James Powers, J. J. Williams, and Thomas Quiner. The third unit numbered John Gordon, J. W. Brockett, Newton Warren, H. Bishop, Charles Long, Charles Corderio, and Moses Aarons. The fourth had four men in the party, R. R. Whitney, Harry Cooper, David Aken, and John Boyle. The fifth party had as members, Charles Blackwell, Thomas McLaren, Henry Thomas, D. G. Tallent, Mrs. Annie D. Tallent, and their son, Robert E. Tallent.

The train averaged from fifteen to twenty miles a day, which was a very good record considering the fact that they were picking a trail over new country and had cattle for draft animals. Everything went well until the party left the village of Norfolk, Nebraska, when one of the members became seriously ill or homesick, and decided that he would return to civilization, which he did. Soon thereafter the train reached O'Neill, Nebraska, which was the farthest outpost of civilization at that time and residents there tried to turn the party back, urging that any further advance into Indian territory would be suicide.

These pleadings were unheeded and the party proceeded on its way. Two days later they came upon a party of United States surveyors who had been sent out to establish the Nebraska State line, but were forced to abandon a part of the work because of Indians. The surveyors urged the expedition to return, saying that the Sioux Indians were on the warpath and would not permit any invasion of their territory. Despite these added warnings the train again set out and after three weeks' travel they reached a point southeast of the Black Hills on the Niobrara River. The oxen were weary, the men were tired, and the weather was chilly, but no talk of return was sounded by any of the party. They were now beyond the protection of the law and in hostile Indian territory. Obedience to the leader was essential to the safety of the expedition.

The river was crossed and a course north and west was followed, finally making intersection with the Fort Randall Government road. Here they saw a small detachment of government cavalry passing along the road to the westward, but they were not discovered. They proceeded on their way, using extreme precautions against a night attack, having night guards watch the stock.

The limited diet and cooking facilities soon resulted in sickness and a number of the party became seriously ill. The sickness also brought about an attack of homesickness to some members and Eaf. Witcher decided that he would return. He parceled out his belongings to other members and prepared to depart for the East. A council was called and a debate followed in which a set of resolutions was drawn up which declared that it would be treasonable for any of the members to leave the group and spread the news of the expedition in civilization; a penalty was added that the offender should be disarmed and placed under guard until he changed his mind about deserting. Eaf. changed his mind and became reconciled in time to this new ruling.

Before reaching White River, water became scarce, which finally necessitated the unloading of one wagon and packing it with blocks of ice which was melted from time to time as it became necessary for use. This ice was carried for miles through the Bad Lands. One man was still too ill to attend to camp duties, and for several days he did nothing but lie in bed in a wagon and moan. Upon reaching Bad River there was a consultation concerning him and it was suggested that the party stop for a few days in the hope that rest would aid in his recovery. This was finally voted down on the theory that a stop in the most dangerous region traversed on the trip would probably endanger the entire group, and the sick man could still be comfortable in the wagon. After several days of suffering he died and a halt of one day was made for the last rites over the body of Moses Aarons. J. J. Williams, a skilled carpenter, shaped a coffin, a grave was dug, and the body placed beneath the sod. A wooden cross was erected and on it the following inscription read: "Died here on the 27th of November,

1874, on his way to the Black Hills, Moses Aarons, aged 32 years. May he rest in peace."

The party had its first glimpse of the Black Hills, a long dark outline against the sky, on November 31. This was at the mouth of Elk Creek where it empties into the Cheyenne.

The Hills were entered on December 9 at a point about four miles below the present site of Sturgis, at which point the party took dinner in the midst of a howling snowstorm. Here they found the trail of the Custer Expedition in July and August of that year, where it had left the Hills. They followed this trail into the heart of the Hills, arriving on French Creek, near Custer, on December 23, 1874.

Camp was established and plans were made for a permanent post. The following day was devoted to laundry, baths, patching equipment, and overhauling gear of all kinds, in preparation for a long stay. During the ensuing two weeks work was started on a stockade and fourteen days later it was ready for occupancy. This structure became known in history as the "Gordon stockade." It was built of heavy pine logs thirteen feet long, set close together vertically, three feet in the ground. When completed it formed an enclosure about eighty feet square. Bastions were built at the corners, standing out six feet from the walls and portholes were placed along the walls at intervals of about eight feet. Within the stockade were built seven log cabins, three on each side and one opposite the gate.

During this time there had been some prospecting in the stream and gold had been found at many points. After the stockade was completed, a rocker was constructed and sufficient gold was rocked out to prove that it was there in paying quantities. When sufficient gold had been recovered to make a good showing, John Gordon and Eaf. Witcher were selected to take it out and prove to Collins and the world in general that a strike had been made. These two men left on February 6, 1875, and twenty-three days later they arrived in Sioux City. Newspapers broadcasted the news, people were again excited about the region, and the Black Hills was the topic of discussion throughout the middle west.

Gordon and Witcher organized a second expedition to join the original party and started for the Hills, but this train was intercepted by the militia and turned back before reaching its destination.

The remainder of the party, who had remained at the stockade, worked streams for gold, built better shelters, and otherwise occupied themselves until spring, and as there had been no interference from the outside because of their invasion of the reservation, they relaxed their vigilance. When spring arrived, Blackwell and McLaren prepared to leave for Fort Laramie and on February 14 they departed, but had a mishap and returned to camp the same evening. They repaired their outfit, started again, and finally reached the outside settlements. They never returned to the Black Hills.

The fever of departure seemed to have spread as on March 6, four others, Newton Warren, D. McDonald (Red Dan), J. J. Williams, and Henry Thomas, departed for Fort Laramie. Their desertion left but eighteen of the original party in camp. Not having any reinforcements in the arrival of other pioneers to augment the party, the situation was not at all enviable.

The month of April opened with a heavy snowstorm, almost approaching a blizzard, and before it was over, four men rode into the stockade. It was at first thought that they were the vanguard of another party, but this hope was soon dispelled. Two were government troopers and the other two, J. J. Williams and Dan McDonald, were also rigged out in military attire.

The mystery of their return was soon explained. The party of four which last departed had reached Fort Laramie, where two of them were permitted to proceed on their journey and the other two were retained to guide the troops back to the stockade. These two led a troop of the Second United States Cavalry into the Hills for the purpose of removing the invaders from the reservation. Formal arrests were made and all were given twenty-four hours in which to prepare to leave. The exodus started on April 7, and the cavalcade wended its way southward, via the Red Cloud Agency and on to Fort Laramie, where the members under arrest were released without parole, and given transportation to Cheyenne, Wyoming. At that point the party disbanded. Thus terminated the Gordon Expedition of gold seekers to the Black Hills.

VIII

HIDE AND SEEK WITH THE SOLDIERS

EARLY comers into the Black Hills resorted to all kinds of devices to get across the government Indian reservations to reach the gold diggings, according to Robert James of Deadwood, who was a member of the second Gordon expedition, which attempted to get into the Black Hills before the government had concluded a treaty with the Indians.

This party, composed of 148 men and two women, under the leadership of John Gordon, crossed the Missouri River on April 25, 1875, with Fred T. Evans of Sioux City, Iowa, later of Hot Springs, South Dakota, in charge of transportation, although there were several private outfits in the party.

The party made its way along the Nebraska side as far as they could, for unless they were on government land the soldiers could not turn them back, even if they did discover them. There was a strip of land near the Spotted Tail Agency in northwestern Nebraska that had never been ceded to the government by the Indians, over which they had jurisdiction.

"As soon as our party set foot on this strip of land," said Mr. James, "they nabbed us. The soldiers were headed by Captain Walker from Ft. Randall, who ordered us back, but we rebelled. We did sign an agreement to cross the Niobrara River on the old Ft. Randall and Spotted Tail road, and while we were going back we wanted an escort to take Fred Evans to Ft. Randall to get permission to make a permanent camp until the matter was settled.

"Argument started when the outfit, its teams in a mile long string, began to cross the river. About half refused to go. The others were escorted to Ft. Randall by mounted soldiers.

"Our party went into camp and for two or three days we

[29]

watched the soldiers through field glasses. Others of the party were brought back and we sent word that we wouldn't move unless they took us as prisoners. We refused to get the mules or harness them, so that Captain Walker had to detail men of his own to do that. We stampeded the mules to antagonize the soldiers," said Mr. James.

After some delay, Captain Mills, a superior of Captain Walker, arrived on the scene and he ordered everything burned. On the 25th of May, the entire expedition was surrounded, seized, and valuable merchandise, supplies, everything they had, was burned, with the exception of one wagon, that of Mrs. Brockett, one of the two women in the party, who refused to get down from her load of goods. Threats and cajolery, alike had no effect upon her, and at last, the commander was forced to turn her toward the east and let her go.

The others of the party were marched back across the river and admonished never to try to enter the country again as trespassers. Gordon was taken to Omaha, where he was tried and later released.

James, with two or three others, got through the guard and met Collins, a newspaperman from Sioux City, and made new plans for getting into the gold country, after the treaty with the Indians would be signed. They planned to come in February, 1876, but because of the bad weather, and later other matters, did not get here until July, 1876.

"I spent 16 years in mining and had the best time of my life, even if it didn't pay in money," said Mr. James. "Deadwood was wild but I always endeavored to stay where I thought I belonged and never went with the tough element. I have stayed here all the time since 1876." Mr. James died in 1934.

It was estimated that $5,000 worth of the latest improved firearms were burned in that questionable destruction related by Mr. James.

IX

TRAIL BLAZERS IN 1875

On the second day after my arrival in Deadwood I met on lower Main Street an old Montana friend, James Sutherland, from Eldorado Bar. He informed me that my old partner, William Smith, from Cave Gulch, Montana, was here, and that he came in the summer of '75. Pointing to a clump of trees in the now Second Ward, Deadwood, he said, "You will find his tent in that bunch of timber." Going as directed, I found my old friend in a large wall tent but somewhat indisposed from an attack of rheumatism resulting from exposure while making a trip to Cheyenne during the previous winter. Here was a man who had passed middle age, well educated, well informed, a practical miner, of strict integrity and unquestionable veracity. From this man I received more authentic information regarding the discoveries made in Whitewood and Deadwood gulches and the locating of placer claims and the townsites of Deadwood and Central, than I have since learned from all other sources.

Mr. Smith informed me that he, with John Kane and three other men whom I did not know, left Cave Gulch twelve miles from Helena, Mont., in the month of August, 1875. They were equipped with saddle horses, pack animals, tent, rifles, and about four months' provisions. They traveled by compass a southeasterly course for the Black Hills, coming straight through without any interruption whatever. They saw neither white men nor Indians. They reached the Black Hills and camped on the ground that was afterwards Crook City townsite, ten miles from Deadwood, on the fifth day of September.

There they saw no signs to indicate that either Indians or white men had ever been there. The next day they followed up the stream as far as it was possible to go with their pack horses, struck off south of the creek and came to the head of a small creek afterwards known as Smith Gulch. Mr. Smith did not say that the gulch was named for him, but others did say so later.

They came down that gulch and struck the main stream, which they called "Whitewood" on account of the thick growth of cottonwood timber, and there went into camp at the mouth of Spruce Gulch now in the First Ward of Deadwood. The next day, the seventh, they prospected and discovered gold.

It had been said, and is believed by many, that Frank Bryant, John Pearson and others, had been there and had made the first discovery of gold in that gulch in 1875. This report I do not credit. I have no recollection of Smith saying that his party made the first discovery. However, I inferred from his statements that they did so, and that his partners staked Discovery and the claims adjoining it. He said that he went up the gulch half a mile and staked a claim just below the junction of the two creeks, Whitewood and Deadwood, where his tent was located when I found him.

The second day after staking their claims they packed and moved on up Deadwood Gulch, literally chopping their way through fallen timber and thick undergrowth, to the mouth of Black Tail Gulch. There they found another party, known as the Blanchard party. The members of this party were A. S. Blanchard, Tom Patterson, H. A. Albien, John Verpont, and a member of the Custer expedition in 1874, whose name was lost. They came from Custer. John Verpont, a blacksmith, made the first discovery of gold in Deadwood Gulch on September 6th, 1875, obtaining then half a teaspoonful of gold dust. This party having made the first discovery of gold in Deadwood Gulch, were entitled to an extra claim for making discovery, and the preferences in selecting their locations. So the number of locations corresponding to the number of men in both parties, and one extra claim, were staked according to Montana Gulch mining rules, 300 feet up and down the gulch from Discovery. While the full number of claims were staked for safety, they were not apportioned to each man until January, 1876.

With one exception, all records of these discoveries and naming of gulches and the townsites have long since been lost or destroyed in the big fire of 1879. This exception is found in a fragment of the records now in the office of the Register of Deeds for Lawrence

County, which states that on April 28, 1876, A. S. Blanchard sold to B. E. Murphy, placer claim No. 1 above Discovery in Deadwood Gulch for $1,500. I have recently learned that Discovery claim in Deadwood Gulch was owned by Hildebrand, and No. 1 below Discovery was owned by Verpont. James Brown of Deadwood, who is yet alive, obtained No. 9 above Discovery, Lardner No. 10, French Bryant No. 11 and also No. 12 by purchase. John Bryant owned No. 13, on which he was killed in a pistol duel, as was his adversary, William Adams, reporter of the *Salt Lake Tribune*.

Therefore, it can safely be assumed that the Blanchard party is the one that came into the gulch from the south, and were on the ground when the Smith party arrived. I am fully convinced that the Smith party broke the trail from Montana to the Black Hills in August, 1875, made the first discovery of gold in Whitewood Gulch and named the gulch on the seventh of September, 1875; and that the Blanchard party from Custer made the first discovery of gold in Deadwood Gulch, September 6th, 1875; and that the two parties together named both Deadwood and Black Tail gulches.

All these activities which have been related transpired before the middle of September, 1875. A few days later, the same month, the Gay party arrived. I have forgotten their number, but there were only a few men. These went up Deadwood Gulch and located where the town of Gayville was started, and further up the gulch. No other parties came during that month.

Some time in October, the Lardner party consisting of a considerable number of men came in and located their claims still further up, where the town of Central City, two miles from Deadwood, was afterwards started.

It has frequently, though erroneously in my opinion, been stated that the Lardner and Bryant parties were the first discoverers and named creeks, Whitewood from its white timber, Deadwood from the enormous amount of dead timber in the gulch and on the mountain sides, and Black Tail Gulch because of the great herds of black tail deer seen there at that time.

Mr. Smith made no mention of any other parties or men coming into the northern Hills until January, 1876. These first comers of '76 numbered about thirty to forty men. As winter was on they did very little in the way of prospecting, devoting their time to the erection of log cabins and making comfortable winter quarters. They found no difficulty in reaching an agreement regarding the length and breadth of their mining locations which were to be 300 feet along the gulch with breadth from rim rock to rim rock on the sides. They also amicably agreed upon a code of placer mining laws suitable for governing their future mining operations as well as for the safeguarding of their priority rights.

Notwithstanding that all of these preliminary matters affecting their future operations had been adjusted and settled in a way satisfactory to all concerned, it was apparent that a feeling of unrest and insecurity pervaded the camp. They realized that they were violators of not only the Indian treaties but also of the laws of their own government, having crept into the Hills in defiance of governmental orders. They felt that at best they were up against an intricate and dangerous situation.

Uncertain as to what would be the attitude of the Federal Government or that of hostile tribes of Indians, this was the time for calm reflection. It was obvious that without protection from some source they would be helpless and entirely unable to develop their mines after having secured their choice of everything in sight. So now these venturesome little parties of lucky sooners were growing anxious to see a rush of mining immigrants to the Hills with the coming spring. Although they had made ample preparations for winter comfort, they had let their stock of provisions dwindle and were entirely out. Wild game was abundant and easily available, but they must have flour, bacon, and other necessities for getting through the winter which was now being keenly felt.

The Smith party being entirely out of provisions, Smith was selected as the best and safest man to make the trip to Cheyenne to get a supply of food. This he did with a saddle horse and two pack horses, returning with a supply ample to carry his party through the winter, after having several weeks of the hardest time of his life in keeping on the trails, bucking snowdrifts, and battling the elements, which injured his health, no doubt for life.

Bill Gay made a trip to the Spotted Tail Agency for supplies about the same time. He, with another party, returned with a wagon loaded with provisions.

While Smith was absent on his trip in January the miners held a meeting, organized and apportioned their claims. Lardner was elected recorder. Smith said that in the eagerness of some of the party to get near as possible to the Discovery claim, they took advantage of his absence and crowded him down to No. 5 below Discovery. He accepted it although if he had been present he would have selected a different claim.

About the first week in January several parties from the southern Hills arrived in Deadwood Gulch and before the month was gone, practically every vacant foot of ground in the gulch had been located and duly recorded. In February and March there were a large number of prospectors from the southern Hills and some from other states. Every foot of placer ground in Deadwood and Whitewood gulches was located.

Smith said that fortunately for the first comers they had organized and drafted and placed on record a code of the mining laws specifying the size of the claims and rules governing their mining operations. This wise policy, he said, undoubtedly saved them much trouble, if not bloodshed, as there were a large number of disappointed later comers who favored cutting down the size of the locations to provide more claims. They demanded that this be done. There were too many, however, who had already located and recorded their claims who, naturally, were not in favor of this unreasonable proposition. It was flatly rejected and the matter quickly settled. Smith made no mention of a miners' meeting being called for that purpose. Many of those who were disappointed in getting in on the ground floor purchased claims outright from the original locators and others purchased undivided interests. A large number of the original locators disposed of their claims before any development was made on them.

Having had the original records for a time in my possession, which were copied and the copy subsequently lost, I am enabled to say that more than half of the miners who took out the gold from Deadwood Gulch purchased their claims from others, and can name more than a dozen claims below Discovery in Deadwood Gulch that changed ownership before mining operations were well under way.

With but one exception, all of the hundreds of successful locators who had secured practically all the placer claims along Whitewood and Deadwood creeks and adjacent gulches, were greatly pleased to see the thousands of immigrants pouring in and gave them encouragement in securing lots and building up a town. This exception was the owners of Numbers 24 and 25 below Discovery, namely Pat Constantine and Company, of whom I shall make further mention. The first miners had, sometime previous to the laying out of a townsite, selected the only suitable area which was at the junction of Whitewood and Deadwood gulches, where it was afterwards located by Lee, Brown and Williams. These locators had secured two claims on Deadwood Gulch and two opposite them on Whitewood Gulch, and, as I remember it, were the owners of a block of ground 600 feet along the two streams and from hillside to hillside. The Deadwood townsite was laid out and platted by these three claim owners, all of whom selected for themselves choice corners and other desirable lots, and as I understood it, reserved the right to operate their mines.

J. J. Williams did sink a shaft twenty-two feet to bedrock back of Main Street at the end of Gold Street and did considerable mining there in 1877 but they were so handicapped by town buildings that they abandoned the project and filled the shaft. These owners evidently expected to, and undoubtedly did realize more money from their town property than they could have done otherwise had they so desired, or had they been legally able to prevent continuance of the tremendous building boom which was well under way.

Some weeks before the townsite was laid out these claim owners well knew that they held not even a squatter right, and therefore could not legally obstruct the work of others, although some of them did so by digging ditches and building water flumes and piling logs in the streets. Mr. Smith said that he took no part in the matter of town building, nor made any objection to the location of lots all around him on his ground, as it was his intention to sell his mining claims and he was at that time negotiating a sale which was consummated soon after my interview with him. His Deadwood Gulch claims were sold to Neill, Wisner and Company and the one in town, as I remember it, was sold to Spencer and Norton. He received fair prices and probably realized more from the sales than he would have done had he employed others to develop the claims.

Here I shall digress to speak of the personality of this man Smith. He was of good judgment and took few risks in money matters. He believed as did the old Missouri gentleman that "A bird in the hand was noblest work of God." While he was an ardent admirer of President Grant, he was not expecting the government to show any leniency in the matter of trespassing upon an Indian Reservation. In that conclusion of Mr. Smith I heartily concurred. I fully expected that a regiment of United States soldiers would give us a call at an early date; and I am yet firm in the belief that if the Indians had remained quiet and had not engaged in barbarous massacre of the white people who came upon their reservation, that every white man would have been ordered during the summer of '76 to vacate the Black Hills region and would not have remained long defying the order. That was the view of both of us at that time.

Mr. Smith, being well supplied with money after making his sales, quietly departed for San Francisco where he purchased valuable property on Montgomery Street from whence he last wrote me.

In getting back to the genesis of Deadwood it may be said that although it is generally believed that "there is nothing in a name," it is doubtful if there could be found another name so laden with thrilling thoughts, or the mention of which would so vividly open to the mind a panorama of revelry, wild ruffianism and tragedy, as does the name of Deadwood. Many and varied are the stories which have been told and written concerning the origin, early life and unparalleled growth of this famous old city. Born out of wedlock, so to speak, upon the western wilds, it was no wonder that it was destined to become famous as an outlaw city. Its destiny followed as a natural consequence the fact that it had no legal status, being from the start peopled by an aggregation of resolute invaders, without vestige of legal or moral right to enter; but lured by gold, they did stealthily and forcibly enter, despite the protests of its lawful owners, the Indians, and in defiance of a special restraining order issued by the supreme authority of their own government. Here they found themselves foot-loose in a chance world, free to act as their fancy dictated. Under the protection of no government, they were subject to no law save that of self preservation. Even that too often proved to be inadequate for protection of the weak and innocent against the abuses and brutalities of the evil minded, nowithstanding that the latent power of the venal element was not comparable to that of the upright citizens comprising the bulk of that immense throng of stirring humanity.

The minority element, however, was in evidence at all times and at all hours, both day and night, plying their nefarious schemes and vocations, looking for suckers, seeking and taking all possible advantages of easy marks. The underworld element, composed of the proprietors and operators of gambling halls, bawdy houses and other dives and sure thing enterprises, by their never ceasing vocal and instrumental noises, kept the new city in continuous uproar.

Such was the founding of the new city which, as if by magic, suddenly sprang into existence in the wilds of this unexplored region and by chance was christened Deadwood. Such were the prevailing conditions here when I came in the spring of 1876. Here was the city which, but a few weeks before, had as a nucleus, two saloons and less than a dozen buildings which had now increased to hundreds, including log cabins and shacks; and the score or two of people had now reached well up into the thousands. This great mass of stirring humanity, seen daily and nightly within the confines of this new city, were likened to a disbanded army, each man going when and where he pleased with no one to direct him and none to say nay. A great majority of this vast number of fortune seekers conducted themselves in an orderly and gentlemanly manner. Hundreds of them were disciplined soldiers who had served in the contending armies of the great Civil War, and truly it can be said that, aside from the fakirs, rounders, drunkards, and other turbulent elements of the underworld who were day and night holding full sway on Main Street and were keeping the town in a continuous uproar, there was never before nor will there ever again be a more sympathetic, good-natured, and harmonious aggregation of people thrown together in a space so limited as were these Black Hills pioneers of '76.

They evidently had come to this new country with the one object in view, that of bettering their financial conditions in honorable ways, and were apparently glad to meet and converse with their fellowmen, seemingly without any distrust of each other. No formal introductions were necessary in leading up to friendly acquaintance-ship. A pleasant salutation or its Indian equivalent, "How" sufficed as a formal introduction. There appeared to be a sympathetic good-fellowship pervading the main body of this great multitude of strangers in a strange land. The camp fire of any one party was free to as many others as cared to utilize it. On many occasions the scant stock of provisions of one party was shared with others.

I am stating these facts to show the estimate I have placed upon the open-heartedness and generosity of these pioneers of '76. There were, of course, many exceptions to this general rule. For some weeks during the big rush, the early morning stillness would be broken by a voice crying out "O Joe," which would be taken up in various parts and passed along by possessors of healthy lungs until it finally died out. Whether Joe's whereabouts was located or he was given up as lost, this deponent knoweth not.

X

ALLEGED PREHISTORIC MINING OPERATIONS

SINCE the unauthorized appropriation and occupancy of the Black Hills by the white people over sixty years ago, this great wealth giving storehouse of nature has been explored, prospected, and partially developed throughout all its areas. The explorations and developments were carried on chiefly through a system of scientific methods through which many important and valuable discoveries, both on and below the earth's surface, have been made. Notwithstanding these many years of occupation and the rich discoveries, only one discovery of historical importance has been made upon which can be based belief that any mining operations had been carried on in these Black Hills by white people prior to General Custer's expedition through them in 1874. Even that one, known as the "Thoen Stone Discovery," affords no clue as to where mining operations had been carried on, leaving that important phase wholly to conjecture.

The writer does not dispute nor doubt that gold has been taken from the gulches of these hills in times long past. However, I do take issue with those who have asserted that discoveries of old mining operations—such as shafts sunken in gulches, tunnels here and there in gulches and on hillsides—have been found which were not made by prospectors and miners in 1875 and 1876. The alleged location of only one of such alleged discoveries in the Black Hills proper has been published. This was purported to be in Rutabaga Gulch, where there is no sign whatever of a tunnel nor of gold. This writer, has had sixty-three years residence in these Hills, during the first three of which I traversed most of the gulches where gold was found, and conversed with many miners; and subsequently, besides making personal investigations, made numerous inquiries of other old timers regarding such purported discoveries of old mining operations. In not a single instance have I seen or heard from others anything confirmative of such reports. It is my firm belief that there has not been found any convincing evidence to show that there were ever any mining operations carried on in the Black Hills at any time prior to 1874, except as disclosed by the "Thoen Stone" and possibly the story related by Judge Maguire, Indian legends, prating prospectors, credulous newspaper reporters and misinformed historians to the contrary notwithstanding.

Two such erroneous reports of discoveries current throughout the Hills during pioneer days that have found their way into print and even into histories of the Black Hills, have been discussed in the chapter on, "Trail Blazers in 1875."

As to when discoveries of gold in Whitewood and Deadwood gulches were made and who made them, I am positive that the Smith party of five men who blazed the trail from Montana to the Black Hills in August and September, 1875, made the first discovery of gold in Whitewood Gulch on September 7th, and that the Blanchard party coming from Custer made the first discovery of gold in Deadwood Gulch on September 6th, 1875.

XI

MY FIRST TRIP TO THE HILLS

(By Captain C. V. Gardner)

WHEN, on the 24th day of February, 1876, I consulted the superintendent of the Union Pacific Railroad in regard to the shipment of a carload of goods to Cheyenne, en route to the Black Hills, he asked me if I were sure gold in commercial quantities existed in that wild region. I replied that I had no information except what I had read in the Omaha and Sioux City papers, according to which one might almost expect to pluck gold nuggets from the Hill's pine trees. The gentleman warned me that I was taking a long chance, but I replied that all business enterprises involved taking chances and then, finding me determined, he kindly did what he could to help me in my adventure.

Editor Rosewater of the *Omaha Bee* made extended mention of the shipment at the time, not only in the news columns, but editorially, and a short time ago the present editor of the *Bee*, referring to the old files of the paper, dug up the story of the first carload of goods shipped over the Union Pacific for the Black Hills and commented on the changes fifty years had made.

On arriving at Cheyenne, I found the city full of gold seekers, but all waiting for more definite knowledge of conditions. Many were coming out, all swearing there was no gold in the Black Hills, and few were going in. Desiring more information as to conditions before taking the chances of shipping the goods, I determined to make a hasty trip to the Hills. While waiting at Cheyenne a few days, I made arrangements with a party known as "Deaf Thompson" to join me in the enterprise by enlarging the shipment, he agreeing to put up goods to the amount of 35,000 pounds.

I took the stagecoach to Fort Laramie, 100 miles distant north, that being then the "jumping-off" place of civilization. On arriving there I found no parties who were going to the Black Hills. I determined to walk the distance, about 150 miles, and had even made arrangements with the landlord for four days' rations, which I thought would get me through, providing the Indians did not get my scalp. But just before I started I encountered a mail man who was about to leave for Red Cloud agency, and finding that this would be a step on my way to the Hills, I went with him. I asked him what time we should arrive at the agency and he said, "If we have good luck, we ought to be there at eight o'clock tonight."

It was a bright, warm day, but at about four o'clock in the afternoon the wind chopped round into the northwest and by five o'clock it commenced to snow. It increased in volume, and also the wind, and before night set in a furious blizzard was in full force, such as only many old-timers have seen in this western country. As darkness came the storm increased in violence and we could make but slow progress. We finally lost the trail in the darkness. Fortunately, at about eight o'clock in the evening, our horses ran into an abandoned log cabin. We unhitched them and took them inside, where we found a chimney but no fuel. After feeding the team part of the hay in the wagon, we made a bed of the rest and passed the night as best we could, with one horse blanket over and one under us. The next morning dawned bright and clear though crisp, and we made the agency about ten o'clock.

I asked the Indian agent to help me secure a guide to the Black Hills. He was exceedingly doubtful about it.

"A guide is hard to find," said he, "and even if you find one, the chances of your getting through are about three to ten. Most of the Indians are here, but many renegades are out and if they catch you they will show you no mercy." I assured him, however, that it was "ground hog case" and, after a day or two he found a half-breed who agreed to take me through, providing that I paid him $25 and give him the profits on three or four hundred letters which were waiting to go to Custer, the postage on which at that time was 25 cents apiece.

Desiring to take as few chances as possible, we decided to leave at night. At midnight we had our horses loaded and hitched in the rear of the agency. After a hearty meal we slipped away from the agency into the darkness and rode all night. At sunrise we made a hasty meal and then rode all day and camped at night in a deep canyon, picketed our horses, and wrapped lariats from our saddle horses about our wrists as we slept, so in case of alarm we could move rapidly. The next afternoon we reached the place since known as Buffalo Gap and took the trail for Custer, arriving at a place known as Point Rocks at about ten o'clock at night and the next day made Custer. This is a hasty sketch of my first trip to the Black Hills.

XII

MY ARRIVAL IN THE BLACK HILLS

I EMBARKED at St. Louis, Mo., for Fort Pierre, on a Missouri
River steamer that was bound for Fort Benton, Montana. General
Terry and his seventeen-year-old son, George, were on the same
steamer, bound for the mouth of the Yellowstone River to meet
General Custer. George and I became good friends and I afterwards
wrote him at his home in New York all I knew about the Black
Hills.

I arrived at Fort Pierre on the Missouri River two hundred
miles east of the Black Hills, in April of 1876, the day after a
wagon train had left there for the Hills, so I was detained for several days at that cheerless post, awaiting the arrival of the next
wagon train that was en route from Sioux City.

There was quite a large number of Indians at Fort Pierre at
that time, loafing around during the day and at night holding noisy
demonstrations. Whether these were war dances, religious revivals,
or political rallies, I was not informed.

Comfortably located in new tents at the mouth of Bad River
at Fort Pierre, were about fifty men from the state of Pennsylvania.
This party was thoroughly equipped with all the essentials for camp
life and for home making, from tin cups to grindstones. Evidently
they had started for the new gold fields on a purely business venture with probably no thought at the time of any contingency
arising which might involve them in trouble with Indians over the
right of way across the Bad Lands country, and they were wholly
unprepared for meeting any such emergencies. This very important
matter not having been previously considered they had neglected to
bring with them a supply of war munitions which at that time
were prime essentials in the settlement of Indian difficulties.

[45]

This party had intended to go on west with the wagon train but was deterred from doing so by hearing from another party of men to whom they had given shelter in their tents, some very discouraging reports of Indian activities. The party, which had just returned from Rapid City in the Hills, told some very shocking stories of seeing fresh graves all along the route to that place, and that as far up Rapid Creek as they had gone the graves of white men who had been murdered by Indians were seen on both sides. So the eastern men changed their plans and decided to build boats and go back down the river.

The men from Rapid City, whose business eastward was much more pressing, decided to float down on cottonwood logs. Two logs lashed together sufficed for two passengers. Although the "Big Muddy" was lashing its shores, it held no terrors for these men. I witnessed a touching departure. Four men on four short logs together with a heavy trunk, and below their boot tops in icy water, went whirling down the stream for their final destination, which I presumed was the Gulf of Mexico. Although I had at the time a fine Winchester rifle, I purchased another from them, as they were unable to take it.

While I gave but little credence to the exaggerated reports given out by the excited men who came from Rapid City, I learned before I reached that city that their stories were not founded wholly upon imagination. The Indians had really murdered a number of white men along the route and their graves were in evidence. At the time the men were at Rapid City the Indians were numerous and active in that vicinity, trying out the new needle guns with which they had been amply supplied either by Uncle Sam or other agencies. They were doing some very reckless and indiscriminate shooting, while engaged in their early spring roundup of American horses, which they were claiming by right of discovery and appropriation.

When the belated train from Sioux City arrived at Fort Pierre, I fell in with it, armed and provisioned for the summer, and was soon on my way to the Hills. Our train consisted of about twenty wagons and nearly one hundred men, no women or children. When strung out on the plains it certainly made a formidable showing. If viewed from distant hill tops, as it undoubtedly was, it might have been mistaken for General Crook's army.

MY ARRIVAL IN THE BLACK HILLS

We moved along without incident for several days. There were two men on horseback who went far ahead of the wagons, as did also a very large footman, whose name was Campbell.

One afternoon, as we were approaching a point on the road known as Grindstone Buttes, we saw coming back towards us, abreast and at top speed, the two horsemen and Campbell. Their report was submitted in short order. They had discovered in a large valley beyond the bluffs an Indian village of considerable size, but had neglected to risk a second look in making an estimate of the number of its inhabitants. There was now but one thing to be done, and without parleying the train moved on.

On approaching the bluffs we realized that the picture had not been overdrawn by our scouts. There they were, the tepees looming up in the distance like shocks in an Iowa cornfield, yet we saw no Indians. In sizing up the village the most conservative estimate that I was able to make was one hundred braves. The situation, however, was not discouraging, as we had more than ninety men.

Our wagons were quickly thrown in a circle with the horses all inside. The captain of the train made a call for every man who had a gun to come forward. Previous to this call some of the knowing ones who were familiar with Indian tactics, gave out the startling information that the Reds, before our approach, had rushed across the valley and were then ensconced under the bluffs awaiting our descent into the valley. This would give them a decided advantage in executing their plans for a general slaughter of our party.

We disappointed them in this ruse and were now ready to line up over the bluffs. I gave my extra gun and ammunition to a young man who had none, and we fell into line. And now, to my great surprise and disappointment, only about one-third of our invincible force walked out into the open; and at least one-third had such an array of ante-bellum antiques and heirlooms for shooting irons, as I had never before seen.

Not until this time had I realized the gravity of the situation, of being right in the heart of the danger zone with not to exceed twenty-five effective rifles, with a good part of them single shots, to face at least one hundred warriors armed with needle guns. The situation was by no means exhilarating. I thought of the men who had gone down the river.

However, as we had no river to jump into and no woods to take to, our only alternative was to go forward to give battle. This we were proceeding to do and had crept up to within a few yards of the bluffs, all ready to rise up for the onslaught when two of our bravest, not to say foolhardy men, in their anxiety to get in the first shots, called out, "No Indians." Had there been any Indians there those two men would have gone over the wall with two of the best rifles in the outfit. The reds had given us the slip and the shock of disappointment to some of our militant heroes was keenly felt.

At this juncture three of the reds emerged from the village and came straight towards us. They were two very old men and a small boy. Through an interpreter we were informed that all their party, except themselves, had gone hunting back over the hill in an opposite direction from us. This information was of course accepted for what we thought it to be worth. It was my opinion and that of others, that they were in that locality for the purpose of doing the same as they had been doing on former occasions—ambushing and murdering small parties of white men. They were never known to attack a party of whites anywhere near their equal. They probably had been apprised by scouts of our approach and in view of our numbers had decided to retire back of their camp and watch our movements.

This opinion was confirmed by the fact that they made no attempt that night to stampede our stock. Evidently they were afraid to tackle us. However, had they known our actual fighting strength, they might have given up their search for jack rabbits and turned their attention to bigger game.

Here in our party were nearly one hundred men, no doubt as courageous as any who came to the Hills, who would have been nearly helpless in resisting an attack by any considerable number of Indians. This party was a fair representation of the throngs who came trusting to luck, by which nearly all were certainly favored, not only in reaching Deadwood, but in not being molested after their arrival. Our people, though numbered by thousands, were wholly unorganized and with a small percentage equipped with arms for making a good defense. The thought has many times occurred to me that it would have taken but a fraction of such a

force as Sitting Bull hurled against Custer to clean up Deadwood
and leave it in ashes.

During our trip from Fort Pierre to Rapid City, from four to
six pickets were posted each night far out from camp. This was
deemed necessary in order to give the sleepers ample time to prepare
for action, the guards firing a warning shot should attack on the
camp be made or a prowling Indian be spied. The names of these
guards were called out in alphabetical order. Up to the last night
before reaching Rapid City I had escaped this undesirable duty,
but my name was called when the camp was made on Box Elder
Creek right in the very heart of the danger zone. Here I put in
more than half of the night, which was pitch dark, in watching
near-by bushes and many other objects appearing to be human
forms. Many times, with my Winchester at my shoulder, I watched
for a movement, but as none was discernible I was spared the painful duty of killing a red man and arousing the sleepers. The following day our train pulled into Rapid City. Here we found hundreds
of people who had just arrived from Cheyenne and Sidney. However, they were practically all on the move or preparing to move
northward to Deadwood, the Mecca of all travelers. This was
early in May.

As for myself, I was desirous, before going any further north,
of seeing and examining, to my own satisfaction, the wonderful
"Jenney's Bar" on Rapid Creek. So I stored my stock of eatables
which consisted of more than one hundred pounds of crackers and
other items of lesser importance, in a dirt warehouse. These I
subsequently had brought up to Deadwood, by which time they
had considerably appreciated in value and had also seemingly improved in flavor. After storing these goods, I walked into a store
which was filled with customers and purchased some mining implements. While being waited upon, I inquired if there was any
one present who was going up Rapid Creek. A dark complexioned
man came up and said that he was going that way. I held a short
conversation with the man who appeared to be a gentleman, as I
afterwards found him to be. He gave his name as Edson and said
that he came first to the Hills with the Jenney expedition in 1875
and that he came again and located a placer claim ten miles up
the creek from Rapid City. He stated further that he believed
that he had a good claim but as yet was uncertain as to its value.

[49]

So I very quickly decided to go with him as did also several others of our Pierre party. We had a team and all together we pulled up stream with Edson. A few miles from Rapid City he pointed out Jenney's Bar. There we tarried for a time while I tried panning from several of the most likely prospect holes of which there were many. (These were the supposed graves seen by that retreating party we had met at Fort Pierre.) The results obtained from the pannings were but two to four light colors, so we passed on as all others before us evidently had done. We reached Edson's Bar at dark and went into camp. About four inches of snow fell that night and the next morning, Edson, who, I soon learned, was more of a hunter than he was miner, proposed to take our party a few miles northward where he said ranged a large herd of elk. This proposal was eagerly accepted by everyone excepting myself although I had a fine gun and was not a bad shot. I had come to prospect and not to hunt.

Leaving me behind, the party set out but not with the intention of annihilating the herd as each man agreed to restrict his limit to one elk. After their departure for the woods, I went quite a distance up and down the creek and scraped the bed rock in a number of the prospect holes along its banks, but without obtaining satisfactory results. So I very quickly decided that Rapid Creek was a failure for placer mining, and gave it up. I was now ready to again hit the trail to Deadwood. Our party of hunters returned to camp at dark. They, with but one exception, reported hard luck. However, by having one experienced hunter in the party, they were enabled to bring in one fine large elk that Edson had downed, so we were amply supplied with fresh meat to last us through to Deadwood. Early the next morning we bade farewell to our generous host and struck the Cheyenne trail for Deadwood.

Our next camp was struck on Little Rapid Creek. Here, because of having fresh meat with us, we were surrounded and annoyed the entire night by a numberless pack of howling and threatening wolves or coyotes, or both. They failed, however, to muster courage to attack us. So without further incident we reached our next camp, the mountain range three miles north east of Deadwood. There we found about one hundred men and a like number of animals, as this was the nearest point out from Deadwood where dry grass or other kind of horse feed was available, and also the point where all trails to Deadwood converged.

On the following morning we landed on the Main Street of Deadwood which in reality was the only street in evidence at the time although the townsite had been surveyed and platted previous to our arrival and every plot of twenty by one hundred feet on Main Street had its owner and occupants in log cabins, tents, brush shacks, and even wagons and other means of showing and holding title. Main Street was at the time a triple wagon dirt road. The dirt, however, was soon worked into the consistency of a mortar in which filthy condition it was held for the major part of each season for many years thereafter. This street at the time was jammed to overflowing by thousands of men, a few women and hundreds of teams and wagons, apparently all in a moving mass. The back streets on hillsides, running parallel to Main, were being cleared of timber and brush preparatory to the erection of log cabins and other means of shelter.

Proceeding up Main Street to its southern terminus which was where the City Hall and the Franklin Hotel are now located, I turned west up Shine Street, unloading my luggage and proceeded to construct a shelter of quaking aspens and spruce boughs on the space where the Methodist parsonage now stands. There I spent my first night in the bustling new city of Deadwood. Not being interested in town property at the time, as so many others were, as mining had been my vocation for some years previous, I lost no time in finding the recorder of Lost Mining District, which embraced all gulches and draws. Finding that gentlemanly and obliging official, and arousing him from his noon day nap in his cabin in Central City, he handed me the books and also gave me all the information he could in answer to my questions. He became subsequently my good friend, William Lardner.

I found, by scanning the records, that everything of supposed value in the way of placers had been located and recorded as early as the second week in January. Returning to Deadwood, I next took the trail through the thick underbrush up Whitewood Gulch, finding every claim of three hundred feet along the gulch staked as far up as Whitetail Gulch. There with the assistance of a helper, I sank a shaft to a depth of seven feet to bedrock, obtaining but small color of gold. Returning to Deadwood I erected a small, comfortable log cabin on upper Main Street. While I was not idle at all times, I was so situated that I could take in, both by day and night, the various assortment of alluring sights and scenes brought to view in the bustling new city of Deadwood.

Here I am speaking in a personal way, yet as one who was common with hundreds, yes, thousands of others, who found conditions and opportunities here at that time just as I found them. Everything that was considered to be of any value whatever, as well as much that could be scarcely deemed worthy of consideration, had already been appropriated.

A great many large pine trees were to be seen on both sides of Deadwood Gulch and many smaller trees of pine and spruce in the gulch proper. These were felled and cleared away preparatory to the opening of the mining season, which rendered travel by wagon, and even on horseback, extremely difficult. There were a considerable number of log cabins strung along up the gulch. Many of them had sufficed in affording shelter and comfort to two or more occupants during the winter. One of these, just above Deadwood, was conspicuous in having a large, black bearskin tacked up against it. The bear had been killed near by by one of the occupants of the cabin, by the name of Lobeck, a noted violinist and later a victim of John Barleycorn. I mention this as being the only bear ever killed or seen near the city of Deadwood.

These cabins were covered with poles laid close together with pine or with spruce boughs and a heavy coat of soil on top, which was afterward utilized by many who could procure the seeds, for vegetable gardens. The lumber for the doors, and in some for the floors, was made of whipsaw lumber. There are many who have never seen a whipsaw in motion, so I will explain briefly how it is operated. A pit is dug, over which a framework of timbers is arranged for holding fast a saw log, which is first hewn on two sides. One man stands on top of the frame and draws the saw up and pushes it downward while the man in the pit pushes it upward. There were a few large pine trees as well as a thick growth of small trees and underbrush on both sides of the main street in Deadwood. Lee Street consisted of two slippery foot logs over the creek. The junction of the two streams, Whitewood and Deadwood creeks, as I now remember it, was lower down stream than at present. These waters were clear and contained an abundance of small fish of a bony species. All of these perished during the first days of sluicing in the gulch above.

Sounds of axes, hammers, and saws were heard in all directions. Carpenters and other mechanics were in great demand. Any ordinary wood butcher who could furnish the three essential implements of woodcraft could easily qualify as a carpenter and builder. The new town of Deadwood was rapidly converted into a city of no mean proportions. There were two saw mills within its borders and others on the outskirts. All were working overtime in turning out lumber at stiff prices. In less than a fortnight after these mills were put into operation practically every building had its merchant, and every merchant had something desirable (or undesirable) to be exchanged for coin of the realm at prices fixed by and satisfactory to the merchant.

Almost any old timer, who has a clear memory, could easily arrive at a fair estimate of the number of dispensers of liquid "refreshments" by counting upon his fingers the number of other business places where they were not kept for sale and subtracting that from the total number of town lots on both sides of Main Street.

Young Deadwood now, with its increasing population and two established mail routes and two competitive post offices, was making great strides and tremendous efforts to find a place in the sun and was taking the lead by opening up a world exposition in miniature, with Main Street as its midway. There were no elephants, camels, or yaks procurable. It had, however, in addition to its complement of high class, high bucking bronchos and cayuses, an oversupply of tigers, blind pigs and other dangerous animals, which when once encountered, could never be forgotten. However, they were usually inoffensive and harmless, no matter how closely one approached to them, so long as one refrained from poking a hand in their mouths or twisting their tails.

There were many attractive games, devices and schemes put into operation for the purpose of extracting wealth from the numerous free milling propositions so easily discovered a few feet above the grass roots within the limits of this golden city. These finds were termed, in mining parlance, as "pocket deposit." Some of the more alluring and attractive chance games which appeared to offer (without guarantee) an absolute certainty of securing a much desired homestake at the risk of a few dollars, were being staged by torchlight at intervals along the muddy street, in front of saloons and other business places. They were presided over by oily-tongued individuals whose oratorical attainments and attractive personalities well fitted them for driving a profitable trade in their special line of business, that of opening the eyes of the blind and bringing avaricious mortals to a grievous and humiliating state of repentance.

XIII

GOLD SEEKERS OF '76 FROM MONTANA

THE largest aggregation of stampeders to enter the Black Hills in a single body during the big gold rush of '76, was composed of more than two hundred men. They were adequately equipped with saddle horses, pack horses, and a large wagon train loaded to the guards with provisions and adequate supply of provender for their animals. They also had many useful implements deemed necessary in the development of a new country, whether it be mining, agriculture, or other industry.

This formidable body of Black Hills intruders was made up of miners, farmers, merchants and tradesmen of all kinds to be found in and around Helena, Deer Lodge, and other points in Montana territory. All of them were seasoned westerners with no tenderfeet among them. They were armed with the most effective firearms obtainable, prepared to meet, and no doubt were expecting to meet, strong opposition from the hostile Sioux Indians.

This notable outfit started out the first week of April, 1876. Many of its members had been well known to this writer in the years preceding, as ever-ready stampeders if not practical miners, and like him, had more than once been stricken with that inescapable midwinter stampede epidemic which pervaded every Rocky Mountain gold mining camp. Few of the inhabitants, if any, were immune. So the members of this contingent of Black Hills gold seekers had learned from their bitter experiences in having rushed precipitately from their cozy winter quarters. They had been poorly prepared to undergo the hardships to be encountered in the day and night tramps of floundering through snow drifts in frantic endeavors to reach at the earliest hour possible their destinations, which were usually in the most inaccessible mountain regions, only to meet with grievous disappointment.

[55]

With such experiences as reminders, this huge caravan of Montana argonauts started out amply prepared with all requirements for insuring safety and comfort on the trip. William Langston was elected captain of the company, with Joseph Cook as his assistant. This militant outfit, though it proved to be cumbersome as was evidenced by the number of weeks required in moving through hundreds of miles of trackless forests, came through without notable incidents, until it had reached a point some distance west of "Devils Tower," Wyoming, where the outfit went into camp. While all hands were busily engaged in arranging their stock and camp equipment for the night's rest, they were surprised and fired upon by a large band of Sioux Indians. One of their number, George Miller, was killed. The Reds withdrew immediately before an effective return fire could be made. Miller was buried by the roadside and the Indians harassed the party at intervals until it reached a point east of Sundance Mountains where it went into camp. Here they were again attacked, so fiercely that they were forced to dig a number of rifle pits preparatory to receiving a large, determined force of Sioux Indians, as at that time seemed to be imminent. The Indians, however, apparently had realized that they were up against a dangerous proposition, and left the field.

The party next came in sight of the beautiful Spearfish Valley, and on the 10th day of May pulled up to its final camp grounds where the beautiful Queen City of the Hills is now situated. Although many members of the party plunged immediately into the northern Black Hills in search of gold placer locations, they were soon convinced that everything of value in that line had already been appropriated. The majority of them returned to Spearfish Valley, where nearly the entire Montana party, with a few from other parties, united in the plan of preempting and opening up to settlement the entire Spearfish Valley. This plan was promptly executed. In the meantime they effected a town organization and on the 28th of May laid out the townsite and gave it the name of Spearfish, "Queen City of the Hills."

XIV

THE FIRST NEWSPAPER

IN the winter of 1875-76, W. A. Laughlin and A. W. Merrick purchased a complete printing outfit in Denver and had it shipped by team freight to Custer. In May, '76, it was set up there and they got out a small sheet which (it is said) they called the *Black Hills Weekly Pioneer*. This is not disputed, although it was my belief for many years that the title was suggested and accepted after the plant was set up in Deadwood. The rush to Deadwood from Custer came on like a whirlwind and in less than forty-eight hours after the first issue of the paper Custer was practically depopulated and Laughlin was prostrated with tuberculosis. Captain C. V. Gardner saw the plight they were in and kindly guaranteed payment of the freight, so the plant arrived in Deadwood and was set up the first week in June. On the 8th of June the first issue in Deadwood was published. Joe Kubler who subsequently established the *Custer Chronicle*, was pressman. This was in a small log cabin just back of the Ike Brown store on the narrow alley called "Broadway."

The circumstances which gave me the impression that the title to the paper originated in Deadwood was the fact that quite a number of us gathered there while preparations for getting out the first issue were being made. Then J. W. Matkin said, "Let's name the paper the *Black Hills Pioneer.*" Why would he have made that suggestion if it was already named?

The first, as well as many succeeding issues, was readily sold at twenty-five cents each. The Fourth of July number, an elaborate affair of many pages in the national colors, was completely sold out before the demand was half supplied. The writer, by being on the ground early, procured two copies to send away.

XV

THE METZ FAMILY MURDER

ONE of the most horrifying tragedies which left an indelible
mark on one of the many crimsoned trails leading into the Black
Hills during those stirring days of '76, occurred in the latter part
of April of that year. This was the murder, by the Indians, in Red
Canyon in the southern part of the Hills, of the entire Metz party,
consisting of Mr. and Mrs. Metz, their teamster, whose name was
not learned, and a colored woman, whose name I recall as Rachel
Briggs, though this may be erroneous.

Mr. Metz, a prosperous baker in Laramie, Wyoming, disposed
of his property in that city early in 1876, loaded his wagon with
practically all requisites for establishing a bakery, and with his
group, all of whom were able to travel on foot, arrived in the new
town of Custer City in February, 1876. Here he opened up a bakery,
with the colored woman as an experienced cook, and conducted a
lucrative business until about the middle of April, when the big
rush to Deadwood came on and Custer and Hill City were almost
depopulated.

Instead of joining the rush, Mr. Metz decided to return to
Laramie. On the day he had intended to start from Custer, Scott
Davis arrived from Cheyenne with a mule train of freight. Metz
inquired of him whether he had seen any Indians. Scott informed
him that he had not, but advised him not to go out of the Hills
alone, and to wait until the next day and go with his train on its
return to Cheyenne. Notwithstanding this good advice, Metz let
his anxiety to leave the Hills get the better of his judgment. He
determined to make a start and go out as far as Cheyenne River
Ranch and await the coming of Davis.

The four of them started and found no trouble in reaching the mouth of Red Canyon, where they camped for dinner. They had prepared their meal and were, as was shown by indications later, sitting under a large tree, presumably with no expectation of danger or little thought of Indians being in that vicinity. Suddenly the report of fire arms rang out. Metz fell dead with a rifle bullet through his head and several through his body. It appeared that the other three of the party had either escaped the first volley, or had not been seriously wounded, as they evidently had made a dash for safety. The teamster's body was found about a half mile from the wagon and Mrs. Metz had succeeded in getting still farther away when a rifle bullet passed through her heart.

The next morning, Robert Floorman, who was in charge of a party passing through the Canyon, found the three victims with their bodies mutilated. Mrs. Floorman assisted in preparing the bodies for burial. My recollection is that the late George A. Clark, from whom the writer received the details of the tragedy, had charge of the interment of the victims. I know that he had charge of burial of a goodly number of other victims of the Reds in that vicinity.

The wagons of the party had been ransacked, the trunks and boxes broken up, and the contents scattered about, according to Mr. Clark's information regarding this deplorable affair. It was well known that Mr. Metz had enjoyed prosperous business during his stay in Custer and he probably had with him a large sum of money. It was the belief of many that "Persimmons Bill," well known road agent and murderer, who had spent much of his time about the agencies and was believed to be in league with the Indians, was the leader in this Metz massacre for the loot.

Although diligent search for the body of the colored woman was made at the time, it was not located until several days later, when Captain C. V. Gardner went out from Custer on his way to Cheyenne, accompanied by a number who were leaving the Hills. They made noon camp in the canyon near the site of the murder. On resuming his journey, Captain Gardner took a cut-off trail along the creek. He saw the body of the woman in a small ravine, leaning with her face against the bank and arms back of her neck, in an upright position with an arrow sticking in her back.

The Odd Fellows Lodge of Laramie, of which Metz was a member, sent a party of which the late Herman Bischoff was one, to take the bodies of both Mr. and Mrs. Metz to Laramie where they were given ritual interment by the order. The remains of the driver and the colored woman still repose in Red Canyon.

XVI

THE TRAGEDY OF PINO SPRINGS

IT is a matter of regret that but few of the early pioneers who were in the Black Hills prior to the establishment of newspapers and other agencies for the dissemination of news, kept any record of the many exciting and vitally important events that transpired, both in the Hills and along the trails during that period. Consequently many incidents of a tragic nature, and other very interesting episodes, if not wholly overlooked, were given little publicity afterwards.

One of these is now recalled, of which I have knowledge as I was on the ground shortly after the occurrence and learned the facts from one of the parties who participated in the obsequies which followed. The details, as I now recall them, are as follows:

Some time during the month of April, 1876, a horse freight train was put on the road between Fort Pierre and Rapid City by John Dillon, a wealthy merchant of Fort Pierre, for the purpose of furnishing supplies for the Black Hills trade. While on its first trip west, camp was struck at a point on the road known as Pino Springs. During the night a valuable mare was crippled but was taken along four miles next day and left by the roadside. The train proceeded on its way to the Hills, where the freight was unloaded and the train started on its return trip to Pierre.

On reaching the place where the animal was left, it was found to have so far recovered from its injury as to be able to travel, but for some reason, it was left behind and the train went on to Pino Springs, where an early camp was made.

John Harrison, the train master, then started back with two horses attached to a spring wagon, taking with him three men, one named Edwin Sadler, one known as "Texas Jack," the other H. N. Gardner.

[61]

They caught the mare and started to return to camp. In crossing a narrow valley along which ran a dry creek (it was afterwards called "Deadman Gulch"), which was skirted by small trees and underbrush, close to and paralleling the road for several hundred feet, they were fired upon by Indians at close range and literally shot to pieces. The horses, it appeared, had then run in a circle, one running faster than the other, bringing them back close to the starting point, where they stopped.

The bodies of the men were all found on the wagon, stripped of their apparel, and everything else was taken except the wagon and a song book. It was believed that the men were singing in a group when the fatal volley was fired.

A grave was dug and the bodies of the four unfortunate victims were shrouded in their blankets, placed side by side, covered with earth and left in that lonely spot, soon to be forgotten by the world.

An account of this tragedy may have been published long ago in Black Hills papers, but if so it escaped my notice.

XVII

THE BULLWHACKERS

UP to the middle of June, 1876, much of the freight shipped into the Black Hills was brought in by outfits of two and four horse teams. Large trains of oxen were also used. Hundreds of people who were coming in with their own teams were employed by merchants to haul in their goods. It was not long before long lines of mule and ox trains were seen all along the three routes into the Hills. The larger trains, as I now remember, were those of J. J. Evans, Hornick, Witcher & Sons. Others of importance were Pratt and Ferris, John Dillon, Noah Newbanks, Morris Appel, M. V. Shoun, Hedges, John Isaccs, Captain Dotson, Edgar Brothers (John and Fred).

After these trains, of from six to eight mules and from six to ten yoke of oxen of the long horn Texas variety, came in, it was not unusual to see Main Street completely blocked for hours and even half a day at a time, by one and sometimes two lines of these trains. There would invariably be at least two, and more frequently three, freight wagons heavily loaded and down to their hubs in mud slowly following each long string of oxen, the leaders of which would have a spread of horns from three to four feet. These teams would be so closely jammed together as to practically cut off for many hours all intercourse from one side of the street to the other. More especially was it so for women folks as men could manage to climb over wagons connected or dodge past the lead team; but not so the women as the leaders of these bull trains, after being lashed and goaded by their merciless drivers and tortured by flies, became vicious and dangerous.

These animals, like their overworked drivers, when in action were seldom if ever in agreeable frame of mind, as there was never a more strenuous and exciting occupation than that of the bull-whackers, whose viciousness was freely imparted to the suffering animals under their charge. However, it may be said that some of these drivers were different, especially those who were owners of the animals.

These bullwhackers were provided with instruments of animal torture, which consisted of a hickory staff from four to five feet in length, to which was attached a large leathern whip sixteen to twenty feet in length, with a buckskin thong one or more feet long by half inch wide at the end. The expert manipulator of this implement of torture would first swirl it a few times around over his head and then direct the lash to any particular spot he chose on the animal to be punished, where it would strike with such a force that a sound like the crack of a rifle would follow. The suffering brute could only twist and squirm while the blood would ooze from a wound which would be immediately covered for further punishment by a swarm of flies. These animals were used in the freighting business so long as they were serviceable for that purpose, then sold to be "fleshened up" on green grass and later passed into the hands of Black Hills butchers, thence to the ultimate consumer.

XVIII

EARLY-DAY ATTRACTIONS AND BUSINESS

IN this story I shall endeavor to portray faithfully the many alluring attractions which, in a very brief space of time, sprang into existence on both sides of Main Street along its entire length, and which were kept in active operation, not only in the spring and summer of '76, but as long thereafter as they continued to be sources of revenue to their promoters. Many of these attractions furnished amusement and refreshments for all who chose to patronize them and pay the price; the major part of them, however, were designed chiefly for the purpose of separating the unsophisticated traveler from his roll of currency, without giving anything of value in return.

The first dance hall, or what was known both in Montana and in the Black Hills as "hurdy gurdy house," was opened for business about the first day of May, 1876, in a large, round log house on the corner of Main and Shine streets where the Black Hills Trust and Savings Bank building now stands. This location was at that time a hill eight feet above the present street level. The floor was of sawed lumber. The proprietor of the hall had for a nucleus in making up a floor set, his own wife and daughter. In a very short time, however, he added six other "beauties" and his floor space was crowded nightly with a desirable class of customers. His hastily improvised bar was liberally patronized and altogether everything in connection with his enterprise appeared to be working to his advantage.

But this success was short-lived. The famous, or infamous, "Gem Theater," of which I shall have something to say later, was shortly opened to the public. This soon absorbed the trade of the first dance hall promoter and put him out of business. He either sold or abandoned his building (it was later sold for taxes), and departed for new fields.

Nearly all of the saloons and other business houses at the time of which I speak, were situated north of Lee Street, as the heavy grade between Lee and Shine streets and the hostility of the claim owners of Numbers 24 and 25, had greatly retarded building in that section. There were several saloons on each side of Main Street in the block between Lee and Gold streets. Below the latter, however, both sides of Main Street were occupied chiefly by saloons and various other sporting houses. In going down Main Street in the evening one would see on each side a row of kerosene torch lights.

In front of the houses and crowded around many of the lights were scores of people listening to some fakir or "con man" explain in convincing terms just how easily and quickly one could coin money by investing a few dollars in a game where the chances of winning a handsome sum were five or ten to one in his favor. In going down the street the first of these was "Soapy" Taylor, a rough-visaged individual with a big mouth and brazen lungs, whose sole stock in trade was an ordinary suitcase well filled with small cubes of soap. Each of these was neatly wrapped in paper, and a large percentage of them according to his story, were also wrapped in bills of from one to five dollars. These packages were offered at fifty cents each. While explaining the advantages in favor of the customer, he would reach down without looking, pick up one, unwrap it and show a bill, ofttimes two or three in succession. Some "capper" for his game would then purchase one and he also would find a one or two dollar bill. At this stage of the game some of the outsiders would become interested and the sale would be started. Occasionally some one would draw a prize, but the majority of them got only the soap. So in selling several hundreds of the packages "Soapy" would, by giving away fifty or sixty dollars, realize double the amount.

Farther down, on the corner of Main and Gold streets, was located the "Wide West Saloon," owned by Jim Persate. This was first sheltered by a large tent but it soon gave way to a substantial building. Here was one of the first, if not the first, "faro banks" to be put into operation in the new city of Deadwood. This faro table was presided over by different persons, among whom was a short, pudgy, unattractive French woman known as "Madam Mustache" because of having an abnormal growth of hair on her upper lip, which she appeared to cultivate. She was said to be the proprietress of the bank. Her associate was an individual known as "Big Thumb" Jake who had a thumb of great size. Their game was said to be conducted "on the square," as were, so far as the writer knows, all games of faro, with the percentage, of course, being strongly in favor of their operators. This saloon was also equipped with a bar, poker tables, clubroom, and other gambling devices.

Just across the street was the "Eureka Hall." This was a large frame building which had been hastily constructed as soon as lumber was obtainable. It was provided with a bar in front, with a stage or low platform at the rear, and floor space which was covered by one hundred or more chairs and benches. Upon the stage was constructed a large upright wheel and on this were painted many numbers. There were also a great number of paddles, and on the paddles were painted numbers to correspond with those on the wheel. These paddles were sold to customers at fifty cents each. The investor could take one or as many as he wished. The chairs and seats were usually pretty well filled and the paddles all taken. The operator would give the big wheel a vigorous whirl and after spinning around many times it would stop and the number at the top would be the winning number and the man holding the paddle with the same number would call out "Keno" while many of the others would mutter "Oh, hell." I was not informed as to the percentage of the game. No doubt it was greatly in favor of the operator.

Excellent music was furnished here continuously as far into the night as the crowd of people would justify. It was here that Eugene Holman, an accomplished violinist, and his consort, "Monte Verde," one of the finest singers ever heard in Deadwood, furnished the music. This hall was used later solely as a saloon, dance hall, and gambling house. In that hall I have seen captured criminals who had been traced from other parts of the country, sitting handcuffed beside Deputy U. S. Marshals, the captives waiting for the captors to go broke at the faro bank before being taken to their beds for the night.

Next on the corner of Main and Wall streets was Gus Schugart's

[67]

beer hall and gambling house. Here one could see nearly every night a packed house, with fist fights, knock downs, and gun plays. However, I knew of only one innocent bystander being killed, although this writer barely escaped on one occasion when a cocked revolver fell at my feet and failed to be discharged.

On the opposite corner from Gus's place where the Fairmont Hotel is now located, was "The Melodeon," a well appointed saloon and gambling house with a stage at the rear. Here "Handsome Dick" Brown, first "Deadwood Dick," a comedian, banjo player, and baritone singer, with his consort, Fannie Garrettson, and Ed Shaunessey, entertained packed houses nightly. Dick was in reality the greatest drawing card in the city. He had many up-to-date songs in his repertoire which he would sing to the delight of all who heard him.

One door below "The Melodeon" one man was killed with a prostitute. Three doors below was located the "Bella Union," owned and managed by Bill Nuthall, a well seasoned character, if not a criminal. This theater, saloon, and all-round gambling house, was one of the most disreputable joints on the street. Two men were killed in this joint in quarrels over prostitutes.

Just below the "Bella Union" was the "Saloon No. 10" fitted out with bar, poker tables, and clubroom. This was the saloon where Wild Bill met his death.

"Nutshell Bill" operated his shell game in different saloons on lower Main Street where he caught scores of inexperienced suckers who had never heard of a thimble rig game. Bill had three halves of hickory nutshells which he manipulated on a table. These he placed a few inches apart from each other. Under one of these he put a rubber ball the size of a pea. Then with the tips of his fingers he would move first one and then another. Looking away from the shells he would expose the ball so that everyone who happened to be looking could plainly see which shell it was under. He would then raise his hands from the table and offer to take any bet that anyone would make that he could pick the shell which contained the ball. Everyone looking had seen the ball and, of course, they knew which shell it was under. Invariably there would be at least one who was willing to bet $10 or $50 that he could pick the shell. Bill had manipulated the ball under another shell. A roar of laughter would follow, while the victim of his own folly would quietly withdraw. However, his place would soon be taken by another who was just as eager to make easy money. Of the hundreds of onlookers, not one would dare to interpose in these games, unless in the case of a partner or a particular friend. In such event he would have to make quick time in getting out of the room. Most of these crooks and tricksters were provided with "bouncers" and sluggers. The operators were usually well trained in the art of slugging. I have seen "Nutshell Bill" jump from his seat and pound up men much larger than his size.

On the east side of Main Street, directly opposite "No. 10," was constructed early in June a large, two story frame building. This abominable institution was at first called a "hurdy-gurdy" house but was later known far and wide as the "Gem Theatre." It would require an abler pen than mine to portray anything approaching a true picture of the inside workings of that notorious den of iniquity. By reason of its drawing financial support from so many of the so-called leading citizens of the city, as well as from practically all residents and floaters of the underworld who drifted into the Hills at the time, it very soon won and held for many years, to the everlasting shame of Deadwood, the distinction of being the city's chief attraction, being rebuilt after the big fire. Notwithstanding that churches and theaters had sprung up early in the new town and were fairly well supported, the old "Gem Theatre" outstripped them all and flourished, probably far beyond the wildest dreams of its dissolute and degraded promoter, Al Swearengen.

This indictment is not based merely on the fact of his owning and operating a saloon and dance hall, but more on his brutal methods of operating them. The floor in front was provided with a bar on one side and with seats for waiting patrons and spectators on each side. The rear end of the long building was cut up into small rooms. It was here that he kept under strict surveillance his herd of so-called female employees, when in fact they were on the level of "white slaves." His first installment of these unfortunate creatures were indeed a motley crew, of ungainly features and uncertain ages. However, they carried out their contracts so long as they were physically able to do so. The duties devolving on them was to dance the entire night or just as long as they could secure partners. During the first few weeks it appeared that they were overstocked with partners, as there were many strangers coming in who were desirous of being able to say that they had once danced in a "hurdy-gurdy house." There were also many others who were so exhilarated that they would hang on to their female partners all night, or so long as their pocket change held out. This was true especially of the teamsters known as "bullwhackers." Many of those festive souls would frequently, after unloading their freight, take their teams out to graze for the night and then hike back to the "Gem" to spend the night and also all of their available cash in one way or another under its roof.

Swearengen kept at all times a full crew of understrappers, with Dan Dority as general manager and Johnny Burns as floor manager, and several burly "bouncers" whose duties were to see to it that those who had spent their money, kept quiet or hit the side walks. All of these underlings were of the same low grade of morals as their boss and each, like himself, had his "woman" with the sole privilege of "beating her up" at any and all times that suited his pleasure, which was no uncommon occurrence.

On one occasion as I was passing up the street, I heard a great clash of voices and a shot fired. I waited until others had rushed in and following them, I beheld a man lying on the floor with a bullet hole clear through his head back of his eyes. The woman "Tricksie" had grabbed a pistol while he was beating her and turned the tables on him. A doctor came and ran a probe through his head. However, there were no brains, at least in that section of his skull. A few weeks afterward I met the same man on the street.

Swearengen made frequent trips to the states for female recruits. Those he selected he promised employment in hotels or in respectable families, thus inducing them to accompany him to the Hills, to be landed and stranded in the "Gem Theatre." Such were the stories of many of these unfortunate women. Some of them who refused to submit to Al's absolute and inexorable decree of subservience, and those who failed to measure up to his requirements as classy attractions, were peremptorily discarded and put out, if not forcibly kicked out, on the streets to take refuge in brothels or other places where the management was not wholly devoid of all sense of human feeling.

This vicious institution, in its later years, was conducted principally as a theater, and frequently procured some of the best talent found among traveling attractions. However, it continued to the end in maintaining its notorious record as a defiler of youth, a destroyer of home ties, and a veritable abomination.

I have presented this unpleasant subject at some length, without going further than touching its high points, in endeavoring to give you a partial description of a few of the numerous alluring and misleading attractions which were operated along the entire length of Main Street during the pioneer days of Deadwood. In them, persuasive eloquence, intoxicating liquors, enameled beauties, and stupefying concoctions were freely used in effecting the purposes for which these attractions were designed, namely, separating by foul means inexperienced and incautious individuals from their money; and the degradation and pollution of the pure and undefiled by reducing them to the same depths of infamy which they, the designers, themselves occupied. I will now drop this subject and speak of the many more legitimate business enterprises which came into existence during the spring and summer months of '76.

The first saloon to open for business in Deadwood was a one story rough log house, about 14 x 20 feet, situated on the corner of Main and Gold streets. This was built and owned by Craven Lee and Ike Brown, two of the locators of the townsite. Lee later built and occupied another building two doors east of the south corner of Main and Lee streets, where he had his office as city recorder. Brown soon after opening his saloon, sold in connection with it a small stock of groceries. Over the front door of the store was painted conspicuously a crescent shaped sign "Zion's Cooperative Mercantile Institution" which gave the impression that one or both of them were of the Mormon faith.

These two men appeared to be opposites in temperament and characteristics. Lee appeared to be an easy going, pleasant man to meet, while Brown was quick tempered and hot headed, ever ready for a fight, and did fight on more than one occasion. He served as "sheriff" at the trial of Jack McCall for killing "Wild Bill" Hickok. However his career was short-lived and his lifeless body was brought into his store and prepared for burial on the twenty-first of the following August.

Just who brought in the first stock of groceries I have no clear recollection. There were several stores opened for business at about the same time. Captain C. V. Gardner erected the first frame building which was two stories, on the lot adjoining Brown's store and saloon. He had the largest stock of goods that came in at the time. Bent and Deetkin opened up the first drug store, which was on the east side of Main Street. Dave Holsman opened a clothing store opposite Brown's, on Main Street. This stone-log building he rented of John Beuter who had traded a pair of mules and a wagon for it. Holsman was the only renter that I ever heard of who refused to pay his rent on the ground that the owner had no legal title to the lot. So Beuter sold the lot to him for a small sum rather than put him out or off the earth as many others would have done.

There were quite a number of eating houses opened to the public on Main Street where one could, for the trifling sum of $1.00, get at least a satisfying meal, if not a square one. These meals were served minus pastries or desserts of any kind. No provision was made in these eating places for a resting place for the unfortunate patron who had, in his frantic haste to get here first, left his blanket behind. The sawdust floor had to suffice for his tired frame.

The first real hotel opened where the weary stranger could, in addition to his meals, get for the price of $1.00, a roughly improvised bunk, or if he preferred it, floor space for his blankets, was a two-story frame building which covered the entire lot on which it was erected and conducted by its owner, Charles H. Wagner, who christened it "The Grand Central." The first cook in this first up-to-date hostelry, if my memory is correct, was "Aunt Lou" Marshbanks, a colored woman, who was born a slave and had been educated in a southern kitchen. However, she did not long serve in that position as A. J. Bowie, Superintendent of the Father DeSmet Mine, induced her to resign and accept a like position with less work and increased salary, in the Company's boarding house. Here she reigned as its mistress for many years, and later lived and died on a ranch of her own, liked and respected by all who knew her.

Before the month of July had passed a goodly number of two-story hotels were opened for business, furnishing good meals and ample rooms to accommodate all who could pay the prices, which were not exorbitant when the high cost of provisions was considered. The "Wentworth," a large two-story frame building which was located on the lots now occupied by the Elks building, was built and conducted by J. D. Cornell. The "Custer House," a two-story frame building, was erected on the corner of Main and Lee streets by Scollard and Ammerman, who conducted it for a time, then sold it to other parties who conducted it until the fire of '79. The "I. X. L. Hotel" was owned and conducted by Van Danaker.

North of, and adjoining the "Custer House" on Main Street, was a theater building owned by a stock company (not incorporated), built to accommodate Jack Langrishe, a versatile comedian and tragedian, and give the community the privilege of seeing a first-class theatrical performance in the new town. Jack was well known to all westerners as a highly rated actor and theatrical manager, and also as a comical writer. He had been known to reach the acme of his profession, at least so far as going flat broke goes. Such was his condition when he arrived in Deadwood. Most all old westerners here knew how to appreciate and sympathize with this versatile genius. However, Jack did not drift into Deadwood, as did many other notable personages. He came in as a first class stage passenger, leaving such of his paraphernalia as could not be packed in trunks "in soak" in Cheyenne. He brought with him a cast of high grade talent such as Jimmy Martin, Jimmy Griffith, and others of equal talent. He met here a number of those who had given him support when he first appeared on the stage in Denver in the sixties. Among these was this writer's Montana roommate during the winter of '70-'71, Edwin R. "Windy" Collins, who was born in New York City and practically educated on the stage, who could carry through his role in any Shakespearian play.

Langrishe, however, not being able to bring with him such of his scenery and stage settings as was indispensable in launching his show, was compelled to employ J. N. Robison, a first-class painter, decorator and scenic artist, to fit him out with a full set of scenery, and stage trappings from drop curtains to all minor requisites in staging his show. After overcoming the many perplexing difficulties met in getting his stage settings arranged, Jack finally opened his theater to a waiting and impatient public some time in July, at moderate prices, $1.50 for the house where sitting or standing room was available.

While his repertoire of plays was not strictly up-to-date, they were good and gave satisfaction to packed houses. After playing for a few weeks he closed the house, turned his attention to gold mining, and took a losing chance in the Big Horn Mountain Stampede, one of the many exciting and expensive fizzles of '76. The theater building was later utilized as a saloon known as the "Senate" and was conducted for a time by Mann and Manning. It was one of the liveliest institutions of the time, where numerous exciting episodes were frequently staged, altho I can recall no fatalities occurring in that particular resort. There were, however, on several occasions, exhibitions of playful gun maneuvers which reminded the spectators that they were badly in need of fresh air, and some of them were not averse to walking over others to obtain it. It was here that the reputed "mankiller" Johnnie Varnes, presided at one of the faro layouts, and where he and the corpulent Charley Storms, another noted gambler, engaged in a dispute over a card game which resulted in a pistol duel on Main Street. It ended in a bloodless affair so far as the combatants were concerned, but not so fortunately for Joe Ludwig, an innocent bystander, who received a severe flesh wound.

Hardly a day or night passed during the spring and summer months without contributing something in the way of intensely interesting and exciting episodes, dramatic and ludicrous, not always of a tragic nature. People were constantly kept in a state of expectancy and wondering what would happen next.

Many of that great army of the unemployed, who were camped all over the town and on the hillsides, would scarcely spare the time to stir up their camp fires and prepare their scanty meals of flap jacks, bacon, beans, and black coffee of uncertain vintage. This they hurriedly ate and hastened to Main Street fearing that they might miss witnessing some interesting episode. Apparently every man who came to the Black Hills did so for the purpose of getting out of the trip all that there was in it, and many there were who got more than they had expected or bargained for. Main Street in Deadwood appeared to offer the best opportunities in the line of attractions. Street fights, knock downs, gun plays, and occasional gun shots and blood lettings occurred frequently. The throwing or kicking out on the streets, by bartenders, of men who, after spending all their money, would call for drinks and even "set 'em up" to their pals while knowing that they had not a cent to pay the bill, was a common occurrence. Oftentimes compromises were effected and bloody noses averted by the irate barkeeper becoming the possessor of a gold ring or a diamond stick pin; not infrequently a gold or silver watch would change ownership, at the price of one or a few drinks of "rot-gut," so-called cocktails. In this way many misunderstandings which might have developed into serious difficulties were satisfactorily adjusted, at least so far as the bartender was concerned. Many times, in the fullness of his heart, he would proffer an extra drink or two to his unfortunate customer. It may safely be asserted that none who followed the practice of dealing out spirituous liquors over the bar of a saloon retired from the business with as clean hands and a conscience as clear as when he entered it. It is well known to all old timers that no less than ninety per cent of those who followed the profession of retailing intoxicating liquors over the bar in the principal towns in the Black Hills, lived openly and apparently shamelessly with a low class of prostitutes. This vicious practice was by no means confined to bartenders. Many of the leading business and professional men were equally guilty.

XIX

THE FIRST SAWMILLS

Up to the middle of June, '76, practically every house built in Deadwood was constructed of logs, some rough and some hewn, although there had been much whipsawed lumber turned out at and around Central City. This, however, was used up chiefly in construction of sluice boxes for placer mining. These boxes were made of inch lumber twelve feet in length and twelve inches wide.

The bottom was dressed down from twelve inches at the upper to ten inches at the lower end so that the small end of one would fit tightly, without nailing, into the large end of the one below. By fitting them together thus they could be easily moved.

About the first of June three sawmills were shipped in and were immediately put into operation. One of these was located in "Elizabethtown," now the first ward in Deadwood. It was owned by Dudley and Caldwell, two real gentlemen. Another sawmill was put in operation about the same time in the present fourth ward, where the county court house and jail now stand. This was owned by Boughton and Berry. The third mill was west of the present Northwestern round house.

These mills, it was said, turned out daily about twenty thousand feet of lumber for some time thereafter, as timber was abundant and easily available at that time. With this supply of lumber within easy reach, Deadwood was soon built up with one and two story frame buildings. Within a very short time after these mills were put in operation several others were located in the heavy forest which then surrounded Deadwood and ever since lumber has been plentiful at reasonable prices. It was in that first year of occupation of the Black Hills by white men that the destruction of their magnificent forests, their crowning grandeur, had its inception.

XX

BEEF CATTLE FOR BLACK HILLS MARKETS

SEVERAL droves of beef cattle were brought into the Hills during the summer of '76 to supply fresh meat. This was, at the time, an extremely hazardous undertaking, as the Indians were at all times on the alert for droves of animals. Knowing that it was impossible for the owners of these droves to employ a sufficient number of herders to protect them against any considerable number of raiders, the Indians were ever ready to swoop down on them.

Mark V. Boughton, the sawmill owner, brought the first drove of cattle to the Hills, reaching here without interference. He located his herd on lower False Bottom Creek, about twenty miles north of Deadwood. The wily Reds soon discovered this location and his utter lack of defense. Shortly after his arrival they swooped down upon his herd, and after killing the herder, stampeded and cleaned out the herd, leaving him practically broke.

Capt. Oliver Dotson, a former steamboat captain who first came to the Hills in January, '76, returned to Nebraska where he procured an ox train of nearly one hundred head of fine cattle and brought in a heavy shipment of freight for the merchants. After unloading his cargo he also took his cattle to lower False Bottom Creek, and his herd, like Boughton's, became easy prey to the marauding Reds who took possession and escaped with the entire herd.

John and Rasse Deffenbach, brothers, succeeded in reaching the Hills in '76 from Colorado with a drove of cattle and a band of horses. They located in the Spearfish Valley and soon developed a profitable business by supplying the butchers in the mining towns with a choice grade of fresh meat for their "sowbelly" and beans customers, of whom the writer was one. They soon afterwards

[77]

moved their herd and camp over into the Belle Fourche Valley where they located a large tract and established the V. M. cattle ranch, but very soon thereafter sold the outfit to Clark and Plum, other cattlemen. The Deffenbachs soon gathered up another herd of about three hundred cattle and a number of horses, and finding a suitable location on Sweet Water Creek, Wyoming, near the Bear Lodge Mountains, they decided to establish another stock ranch in that valley. They were just getting fairly established in their new home when a band of Redskins swooped down on the party in charge of the herd, killing John Deffenbach, the older brother, throwing his body into a washout, and stampeding the entire herd. Rasse Deffenbach was at the time in the Deadwood hospital with a broken leg. A party led by Dan Deffenbach, a younger brother, started in pursuit of the marauding Indians, overtook and engaged them in battle. A man named Rhodes was killed in the fight, as were also several of the Indians, and a few horses were recovered. It was in that vicinity that this writer saw John Deffenbach with his herd of cattle, on his way to and from the mythical Wolfe Mountain gold region. That occurred in the latter part of November, 1876, before they had established their stock ranch on Sweet Water Creek.

Some time in the latter part of March, '76, a party of seventy-five or eighty men, known as the Ward party, started from Bismarck, North Dakota, for the Hills. The two Ward brothers and a man named Collins brought along a herd of cattle. The party reached Grand River without any interference. Their good luck ended there as a large band of Indians swooped down on the herd and succeeded in stampeding and getting away with most of the stock. They also gave battle to the whites, shooting one of the Ward brothers, William as I recall, in the thigh. He lived to reach Crook City but finally died of the wound. Collins was wounded also but recovered. A man named Sam Wells was shot in the knee.

The party pulled into Crook City about the middle of April, 1876. A number of friends and acquaintances of the writer were members of the Ward party. Among them were Ed Wolff and Richard W. Clark, who in later years was given the appellation of "Deadwood Dick," and others whose names I have forgotten. Crook City, which is now but a memory, was in the spring months of '76 a lively town of one thousand or more inhabitants. Here numerous tragedies and fatalities occurred. There was but little more than a mere prospect of gold found in Whitewood Gulch at Crook City, nor for six miles up the gulch towards Deadwood, nine miles distant.

It was here in Crook City that the first real duel occurred which was on the Fourth of July, between Tom Moore, with a needle gun, and Jim Shannon, with a Sharps rifle, in which the latter was killed instantly, while Moore was untouched. He was given a trial by an improvised jury and was promptly acquitted, as he should have been, according to the evidence adduced in the case.

XXI

POTATO CREEK RUSH

COMPARATIVELY few of that great crowd of fortune hunters who flocked to the Black Hills during the big spring rush of '76 had had any practical experience in gold mining or in prospecting. Many of them, however, came here with the intention of engaging in that precarious business and plunged into it with the same self-reliance and determination as did professional miners. Consequently, the entire Black Hills country was overrun and thoroughly explored that season by amateur prospectors. Scarcely a creek, dry gulch, bar, or even a hillside could afterwards be found that did not bear ample evidence of having been severely gouged by these vigorous prospectors searching for gold placers.

During this time reports of important discoveries were coming into Deadwood with such frequency as to keep many here on the alert and their cupidity intensified. Although many of these reports were based upon actual discoveries of gold and were given out and passed along in good faith, they were misleading as the properties, when developed, were found to be worthless.

However, there were a few exceptions to those general conditions. The one most notable at the time was when, early in the spring, the report of a rich discovery of gold came in from a small placer gulch twenty miles west of Deadwood, known afterwards as "Potato Creek." This report, accompanied as it was by a liberal display of gold nuggets, required no further proof to verify it. The word "potato" when mentioned in connection with gold nuggets, appeared to have a magical effect, for where could there be found a "tenderfoot" or anyone else who didn't know something, in fact, everything about potato digging. So now, why not nugget digging when the two were so closely connected as they were in this case?

Whether they were inspired by this or other considerations, many campers, on receipt of this encouraging report, banked their fires and made a hasty movement in the direction of the new discovery, all hoping to reach there in time to get in on the ground floor. But alas, their hopes were soon dispelled, as the fortunate discoverers and owners of these bonanza nugget claims had very wisely taken the precaution, before announcing their find to the world, to surround themselves with every legal protection afforded by local mining laws, forestalling any attempts which might be made by outsiders to secure a foothold in the gulch. Not only were all placers being securely held, but also all quartz locations above and around the gulch were in the possession of the lucky parties who were first on the ground.

So the nearest approach to the "ground floor" to be had by those coming later, consisted in the privilege of ground space for spreading their blankets during their brief sojourn in the new camp. And even in the grant of this concession, there was found no guarantee of consolation or comfort in that rigorous season of the year.

So the majority were back the next day in Deadwood, their base of operations. A few, however, remained at Potato Creek and joined in the search which was instituted at that time and continued for many years in the effort to locate the "mother lode." But the maternal source of these precious yellow beauties had apparently disappeared without leaving any trace of its whereabouts.

It has been asserted, and believed by many, that the name Potato Creek was given it in a comparison of digging potatoes with digging nuggets. But this, according to the statement of the late Jim Carney, was an erroneous conclusion. His story ran like this:

Early in the spring of '76, three others and himself arrived at Potato Creek, hungry and tired. Taking from their pack the potato sack, their chief source of sustenance, and shaking it, one potato fell to the ground. While he was engaged in dividing it into four equal parts, one of the party asked for the name of the creek. Another answered, "It has no name." Then Carney said, "I name it Potato Creek in memory of this bountiful feast." And so it went at that.

Besides the fame acquired from being the home of nearly all

[81]

gold nuggets of any consequence found in the Black Hills, Potato Creek holds at least another, though less enviable claim to notoriety, in the fact that it was here that a nefarious scheme was concocted which resulted in the organization of an intrepid gang of highwaymen whose operations will be related, as I now recall them, in another article.

XXII

KILLING OF JIMMY IRON BY INDIANS

DURING the first three months following the big gold rush into the Black Hills in 1876, food for live stock in the inland towns of the northern Hills was, with the exception of isolated patches of dry grass, wholly unavailable. After the three thousand or more head of horses, mules, burros, oxen and cows were relieved of their burdens, they were immediately taken to Centennial Valley, eight miles from Deadwood and placed in herds to be kept together during the day, then rounded up and corralled at night. This was done without guarantee against their loss from any cause.

There were, however, a few freighters who had forestalled this contingency by bringing with them surplus oats, and these were prepared to keep and put their teams at work in the towns. A few had the forethought to bring scythes with them and those who did were soon in the valleys at work mowing and raking up both new and old grass and weeds. All of this was relished and devoured by the stock kept in town. This kind of trashy provender was in great demand, and brought fabulous prices in keeping with the price of team work.

The hay making industry was carried on extensively throughout the summer by different parties, but all were united in one purpose: this was resisting assaults by the numerous roving bands of Indians. It was well known that they were keeping watchful eyes on the whites with the intention of making a killing and getting away with the stock as soon as they were offered opportunity for doing so without the danger of losing their own blood on the hay fields. The various crews of hay makers, being well aware of the intentions of the Reds, kept in touch with each other and employed one of their most experienced and fearless scouts, Jimmy Iron, to post himself each day upon an elevated point, where he was able, with the aid of a field glass, to make survey of the surrounding country preparatory to sounding an alarm of danger if a band of Indians appeared in sight.

This precautionary measure was maintained without an incident for some time. However, it appeared that the Reds had been employing the same methods of surveillance and had espied Jimmy. By watching his movements they noted that he had followed the same route each morning, so placed one of their number within easy range of the trail. When Jimmy approached, the Red shot and he was killed on the spot.

This was a sad blow to his fellow scouts and many friends. He was buried where he fell. Some years later a small monument of stone was placed over his grave by one of his fellow scouts and close friends, John T. Spaulding, "Buckskin Johnny," the recognized chief of scouts. He was the one seen in 1876 and spoken of by Mrs. Tallent in her history, as "Buckskin," though she never learned his name. Jimmy Iron was recognized by his friends as an intrepid Indian fighter who had had some narrow escapes.

On one occasion, while scouting in the southern Hills as Captain Jack Crawford's right bower, as he was coming around a point of rocks he met face to face with an old Indian scout, one who was quick to realize that he was at a disadvantage. He put out his hand with the friendly greeting, "How, kola, how?" This ruse apparently threw Jimmy off guard for the moment. Quick as a flash the old buck fired a pistol shot through his blanket which struck Jimmy on one side of his breast but failed to down him.

It was now his move, and the next minute the red trickster lay dead at the feet of his intended victim. The ball had struck and buried itself in a Bible which Jimmy's mother had given him together with her blessing when he left his home never to return.

XXIII

DEATH OF CHARLES NOLIN, MAIL CARRIER

UNTIL February, 1877, when the Black Hills were formally thrown open to settlement, they were in fact a part of the Sioux Indian Reservation. Therefore the Federal Government could not make any arrangement for handling mail to and from the Hills.

The earliest service was by entrusting mail arriving at the three chief ports of entry into the Hills, Cheyenne, Wyoming, Sidney, Nebraska, and Pierre, Dakota, to freight trains or other parties going to the Hills, to be distributed as might be under the conditions. A little later service was by volunteer carriers and postmasters. One such carrier, Charles Nolin, lost his life in the service.

Shortly after the middle of June, two improvised post offices were established in Deadwood for the receiving and distribution of mail matter. One of the two self-constituted "postmasters" located his office in Capt. C. V. Gardner's store on the west side of Main Street, while the other located on the east side of Main Street in Sheldon's store. For a month or two they received and delivered letters brought to them by volunteer carriers, at the price of fifty cents for each letter.

It was generally reported that the carriers who risked their lives and spent about two weeks in making dangerous trips to and from Sidney and Fort Pierre, received twenty-five cents for each letter delivered. The "postmaster" kept twenty-five cents for each letter and for his trouble in handling them and in dividing the service charge. A long row of letter customers was to be seen each day lined up along the street from each of these so-called post offices. No complaint was heard as to the cost of the letters. What disposition was made of the uncalled-for letters was never disclosed, but was left for conjecture.

[85]

PIONEER DAYS IN THE BLACK HILLS

The generally accepted statement of facts concerning the death of Charles Nolin, volunteer mail carrier, is as follows:

One day early in August, 1876, the date not definitely established, Nolin, with his load of mail, joined near the present site of Rapid City, a caravan, known as the Schofield Freighting Outfit, en route to Deadwood. Toward evening they reached the top of the hill about a mile and a half southeast of the present city of Sturgis. Nolin, anxious to reach Deadwood that night, left the party there and hurried on. Apparently Indians were watching the party, as Nolin was killed by them within two miles of the point where he left the caravan, on the outer edge of Sturgis as it is now, near three large oak trees where the trail from Pierre and Sidney crossed a little creek, which the pioneers named Deadman Creek. Apparently the Indians were hiding under the creek banks. The freighters heard the shooting. When they reached the place they found he had been shot and scalped by Indians. The mail had been scattered about. They buried the body near the place where it was found. The burial was hasty and the grave shallow. Later another freighter, E. L. Carl, noticed that coyotes had dug open the grave, and filled it with heavy rocks. Thus the body remained until 1880, when the remains were disinterred and buried in Bear Butte Cemetery near Sturgis.

One afternoon in the month of August, 1876, in company with my companion in many hikes over the northern Hills, I was coming up lower Main Street, when we met a large, fine-looking man of apparently twenty-five or twenty-eight years, who had a leather pouch strapped upon his shoulders. I asked him what mail route he was serving. He answered, "The Fort Pierre mail route." I noticed that he was a man of pleasing appearance. I said, "I should think it would not pay you for the terrible risk of life you are taking." He said, "While it certainly is a dangerous and strenuous business, I have made two hundred dollars per month at it." My companion spoke up and said, "I wish to God that I could strike a job like that." The man said, "You can have this one after I make this trip. It is my last one. I am going back home."

I then asked him where his home was. He gave the name of a town in the state of Indiana. I then asked him if he was making his trips on foot. He said, "Yes, that is the only way I could make them. I travel altogether after dark and lay off from the road under sage and other brush all through the long days. It's wearing me out and I am tired of the job." So he bid us good-bye and passed on, leaving the impression that he was a gentleman of more than ordinary intelligence.

A short time after this conversation, the news reached Deadwood that the Pierre mail carrier had been killed by Indians on the road between Rapid City and Crook City. My recollection is that the published accounts stated that he was bringing in mail from Pierre. Other writers state that he was carrying mail from Sidney, Nebraska. The Pierre and Sidney trails converged near the present location of Rapid City.

I never saw nor heard of that volunteer mail carrier after our conversation on the street in Deadwood, and have always believed that it was he whose death was reported shortly thereafter. If this supposition is correct, as only one such death of a mail carrier was reported, it was Charles Nolin and he was a Deadwood-Pierre mail carrier. Other accounts say that he was a carrier from Sidney, Nebr.

For over half a century the place where Charles Nolin met death was marked only by a pile of boulders, erected by those who had knowledge of the tragedy. Then the Society of Black Hills Pioneers and citizens of Sturgis sponsored a movement for erection of a monument near the spot. This is constructed of various ornamental rocks gathered from various sources in the Hills. It was dedicated by the Black Hills Pioneers on Memorial Day, May 30, 1932, with impressive ceremonies, several thousand people from all parts of the Hills being present.

About the time of the death of Charles Nolin, or shortly before, Charley Utter and others established the Seymour and Utter Pony Express-Mail Service, first between Deadwood and Fort Laramie, Wyoming, and later Sidney, Nebraska. One of his associates, who rode between Deadwood and Sidney, was Herbert Rockefellow, known as "Rocky." This service was continued for several months. The skilful riders, with relays of swift ponies, traveling mostly by night, gave excellent service. I was very well acquainted with Charley Utter, whose abode adjoined mine in Deadwood Gulch, and I never heard of his losing a horse or man in the business. Later this pony express business passed into other hands who gave less satisfactory service, and the transportation of mail was turned over to the Cheyenne and Black Hills Stage Company, which had then become well established. This service was continued until the Hills were opened for settlement and regular government mail service established in the spring of 1877.

XXIV

THE RISE AND FALL OF GALENA MINING CAMP

EARLY in the spring of 1876, after Whitewood and Deadwood creeks, and their tributary streams, as well as all dry gulches surrounding them, had been staked and duly recorded as gold placer properties, the great overflow of fortune hunters spread out through the Hills in search of unclaimed territory.

One of the first, also one of the most promising streams, afterwards known as Bear Butte Creek, some eight or ten miles east of Deadwood, was discovered. It was quickly overrun by scores of excited prospectors, and was immediately staked from source to outlet and recorded as placer mining property.

Discoveries of gold were made on many claims for ten or twelve miles along the stream. Some very encouraging, though eventually disappointing, discoveries of gold were made at numerous points in the gulch. Bear Butte Creek, as a placer proposition, soon proved to be a dismal failure. Many of the disappointed searchers, undismayed, turned their attention to another phase of the mining industry, that of seeking ledges of gold bearing ores, and a number of them were amply rewarded for their endeavors. These were found along the mountain side facing the creek on the south, at different points. Adjacent to the point where the town of Galena was afterwards located were many very promising outcroppings of lead and silver ores with a lesser showing of gold ores.

As remembered by the writer, who personally knew most of the locations in that area, the first of the many locations made on that huge mountain side, and filed for record, and the one which ultimately put the Galena district on the map as a mining center second only to the great Homestake area, was made by Frank Cochrane, and was given a name which was on the tips of many tongues at the time, namely "Sitting Bull." Adjoining the Sitting Bull and next in order came the "Florence," the "Merritt No. 1" and "Merritt No. 2" by H. N. Merritt and brother. Others followed at later dates including the "General Crook," "Alex" and the "Chub" Lee, the "Cora" by W. W. Andrews, the "Emma" by James Conzette, the "El Refugio" by W. H. Franklin, the "Hester" by A. E. Collins, and the "New Years" by N. Primrose.

The Richmond location which adjoined the Sitting Bull on the south, which eventually became a stumbling block for its encroaching neighbor, the Sitting Bull, was located and owned by Mike Dugan and others. It eventually brought its neighbor into disrepute, and its numerous employees into enforced idleness. Robert Floorman, a placer miner who had been operating with indifferent success a placer claim in Deadwood gulch, became discouraged and went out to Galena and purchased the Sitting Bull and the Florence, and the two claims were developed under his management. A considerable amount of high grade silver ore and much lead ore with light bearings of gold were extracted from the two claims, and shipped by bull trains to Denver. It was soon realized, however, that the cost of transportation, together with other expenses, by far exceeded the value of the ore, and the shipments were discontinued. For a brief period quiet prevailed in the new mining camp.

Soon after these unsuccessful operations had been tried out at Galena, there drifted into Deadwood, from "somewhere" an elderly gentleman whose name was J. S. Davey, with his wife and son Frank. This enterprising gentleman first started a cracker factory but quickly abandoned the project. He then went out to Galena and leased of Robert Floorman the two claims above mentioned and immediately proceeded to construct near the mouth of the Sitting Bull tunnel a "baby" smelter. From that time forth and ever after if not theretofore, he was known as "Colonel Davey." As to how he became possessed of that enviable military title, the writer was never informed.

The colonel's "baby" promised to be a money maker right from the start. Soon the colonel was able to, and did purchase the two claims of Floorman. While huge bodies of high grade silver and steel galena ore, streaked with narrow seams of gold ore, were being opened up and developed in the Sitting Bull, the colonel was having constructed a much larger plant, with sufficient capacity for treating, not only the output of his own mines but also much of the ores extracted from other mines in that locality.

Thenceforth, for two or three years, the Sitting Bull mine was making rapid strides in its efforts to reach and go over the top as one of the greatest silver mines. There lay before the colonel for extraction within two thousand feet of the ore trend in the Sitting Bull mine, a body of ore estimated to value sixty million dollars. This information came from a friend of the writer who was present when two representatives of eastern capitalists were being shown through the mines, doubtless making close examination of everything in sight, though apparently in a casual way, as they evinced little concern. However, before taking their departure, one of the men ventured to remark, "You have, at present, colonel, a fine showing for a mine; we hope it may not grow less so. I presume that it would require a considerable sum of money to break your hold on it." "Indeed it would," replied the colonel. "Would three hundred thousand be considered?" ventured the stranger as he turned to leave. At that the colonel's five foot eight increased to six feet, as he gave vent to an expression which indicated that it might be considered, but as an insult to his intelligence. The two strangers who evidently had come for the purpose of bonding, or buying the mine, took their departure and were seen no more in that locality. Though a goodly number of other locations in the vicinity of the Sitting Bull mine were being opened up with wonderful showings of steel galena ores, that particular mine was the object of most admiration, and its conceited owner was recognized as the "man of the hour."

It was the colonel, or "de Cunnel," according to the linguistic twist of the different tongues heard in all conversation in that fast growing, one man town. The colonel seemingly was monarch of all he surveyed, and he was doing no small amount of surveying. He spent money lavishly in augmenting his industries, and in building up the town, which increased in population to nearly one thousand inhabitants. Truly the town of Galena was "booming." However, like many other mining towns, it was short lived. This unfortunate ending was not due to any failure of the mines. It was due to two other causes: first, prolonged litigation by mine claimants; second, the ultimate demonetization of silver, and drop in value.

The owners of the Richmond location, which lay on the apex of the mountain about five hundred feet above the ore body, believed it could be reached at a much lesser depth than that which they afterward learned, by Davey's workings, to be the real depth. They had reached a depth of about one hundred feet when their operations were discontinued. Colonel Davey had now reached the end of the Sitting Bull location, with the intention of following up his ore body as he undoubtedly believed that he had the right to do. However, the owners of the Richmond body took a different view of the matter, and warned him against making further operations under the side line of their claims. The colonel had a copy of the mining laws which, as he understood them, gave him the right to follow his ore vein along its dip, continuously, and he refused to halt. He was enjoined, and a great, prolonged legal battle of mining giants was precipitated.

The three owners of the Richmond mine were without money for maintaining their suit. However, they were not long in finding a New York millionaire who, for a controlling interest in their mine, was willing to, and did meet, all requirements found to be necessary in fighting their case through the courts to its ultimate finish. Both sides in the controversy lined up with a brilliant array of the best legal talent to be obtained. Apparently they were fortified with all high court mining case decisions that had been handed down during the past one hundred years. Most of the decisions, however, appeared to have been made in disputes over vertical foundations. The Sitting Bull mine was in a flat formation and Davey claimed that he was following the dip of the formation. Numerous surveys by civil engineers were made before and during the trial of the case. It was found, and conceded by all that, while the trend of the Davey ore body was south, seventeen degrees east, on a six per cent grade, the main dip of the foot wall and cap rock was east, two degrees north, on a fifteen per cent grade. So after a long and bitter struggle in which there probably was more money spent than both mines were worth, with the colonel pretty well broken up financially, the case was decided in favor of the Richmond claimants. The new owner later on became the owner of both mines, but very little in the way of development has been done or attempted since the depreciation of silver.

Several intermittent, though ineffectual, efforts to again put the mine on a paying basis, have been made at different times since its change of ownership. The loss of this great body of high grade ores, together with the many thousands of dollars spent in determination to establish his legal right to its ownership, certainly fell as a crushing blow upon the shoulders of its erstwhile owner. This loss, great as it was, was but one of the two heavy losses suffered by Colonel Davey during the years of his prosperity. Another loss, occasioned by his own folly, contributed largely to depletion of the colonel's fast waning financial resources, and certainly must have created a feeling of regret.

Being desirous of emulating the methods successfully employed by managers of other great mines in the protection and augmentation of their legitimate holdings, as well as for sinister purposes, the colonel secured the services of an ambitious gunman known as Billy Thacker. That there were motives in this action, other than legitimate protection of life or property, was indicated by developments.

It appeared that, while drifting along the ore vein in the Sitting Bull mine, the colonel noticed that the richest part of the great vein was bearing strongly to the southeast with a tendency to pass under a portion of a mining claim which was owned by, and was being scratched on top several hundred feet above the vein, by one Jack Gorman. Therefore this claim must be secured by the colonel to prevent a conflict in that direction. An offer (the amount unknown to this writer) was made and was rejected by Gorman. Increased offers made by the colonel to Gorman were promptly rejected. The claim was not for sale. Gorman preferred to hold on to what might prove to be a great mine, and flatly refused to sell to Davey. Thus hard feelings were engendered and something out of the ordinary must be done. On more than one occasion, in the Black Hills, it was proven that a sure way to get a mining claim was to first "get" the owner. Whether or not this was the plan the colonel had in mind is not known. It is known that it was the plan adopted and consummated by his willing tool, Thacker, who was anxious to gain notoriety as a dangerous two-gun man and killer. In watching for an opportunity to give an exhibition of heroism and do something in the way of earning his salary, Thacker spied the unarmed and unsuspicious quarry, Jack Gorman, coming out of the post office. As Gorman came out with his mail he was stopped by an insulting remark which, it was said, he resented in somewhat vigorous language, sufficiently strong, of course, to justify this dangerous gunman in shooting him down.

The cowardly murderer was arrested and indicted by a grand jury on charge of first degree murder. It was now up to the colonel to bring his money to the rescue. This he did. The best and the trickiest legal talent was procured. The case came up for trial. There were in the Black Hills in those days, continuously loafing around within easy reach of the Court House, two kinds of professional jurors: one kind who could see no reason why a weary pilgrim who had appropriated a cayuse to help him on his way to other parts, should not serve a long term in the penitentiary; the other class could find no reason for punishing a man for shooting down another who was threatening to slap his face. There happened to be in waiting at the time of Thacker's trial, a full panel of this latter class of jurymen, who were willing to render a verdict in accordance with the evidence and the law as given in the instructions of the court. This jury found no difficulty in reaching a verdict of self-defense when it was proven that that great, double-fisted Irishman had actually shaken his fist at the defendant in a threatening manner. Colonel Davey, after footing the bills, soon disposed of his holdings at Galena, and departed as did also the wilful murderer, Thacker.

XXV

FIRST FOURTH OF JULY CELEBRATION IN DEADWOOD

How many, I wonder, are yet here, who gave assistance by pulling on the ropes in the erection of Deadwood's first "Liberty Pole," which was located on the east side of Main Street, opposite Gold Street, from which "Old Glory" was here for the first time flung to the breezes? And how many are yet left of that large assembly who participated in or witnessed the elaborate and impressive ceremonies which were so appropriately conducted as to make our first Fourth of July celebration of "Centennial Day," in 1876, an occasion to be long remembered with pride and pleasure?

The one-hundredth anniversary of our national independence was indeed duly observed by the thousands of people of many nationalities who were massed in the new mining camp of Deadwood on that eventful day. The principal streets were crowded to capacity with stirring humanity. Many eloquent speakers were in evidence. Though throngs were constantly in motion, with all the turbulence with which a Fourth of July celebration would be attended under such conditions, this day passed without a single casualty or other untoward incident worthy of note.

One of the commendable features which gave added zest to the occasion, was the issuance by A. W. Merrick & Co., of an extra sized edition of the *Black Hills Pioneer,* dressed in the national colors. It was replete with laudatory descriptions of surrounding camps, their activities and possibilities, with encomiums for the entire Black Hills in general and Deadwood in particular.

Although many copies were printed of that edition the supply was soon exhausted. I know of none now in Deadwood, though some may have been preserved. It is very regrettable that more have not been preserved, as it would now be very interesting, not only to old timers but to newcomers also.

XXVI

MURDER OF JACK HINCH

On the last of July, 1876, three men were playing poker in Turner's saloon in Gayville; they were Jack Hinch and two men who were at that time partners, John R. Carty, and —— McCarthy. It was at night, and a quarrel and fight resulted. Carty drew a revolver, backed Hinch up into a corner of the room, and was pounding him over the head with it, when McCarthy came up behind him, and reaching around his body, stuck his knife into Hinch, killing him almost instantly. The two then fled. The community was aroused and vowed vengeance on them if caught. Hinch, a quiet, peaceable man, stood high in the esteem of the miners and his death was looked upon as cold blooded murder.

In a day or two Jack Davis, a deputy United States marshal, started out in pursuit of them. Near Laramie City, he overtook Carty, captured and brought him back to Gayville. News of his return with the prisoner spread rapidly, and in a short time the boys were all there. Being on the dead square themselves, they resolved that the prisoner should have a square deal at their hands in his trial. A meeting was organized at which A. H. Simonton was chosen judge, A. B. Chaplin, prosecutor, and Bill Trainor was assigned as counsel for the defense. A jury of twelve men was empaneled, John Kane being one of them. Mrs. Meanar, the first woman in Gayville, was one of the witnesses, John R. Wilson, another. They gave evidence that McCarthy struck the fatal blow.

The defendant's attorney managed his case brilliantly and eloquently. The verdict of the jury was "Not guilty," but the crowd was not satisfied with the finding. Jack Hinch had been murdered. J. R. Carty was known to have been hammering him over the head with his revolver at the time of the killing, and they thought that he should be punished. The jury were of the same opinion, but as they were acting under the statute which provides no punishment of a lesser degree than capital offense, and thought Carty should not be hanged for a murder he had not committed, they acquitted him.

The crowd wanted blood, and were so demonstrative that Jack Davis warned the jury and stood guard over the prisoner all night. The next morning he escorted him to Deadwood, where Carty procured a horse and left the Hills. He never returned.

McCarthy was afterwards arrested, taken to Yankton by the United States marshal, and imprisoned. Witnesses went from Deadwood to Yankton for federal court, John R. Wilson, who had witnessed the killing, being one of them. When the case was called, McCarthy's attorney asked for a continuance to the next term. This motion was granted by the court, and the witnesses who had left homes and business and gone four hundred miles for five cents a mile, when the next term of court convened, had more important business and remained at home. When the case was called, there were no witnesses present. The defense was ready for trial, and the prosecution entered a *nolle prosequi*. McCarthy was discharged, and that was the last ever heard of him in the Hills.

XXVII

PLACER MINING IN DEADWOOD GULCH

WHEN the miners of Deadwood Gulch organized they drafted a code of local mining laws that was deemed suitable for governing their operations under the existing conditions. Lost Mining District was first established. This district, which embraced Deadwood Gulch and its tributary gulches and draws, had all boundaries properly defined, as were all mining locations eligible to record. Placer locations were limited to 300 feet in length along the gulches and their width from "rim rock to rim rock." These locations in Deadwood Gulch had all been measured and were held by the locators prior to the time set for filing of records, which was on January 10, 1876.

There were two channels of washed gravel in Deadwood Gulch, each having at the bottom on the slate "bedrock" a "pay streak," in which was found the placer gold, and the next heaviest wash, black sand, a substance impregnated with iron. The last made of these two channels, resulting from tremendous overflows which occurred at remote periods of time, was the first to be discovered and developed by the miners. It extended along the creek bed in Deadwood and practically all the way up the gulch on the easterly side, ranging from ten to fifteen feet in depth, so that it could be and was worked through open cuts by shoveling the gravel into sluice boxes located above the surface. This channel was exceedingly rich and was easily mined because of having the water on the ground. It was, therefore, quickly worked out, and the miners were not handicapped in working out this channel on the claims now embraced in the city of Deadwood.

There was little gold found in Deadwood in the channel on the west side of the gulch paying more than the expense of mining it, as the bedrock dipped abruptly to the westward and was from twenty to forty feet below the surface where the Franklin Hotel now stands. There being a hill, the channel was forty-five feet deep which necessitated tunneling on a decline and wheeling the dirt up to the water. The claim owners were but small losers because of the surface claimants interfering with placer operations.

In proof of this may be cited that one of the owners of Nos. 24 and 25, William Jackson, who owned a one-fifth interest, after working out the first channel, found employment in the quartz mines, became ill and went broke. Being unable to sell his interest in the Deadwood claims and unable to get a loan from his partners, as they evidently were short also, he finally succeeded in borrowing from this writer five hundred dollars on a mortgage. This loan was not paid when due, nor would it have ever been paid, had they not succeeded in getting their patent through by a decision of the Secretary of the Interior, Kirkwood, and later mulcting the surface occupants out of many thousands of dollars, thereby bringing their practically worthless claims up in value, a close second to No. 2 below Discovery, the richest claim in the gulch.

Having had considerable practical experience in placer mining in Deadwood Gulch, and therefore some knowledge as to the courses taken by these channels as well as to their richness and extent, I am convinced that both gulches, Whitewood and Deadwood, have been greatly overestimated as to their gross output of placer gold, although many of the claims in Deadwood Gulch and a very few in Whitewood Gulch were exceedingly rich in placers.

While coming to the Hills in April, 1876, I made the acquaintance of an old gentleman about sixty-five years of age. I remember his name as Albright, and that he came from Quincy, Illinois. This man appeared to be very eccentric, having but little intercourse with any of the party; although there was another gentleman from the same city, with whom he was messing, Albright had but little to say to him. However, when he learned that I had had some experience in gold mining in Montana he seemed to be interested in the information I gave him, and I found him to be a very affable and desirable companion. I parted with the old man at Rapid City, and lost sight of him for several weeks.

He came to me in June, after the miners had begun taking out gold in Deadwood Gulch, and requested me to go up the gulch as far as Gayville and get prices on all mining claims that were for sale, making my own selection, and he would pay the price; and that he and I should go in together as partners and work the claim. This proposal I readily accepted.

His friend from Quincy had previously informed me that he had on his person $5,000 in currency, and that he was a wealthy, retired business man. So I started out the next day and approached claim owners, thinking surely that some one of them would put a price on his claim. However, I was at least one week too late, as they were working the shallow channel and had cleaned up a lot of the shiny metal, and not one among them would state his price. They told me, however, that the owner of No. 13 below Discovery had just offered his claim for sale. I think his price was $1,000, but the man was not on the claim. I put in some time hunting for him but could not locate him until after his claim was sold. This proved to be fortunate for the old man, as well as myself, as No. 13 proved to be true to its unfortunate reputation.

It happened to be located in a bend in the channel, half a mile above Deadwood, where the slate bedrock was solid and smooth with no depressions or riffles to catch the gold; consequently it never paid much above the cost of development.

At that time there was not a single mining claim in Deadwood Gulch that had its price fixed, though many of them changed ownership afterwards. So my friend, as well as myself, was greatly disappointed. He soon after returned to Quincy and I very readily found work on No. 17 and No. 18 below Discovery, which are now within the city limits of Deadwood. These claims were owned jointly by two men whose names were Smith and Oakes.

Oakes and Smith were both "tenderfeet" as miners. Oakes had been a Wisconsin farmer and Smith evidently had been a city man, a gambler and a beat. Oakes worked steadily while Smith put in most of his time in the city's "Bad Lands." My work was cleaning the bedrock and assisting Oakes in cleaning up and panning out the gold. Up to the 4th of July we cleaned up what I estimated to be, though I did not see it weighed, eight to ten thousand dollars. We had been running along in the shallow channel of No. 17, knowing nothing about the deep channel which, above Deadwood City, was not rich. Oakes believed that we had pretty well cleaned out the two claims. Smith seldom came on the ground. On the second or third day of July they sold two-thirds of their two claims to Wybell and Andrews, retaining the one-third.

I never knew the price they received but think it was about $1,800. They were indebted to their miners several hundred dollars. Smith was indebted to various low characters, men and women, several hundred dollars. They had settled in full with this writer up to the third of July and requested me to remain on the claims that night, and keep watch over them, which I did. The following day, the 4th of July, while the entire populace of the Black Hills were celebrating the first centennial of our independence, Oakes and Smith, well mounted on their fine saddle animals, were making a beeline for other fields and, so far as the writer knows, were never again heard of by any Black Hiller.

On the following day, when Oakes failed to appear at the mine, their departure became known. In order to get the matter settled, a meeting of those to whom they were indebted was called. Then it was discovered that the two men still held a one-third interest in the property, and here is the most interesting part of the story. When it became generally known that there was yet an undivided 100 feet to go to the creditors, they swarmed and settled on the hillside. Several brought legal advisers with them.

Of the many claims presented only those which were well established were recognized, and the total was reduced to about $600. Wybell and Andrews, purchasers of the two-thirds interest, came forward and made an offer to pay off the claims in consideration of the one-third interest being made over to them. The offer was accepted and mining ground of no less value than $2,000 was turned over to them. The two men who thought their mining claims were worked out beat themselves in trying to beat others.

The writer continued working on claims No. 17 and No. 18 during July, August, and part of September, and assisted Mr. Wybell in cleaning up approximately $20,000. During our latest work that fall we ran into the deep channel where the paystreak was immensely rich. It was with much difficulty that we were able to clean up the bedrock, on account of back water, and in taking care of the boulders and gravel which each operator had to keep on his own claim. So the owners of Nos. 17 and 18 planned to have a starting point from which to set their sluice boxes and work up stream, and also to have the large shaft as a receptacle for the rocks and gravel when their mining operations would be resumed in the following spring of '77.

Having cleaned the bedrock just above the proposed large shaft later in the fall of '76, and knowing of its rich yield of gold, I proposed to sink and timber the shaft for the gold to be taken therefrom, the owners to furnish the sluice boxes which were on the ground, and also a "Chinese pump," in case I should find use for it. After some hesitation, my offer was accepted.

A contract was drawn up and signed by both parties, and as early in the spring of '77 as I could get to work, I employed two men to assist me. We chopped and slid down the steep hill a sufficient number of logs to crib the shaft which was to be twenty feet square, and the work began as soon as the ice was out of the water. There being no gold near the surface, everything above eight feet was thrown out on the sides. At that point I found a streak of fine gravel with black sand, about eighteen inches thick, which I put through the boxes and obtained about sixty dollars worth of gold, which was quite encouraging as I was not expecting to find any pay dirt in the first fifteen feet.

The shaft being close to the creek, on reaching the creek level the water gave us trouble until we were compelled to use the pump. The so-called "Chinese pump" was a frame with a windlass at the top over which leather or canvas was built with tin cups attached. This was drawn over the windlass, running on an incline from a sump at the bottom, and the water brought up and dumped on the surface.

Finding that it would be impossible, even with this pump, to keep the water out of our way, I sank the shaft to about twelve feet and after timbering it up abandoned one half next to the creek and carried the other half down to bedrock. Here I was greatly disappointed. According to our cleanup not many feet above the point during our last work in the fall of '76, there should have been at least $200 on this ten by twenty feet bedrock. We found only smooth, solid slate bedrock and I cleaned up another sixty dollars. Being determined to put through the contract even at a loss, I kept the pump running day and night believing that the remaining half of the bedrock would yield double the amount of the first. The season was getting well along and the owners of the mine were growing anxious to put on a full crew which they could not do while my crew was on the job. There being no time limit to my agreement, they offered me $200 to discontinue the work, which I promptly accepted. This put me about one hundred per cent ahead on the deal, while if I had put through the contract I would not have broken even.

The foregoing is presented because it is typical of the experiences of a large percentage of those who engaged in placer mining. Chance was a big factor in determination of the degree of success.

Wybell and Andrews resumed operations on their claims. These two placer claims yielded between forty and fifty thousand dollars. I worked on No. 20 and No. 21 below Discovery, both of which are in the city of Deadwood. These claims were inferior to No. 17 and No. 18. No. 19 was owned by four partners, none of whom realized much more than the cost of operating it. At the deepest point in No. 20 I assisted in taking from the bedrock the skeleton of a pine tree. The heart of the tree, with the limbs and knots, was all that endured through ages, and were still intact. Another discovery calculated to excite wonder was finding driftwood on the hill sides fifteen feet above the surface of the gulch. As to how long the old pine tree had lain under the first and deepest channel of wash gravel in Deadwood Gulch, or how long that driftwood found on the sides of the mountains had lain there undisturbed, I have no knowledge. There were about forty placer mining locations between lower Deadwood Gulch and Central City which produced approximately one million dollars in placer gold.

There were several rich claims in Central City below Saw Pile Gulch, but none above. Though they were all developed, they did not repay their owners the cost of development. Very few claims above the mouth of Bobtail Gulch, on the southeast side, and Blacktail Gulch on the northwest side of Deadwood Gulch, were found to be rich. Both of these side gulches were exceedingly rich in placers.

I had, during my search for a placer claim in June, 1876, met and talked with practically every one of the owners of those claims and was at times on the ground and saw and heard much of their cleanups. They appeared to make no secret of it as they or some of their miners would frequently state the amount openly.

One thing in particular I noticed was that after they had worked out the best channels and had practically gutted their claims, and offered to sell, and did sell them, there was much talk given out as to what had been and what could yet be mined from these claims; but I heard of no large amounts of gold taken out by the last purchasers. No. 1 above Discovery was reported to have yielded $65,000; No. 5, $40,000; and No. 6, $70,000. Nos. 1 and 2 were purchased by the Wheeler Brothers. It was said that they took out and shipped, hauled by four mules, $160,000. That was probably as near the correct figures as could be given. From my own mining experiences in the gulch I am inclined to the belief that there is yet in Deadwood Gulch close to $300,000 worth of gold which could only be reclaimed by ground sluicing on a mammoth scale, requiring several miles of three foot boxes and several hundred inches of water.

Although placer gold was found in Whitewood Gulch, practically all the way from near its source to the valley, a distance of at least fifteen miles, there were but a limited number of claims that paid anything worth while above the cost of mining. There were two very good claims worked out about two miles below the city of Deadwood, and some that paid good wages below the mouth of Gold Run Gulch, which was probably the richest gulch ever discovered in the Black Hills. This is on the present road into Lead, above Pluma. There is also a small gulch tributary to Smith's Gulch which runs into Whitewood Gulch one mile below Deadwood. This little gulch was called Split Tail. It was exceedingly rich in placers but so limited in extent that but little has been said of it in historical accounts of placer mining in the Black Hills.

With all of this million or more dollars worth of gold taken out of Deadwood and Whitewood gulches by placer miners, there were but a very few of the lucky ones who left the Black Hills with any considerable amount of money. Many of them made bad investments and lost out and not a few of them wasted their money, as has ever been the history of mining camps.

XXVIII

"WILD BILL"

In the month of June, 1876, he, in company with Charlie
Utter, "Colorado Charlie," a freighter, Steve Utter, his brother,
Calamity Jane, and "Kittie" Arnold, two female sports, arrived
on horseback in Deadwood. They were seen by this writer, shortly
after arrival.

"Wild Bill," James Butler Hickok, with many other notorious
characters, drifted into Deadwood at a time when turbulent social
conditions had reached their worst stage. Scores of saloons, music
and dance halls, gambling houses and disorderly houses were
running wide open day and night. Yet the conditions were far
from being such as have been painted by some of Wild Bill's
biographers—that decent people scarcely dared to appear on the
street, especially after dark. If there is any pioneer of those days
who felt that he was unsafe, even with every dollar he possessed
in his pocket, in going on the street or into gambling houses or
dance halls as a spectator, I never heard of him. Doubtless there
were robbers and even murderers among those who were conducting the various games of chance, most of which were "skin games."
Though confidence men, they attended strictly to their business
of luring tenderfeet and other suckers into their nets. Although
they caught hundreds that way, I never heard of a gambler or a
fakir reaching into any man's pocket and taking his cash. However, when the spectator, in his eagerness to increase his capital,
took his roll from his pocket, he almost invariably lost sight of it.
As to shooting over games of chance, it seldom occurred. Varnes
and Storm did settle a dispute, supposed to have been over a
game, by salivating Joe Ludwig, an innocent bystander. There
were, however, many disputes over other matters settled with guns
in disreputable houses.

[105]

I have described these conditions to show that, from my point of view as an everyday observer in those memorable days of '76, while there was no question but what the city of Deadwood was at that time in need of better local government, it was not in need of a notorious man-killer as peace officer. There may have been some talk by his friends that he was to receive the appointment as marshal, but if there was such talk, it was not generally known, as I never heard of it. As regards the stories about Johnnie Varnes, a professional gambler whom I knew very well, and Tim Brady, a man I never heard of, conspiring to have Wild Bill killed, it is my opinion that it is without foundation, and has been related by hero worshipers for the purpose of leading readers into belief that their hero was greatly feared by the tough element in Deadwood. One writer states that "Cold Deck Johnnie" gave Jack McCall seven hundred dollars to kill Wild Bill. Another says that he gave him a few drinks of whiskey to do the job. I don't believe that Varnes or any other gambler in the town had any fear of Wild Bill, as he himself was a gambler. Though not a very successful one, it was his only occupation in Deadwood.

In a former story by the writer of some occurrences of those days, the statement was made that Wild Bill was frequently seen while in Deadwood, walking on the street with two six-shooters stuck under the waist band of his pants, with no scabbards in sight, and that he was being followed by his "consort," "Calamity Jane." The latter part of this statement has been disputed by some of his admirers. They contend that Wild Bill would not so lower himself, and that "Colorado Charlie" was her man. Nevertheless, it is a fact that she came to Deadwood with him and others, followed him up and down the streets, accompanied him to and from restaurants, and after he was killed, wailed over his body and invoked maledictions upon the head of his murderer.

Although I had some acquaintance and some business dealings with Colorado Charlie, I am unable to vouch for him further than that in appearance he was as much of a gentleman as Wild Bill. I have always been of the belief that he brought Wild Bill to the Hills and that the latter was indebted to him.

I never, with the exception of one occasion, heard of Wild Bill having a dispute with anyone while in Deadwood, from the middle of June until his death six weeks later. I was told by a friend

whom I considered to be truthful, that he had heard Captain
Massie abuse Wild Bill and dare him to do his worst. Possibly
this did occur and Bill did not wish to kill Massie. That dispute
may have given Massie reason for the remark he made to Anse
Tippie, that "he was afraid Wild Bill would kill him."

Wild Bill had no cabin, but lived in Colorado Charlie's large
tent which was spread in front of the location of the present
Northwestern passenger station, midway between that and the
creek, and not near the Burlington depot as has been erroneously
stated. On the Fourth of July, 1876, twelve shots were fired in
rapid succession at or near his tent, which was about ten rods
from my cabin, with brush between them. Immediately after the
shooting a man came along and I inquired of him as to who was
shooting. He answered that "Wild Bill was showing how he could
trim down a twig." I neglected to ask, nor did he say, whether
or not Bill succeeded in trimming it down. I have wondered if
those twelve shots were his last, and his valedictory to an unappre-
ciative world.

In a recent write-up of Wild Bill, it is stated that in coming
to Deadwood, he remarked to his friends, "Boys, I have a hunch
that this is my last camp and that I will never leave it alive,"
and that he made the statement the evening before his death that
he believed his time on earth was short. These expressions of fear
have been construed by his ardent admirers as presentiment of
his approaching death. Whether or not he actually did thus express
himself, there can be little doubt that such premonitions of death
must have been ever present in his mind. With thousands of people
of all characters and from all directions flocking to Deadwood,
this was the place where he was likely to meet the avenger.

He wandered about from town to town. His greatest solace
was at the card table. He was wise in refusing to sit at a gaming
table with his back to the door, and in being ever on the alert,
ready to defend himself at all times. That he courted sympathy
was evidenced by the gentlemanly manner in which he introduced
himself to Mrs. Tallent on the street in Cheyenne, a few months
before his death, as she relates. "My name is Hickok," he said,
and she bowed in acknowledgment. His next announcement astonished her. "I am called 'Wild Bill,' and you have no doubt heard
of me. Although," he added, "I suppose you have heard nothing

good of me." She candidly answered that she had heard of Wild Bill and that his reputation at least was not at all creditable to him, but perhaps he was not so black as he was painted. "Well, as to that," he replied, "I suppose I am called a red-handed murderer, which I deny. That I have killed men I admit, but never unless in absolute self-defense or in the performance of an official duty. I never in my life took any mean advantage of an enemy. Yet, understand," he added, with a dangerous gleam in his eye, "I never allowed a man to get the drop on me. But perhaps I may yet die with my boots on," he said, his face softening a little. Was this a premonition of the tragic fate that awaited him?

As a final move in his checkered career, Wild Bill found a new field in the Black Hills where his operations were cut short at a poker table on the second day of August, 1876, by the murderous hand of Jack McCall.

Many contradictory statements have been made by different persons who claim to have witnessed the murder of Wild Bill and the arrest of McCall. The writer, though near by on the street at the time, did not witness the killing. As I remember the account of it, as related to me by the late Anse Tippie, the bartender in the saloon where he was killed, who witnessed the affair, it was as follows:

Wild Bill sat at a table in a saloon known as the "Number 10" on lower Main Street, with his back to the front door, the only entrance, engaged in a game of cards with Captain Massie, an old steamboat captain, Con Stapleton and Carl Mann. The only explanation ever offered as to why Wild Bill did not follow his invariable custom, to not sit with his back to the door, is that he sought to make such a change in his final game, but that one of the friends with whom he was playing did not comply with his request to change seats.

Jack McCall walked in, stepped up behind Wild Bill, presented a 45 caliber revolver close to the back of his head and as he fired, said, "Take that, damn you!" He then turned with the smoking revolver in his hand, walked out to where his horse was tied, and attempted to mount. The saddle turned and he fell to the ground. He arose quickly, walked up the street and entered a saloon or store where he was found by Ike Brown and others.

He was then arrested and marched up the street to the Lan-

grishe Theater. No report was current at that time of his resisting
arrest, nor were there "ten men armed with rifles" making the
arrest. He was in custody of three or four men with a good-sized
crowd following. As he passed me on the street, I made a close
survey of him. Although I am not positive as to his apparel, I
now remember him as being below average height, and stoutly
built, wearing buckskin pants and moccasins and a sombrero fully
eighteen inches in width, which was pulled down close over his
eyes. At best, he was a repulsive-looking individual. He showed
no sign of being drunk at the time, as he walked quietly up the
street.

This dastardly assassination of Wild Bill by Jack McCall was
truly deplorable. Even though it was generally known that many
of his long list of killings had been committed with utter disregard
for law and the rights of others, no one amongst the great crowd
of people in Deadwood condoned the cowardly act of McCall.

The murder created a great stir, an unusual sensation amongst
the populace, probably more pronounced than would have been
the case had Wild Bill been the murderer and Jack McCall the
victim, because of Wild Bill being known to many while McCall
had not been heard of except by a few. While Hickok was known
generally as a man killer, there were but few, aside from the
scouts and border rangers, who knew much of the details. So
public sentiment for calling McCall to account for his cowardly
act was strongly manifest at the time.

Although the excitement created by the killing of Wild Bill
had already reached high pitch, it was materially intensified by
a Mexican, racing up Main Street, swinging the gory head of an
Indian warrior, who had been killed in the valley by one of M. V.
Shoun's teamsters, and was decapitated by the Mexican who
claimed that he had killed him, and was endeavoring to sell the
trophy. It was obtained by a druggist who put the head in pickle,
but it was promptly reclaimed by Mr. Shoun, who, after scalping
it, returned the head to the druggist, and gave the scalp to the
man who did the killing.

In accordance with public sentiment, a mass meeting was held
for the purpose of deciding what action should be taken in the
killing of Wild Bill. After the object of the meeting was stated,
W. Y. Kuykendall was made chairman. At that time every man

in the Black Hills knew that he was a trespasser, and there was no legally constituted court to try such cases. Nevertheless, it was felt that something should be done, so a court was improvised for trial of McCall. The chairman appointed a committee of three, one from each district, to select thirty-three names from each district for a jury panel. Those named were James Harrington of Deadwood, Mr. Reed of Gayville and Mr. Coin of Montana City. From the names they presented a jury was selected the next morning, comprising Charles Whitehead, foreman, Ed Burke, John Mann, L. A. Judd, Alexander Thayre, S. S. Hopkins, J. F. Cooper, J. J. Bump, L. D. Bookaw, J. H. Thompson, J. E. Thompson, and K. F. Towle. Col. May was appointed prosecutor, and Judge Miller was assigned counsel for the defense.

McCall's defense, not one "trumped up by his attorneys" as has been asserted by some writers, was that he killed Wild Bill in revenge for the murder of his brother down in Kansas some years prior to that time. No other evidence was submitted by the defendant. The jury and most of those present, accepted McCall's statement as true, and after being out but a short time brought in a verdict of acquittal, which could be consistently returned under the existing conditions, and the general conception then prevailing of a man's moral right to take "a life for a life." Apparently it met with almost unanimous approval of citizens.

It has been asserted by Wild Bill's biographers among other wild statements, that "when the verdict of the jury was read, Col. May, counsel for the prosecution, flew into a paroxysm of wrath." Also, that he called the jury all the vile names that his eloquent tongue could command, and even accused them of "selling out"; that he declared that he could prove that two thousand ounces of gold dust had been secretly weighed out that day for their special benefit. Forty thousand dollars to be paid to twelve jurors for returning the verdict of not guilty! This preposterous tale gave inference that a powerful syndicate of affluent gamblers was backing McCall. The writer did not at the time hear of Col. May making any such statement. If he did so it was in the seclusion of his private apartment and away from the ears of that jury, as there was more than one man amongst them who would have broken a six-shooter over his head without allowing him time to retract the insinuation.

After being acquitted and set free, McCall loitered about the city five or six days and was not "chased out by California Joe and Texas Jack" as has been asserted. He then mounted his shabby pony and rode out past the Mountain Branch in daylight where he was seen passing by Gus Oberg, and went directly to Julesburg, Colorado, where he had lived before, and where Wild Bill also had stayed for a time. It is my opinion that these two men were well acquainted before the tragedy in Deadwood, and that an old grudge led to the climax—the murder of Wild Bill. Be that as it may, McCall reached Julesburg with his pony exhausted and himself broke. Here he entered the employ of a wealthy saloon keeper who knew him well and who owned a large ranch near the town. Harvest was in progress and McCall was sent out with others to the fields where he worked a few days until his employer gave the men a royal feast consisting of everything to be found in the market that appealed to their taste, together with an abundance of whiskey. Some of the harvesters drank to excess and failed to show up on the following day.

The next day found them at work, but McCall was missing. One of the men, who gave the writer this information, remarked to his employer that he believed that Jack had skipped. "Oh, no," said the employer, "Jack wouldn't dare to treat me in that way." However, Jack not only had skipped, but also had taken with him his employer's fine private saddle horse and saddle, and plenty to eat on his journey, which was toward Wyoming. Believing himself to have been fully exonerated for the killing of Wild Bill, and immune from punishment for his crime, he went up the line boasting of having killed the greatest gunman in the world. He was arrested in Wyoming by federal authorities, taken to Yankton, South Dakota, tried and convicted of the murder of Wild Bill, and was hanged on March 1, 1877. At this trial he gave an entirely different reason for the murder, but none of the reasons appear to bear the semblance of truth.

If there were any threats of lynching McCall for the killing of Wild Bill, the writer heard nothing of them. His body was taken from where it fell by men who were strangers to the writer and was prepared for burial. It has been claimed by "Doc" E. T. Pierce, a resident of Rapid City and Hot Springs for many years, recently deceased, that he prepared Wild Bill's body for burial. The writer cannot confirm or dispute this claim.

Reports have been published that this impromptu undertaker, while preparing the body for burial, discovered that it was covered with scars from head to foot. In a statement given out by Mr. Pierce, a short time prior to his death, he says that he did not remove the clothes from the body, as it was clean. This statement is in accordance with the facts as the writer has good reason to believe them to be.

The body was taken over to the big tent on the east side of the creek, near the present site of the Northwestern depot, where it lay in state the following day and where it was viewed by the writer and many others. It was then placed in a neat coffin and taken to South Deadwood, to the first bench north of the gulch where there were already several graves, and was buried close by a large pine stump. Colorado Charlie, who is said to have been a partner of Wild Bill, had a high board placed at the head of the grave with this inscription upon it: "Wild Bill, J. B. Hickok, killed by the assassin Jack McCall, Deadwood City, Black Hills, August 2, 1876. Pard, we will meet again in the happy hunting grounds to part no more. Good-bye. Colorado Charlie, C. H. Utter."

This first cemetery being close in, the ground was later incorporated in the fourth ward of the city. The following year another cemetery was laid out, on a plateau high up on the same hill. In the meantime, a large number of graves had accumulated on the slope below. Most of the bodies were later taken up and reinterred in the new cemetery which was called Mt. Moriah.

On the first of September, 1879, Colorado Charlie returned to Deadwood and on the third of September, he, with this writer, and Lewis Shoenfield, the writer's cabin mate, went with a team and spring wagon to the grave of Wild Bill, which had been opened by the cemetery care-taker, William Austin, a large man, an old soldier who died many years ago at Hot Springs, South Dakota.

Mr. Austin had, after preparing a new grave on Mt. Moriah, opened the first grave of Wild Bill. The four of us took up the body and transferred it to the new grave. Here the box was opened and the lid of the casket was removed. The body down to the hips was exposed. To our great astonishment it appeared to be in a perfect state of preservation. Being perfectly white, it seemed to have a coat of lime finish. The clothes, which were decomposed, had evidently been jolted to the sides while in transit to the new grave, leaving the upper portion of the body exposed. The manifold pleats in the fine linen shirt which he wore showed plainly on his form.

The writer took a stick the size of a cane and tapped many places on the body, face, and head, discovering no soft places anywhere. While the body appeared to be solid, petrified, the sound from the tapping was much the same as would result from the tapping of a wall, and not of solid stone. Some of the party were inclined to believe that the body was in process of petrifaction. Mr. Austin estimated the weight of the casket at five hundred pounds. While it was an extremely heavy load for four able-bodied men to carry up the hill, the writer would not place the weight above four hundred pounds, nor did I concur in the belief that it was a case of petrifaction, though there may have been such cases in existence. It was my belief that it was the result of a natural embalming by percolation of water containing embalming substances, depositing these in the tissues of the body.

After a close examination had been made by the four of us, the lid of the coffin was fastened down and the body of the great gunman, one of the greatest man-killers that the world has ever known, was for the second time lowered into a grave to be covered and lost to view. The wooden headboard was moved to the new grave, where it was practically destroyed by relic hunters whittling off pieces. In 1891, a statue was erected by J. B. Riordan, a sculptor from New York who chanced to be in Deadwood. This consisted of a rock pedestal with inscription, including the name of the sculptor, surmounted by a bust of Wild Bill. This was badly mutilated by relic hunters, and in 1902 another monument was placed over the grave. This is a life-sized Black Hills sandstone figure of Wild Bill. It was sculptured by Alvin Smith in a shop owned by H. W. Guyor, in Deadwood, and was erected in 1903. It also was badly defaced by relic hunters and the weather. It was tightly enclosed for protection with a heavy wire screen, but this was cut open by relic hunters, so it was removed about twenty years ago.

The body of "Calamity Jane" (Mrs. M. E. Burk), who died

at Terry, near Deadwood, on August 1, 1903, was interred in a grave alongside Wild Bill's, at her request.

It has been stated by the acting undertaker who was in charge of the original funeral, that Wild Bill's big Sharps rifle was buried by his side. This statement the writer knows to be incorrect, as he saw the gun in the coffin when it was opened on reinterment. It was not a Sharps rifle, but a carbine, or a short cavalry, fitted into an old-fashioned Kentucky rifle breech, with the name J. B. Hickok engraved in the wood. After his death his personal effects were disposed of, and John Bradley of Spearfish, South Dakota, purchased the Sharps rifle. He used the gun for many years afterwards in hunting for wild game. Subsequently it came into possession of Allen Toomey, of Spearfish, now deceased.

Wild Bill had several revolvers, one of which was a finely carved, ivory-handled Colts forty-four caliber, model of 1850. This gun, he said, was a present from Kit Carson. The gun had been used until it was completely worn out, and when it was fired every chamber would be discharged simultaneously. This fine, though useless revolver, was turned in by Wild Bill to Captain Dotson in part payment of a board bill. Subsequently it came into possession of Laverne Wolfe of Deadwood. He owned two other forty-fours and a small pistol. The whereabouts of these is not definitely known by this writer.

Why many alleged photos of Wild Bill show him as a black-haired brunette is strange. He was a blond, as others, including General Custer who knew him well, have stated. His hair and mustache were of a tawny color.

XXIX

"CALAMITY JANE"

NUMEROUS fictitious and unreasonable, though amusing, stories have been written concerning the life of Martha Cannary, commonly known as "Calamity Jane." It is difficult to cull from this mass of fiction the real facts. The writer has considerable personal knowledge, as she was well known to me during the periods she resided in the Black Hills. Other information has been obtained from sources deemed to be reliable. This account will discredit much of her "own story" of her "life and adventures," published a few years before her death, and many highly fictitious and laudable stories told of her by sensational writers.

She was born in Princeton, Mercer County, Missouri, in 1852. Reports received by the writer deemed to be authentic, state that her father, John Cannary, was a hard drinker and very abusive of his family. Such conditions in early life would not be conducive to development of high character. She had several brothers and sisters who apparently were dropped wholly from her life in later years.

In her life story she states that the family migrated overland from Missouri to Virginia City, Montana, in 1865, and that her mother died at Blackfoot, Mont., in 1866, and her father in Utah in 1867. This is not entirely in accord with the record given the writer by an informant who claimed to have personal knowledge to the effect that the family moved from Missouri to Calamus, Dodge County, Wisconsin, and Martha was known to him as a member of the family there, in 1866. There is some ground for belief, if this information is correct, that Martha ran away from home to escape intolerable conditions and headed into the West, some time between 1866 and 1868, between the ages 14 and 16. In her own life story she gives 1852 as the date of her birth, and her presence in Montana in 1866, at the age of 14.

In a book written by a prominent early-day citizen of Sioux Falls, S. D., Thomas H. Brown, now deceased, it is related that he knew "Calamity Jane" in Confederate Gulch, Mont., in 1866, and that she was then about 20 to 22 years old. He relates an occurrence in which she walked into a store where he was sitting, and ordered some groceries, chiefly expensive canned goods, the purchase price being two ounces of gold dust. She put the goods into a sack, slung it across her shoulder and started out. When requested by the merchant to pay for the goods, she whipped out a six-shooter, and backed out the door, going up the trail to the cabin of a needy miner who was sick with smallpox. When the astonished merchant asked as to who his customer was, a bystander said, "Why that's Calamity Jane. Don't you know her? She is a dangerous woman in action."

The writer was in the vicinity of Confederate Gulch shortly after 1866. I heard the names of many who were, or had been, in that vicinity, with no mention of "Calamity Jane." In view of this and the fact that she was then only 14 years old, and the further fact that in her "own story" she states that she was not given the sobriquet "Calamity Jane" until 1873, it appears that Mr. Brown was misinformed as to the identity of the woman in the incident he relates.

In her "own story," she states that she went from Montana to Utah in the spring of 1866, with her father who died there in 1867, and then went to Wyoming, arriving in the spring of 1868. This agrees with the first absolutely authentic record the writer has obtained as to her whereabouts after leaving home. The late Capt. John P. Belding, former sheriff and deputy United States Marshal in Deadwood, told this writer that he knew her in Cheyenne, Wyoming, in 1868, when the Union Pacific Railroad was being constructed in that section; that she was known there as a "camp follower," so dissolute that she and others of her class were forced to leave the city. At that time she was 16 years of age.

No definite information came to the writer as to her whereabouts for seven years thereafter. In her "own story" she claims that she "joined General Custer as a scout at Ft. Russell, Wyo., in 1870." And that thereafter she was associated with the army in that capacity for several years. Inasmuch as she was only 18 years old in 1870, and there is no report of her having any connection with or service for the army in the official records, those of us who knew her personally may well question her story as to her "connection" with General Custer's army during those years. It is generally conceded by old timers, that she accompanied General Custer's army to the Black Hills in 1874, and also General Crook's expedition to the Hills in 1875. The question is, in what capacity she accompanied the army,—whether as a government scout or a "camp follower." On this point the writer, and many others who knew her subsequently, have very positive opinions.

She made her first appearance in Deadwood in the month of June, 1876, in company with "Kittie" Arnold, "Wild Bill" Hickok, "Colorado Charlie" Utter and his brother, Steve. Calamity was attired in a brand new, elegant, well fitting man's suit of buckskin, with a belt of "arsenals." In her "own story" she states that she met Hickok at Fort Laramie, and that they proceeded to the Black Hills, arriving "about June." Thereafter she was seen frequently in his company, and following him about the streets, during the few weeks he lived after their arrival in Deadwood.

Following her arrival in the Hills, Calamity Jane spent several years in Deadwood and nearby mining towns, figuring conspicuously in the many dance halls, and was ever on the move, apparently without having any settled or permanent location, with the exception of a time in '76 and '77, when she rented and kept a house of her own. She was ready to take hold of any kind of work, as was evidenced by her serving as a "bullwhacker" on more than one trip to Cheyenne in 1876. Although I never happened to witness any of her cruel performances with a twenty-foot bull whip, it was generally conceded that she was an expert with that instrument of animal torture. In her "own story" she tells of such occupation in 1879, between Pierre and Rapid City.

Much has been said concerning the ladies of Deadwood taking an interest in Calamity Jane and teaching her the use of a needle. This I believe to be erroneous, as she was known to use her needle while she was located for a time on Sherman Street. A citizen of Deadwood, who now has gray hair, informed this writer that she made him his first pair of long pants out of a California blanket.

That she was of a kind and sympathetic nature was shown by

her tender ministrations to the suffering, and to the dying little sister of C. H. Robinson of Deadwood. Much has been said and written about Calamity Jane and Kittie Arnold preparing the body of the Reverend Henry Weston Smith, who was murdered, for burial. To this story I give no credence whatever, although I was not present at that time. It was my understanding that Mr. C. E. Hawley, an upright citizen and church member, had charge of the obsequies, and I am sure that he would not have called upon one of those women for their assistance. In her "own story" she makes no mention of any such occurrence.

After the death of Wild Bill, Calamity Jane never appeared to show any preference for any particular one of that numerous element who depended upon the resources of one of her class for the price of a cigar, a drink, a meal, or a stake at "Bank the Wheel."

Calamity was mannish, resourceful, and independent, though plain and unattractive. She appeared to be able to make her way through life. She dressed, after her first appearance in Deadwood, as other women dressed, and although she was the last word in slang, obscenity, and profanity, her deportment on the streets, when sober, was no worse than that of others of her class. In her "own story" of those years in the Hills she relates a number of occurrences in which she played heroic parts. The writer was in close contact with events then transpiring, but heard no reports of the occurrences she relates.

She disappeared from the Hills in 1880. According to her "own story" she went to Wyoming in 1881, "took up a ranch in Montana" in 1882, and kept "a wayside inn where the weary traveler could be accommodated with food, drink or trouble if looked for"; quit Montana in 1883, reaching San Francisco in 1884, then went to Texas where she met Mr. Clinton Burk, a native of Texas, and married him in August, 1885; remained in Texas until 1889, a daughter being born in October, 1887; then went through Boulder, Colo., where "we kept a hotel until 1893, then traveled through Wyoming, Montana, Idaho, Washington, Oregon, and back to Montana and Dakota arriving in Deadwood in October 1895." She returned to Deadwood in company with her husband and a bright appearing little girl of about nine or ten years of age. This child was later sent to the Sisters' Convent School at Sturgis,

[118]

South Dakota, where she received her initial schooling and a moral training, that well prepared her for the journey through life along the paths of purity, Christianity, and usefulness, which she chose to travel, and from which, according to those who claim to know of her present whereabouts, she has never strayed.

Burk soon found employment here as a hack driver, and for several months following proved himself well adapted to the business by making good for his employer. However, he was not long in the business with his employer's money in his pockets, until prosperity got the better of him and he became an embezzler by appearing to trust his customers and making excuses for not turning in cash receipts, until his collections amounted to one hundred and seventy dollars. With this in his pockets he absconded and was never again heard of by either his family or his employer.

Calamity Jane was once more thrown upon her own resources at an age when she was wholly unfitted to take care of herself. However, she soon found a way of making a trip to the eastern states. Much has been written of her activities and escapades while in the East, to which I give but little credence. However, she made the acquaintance of a story writer, to whom she outlined a history of her life. The resourceful writer did the rest, and had this published. She returned to Deadwood, bringing with her a goodly number of her "own story" which she sold in Deadwood, Lead, and surrounding mining camps.

In canvassing the mining camps, she hired a hackman to take her around. The hackman informed me that she had no trouble in disposing of her books. Some miners would give her five dollars, while others would hand her fifty cents. Calamity realized a considerable sum of money from the sale of the books, which was soon dissipated. Once more she was left penniless. While temporarily residing at Terry, a mining camp eight miles west of Deadwood, she was taken suddenly ill and rapidly grew worse. Soon she was beyond the skill of her attending physician, and she died on the first day of August, 1903, lacking one day of being exactly twenty-seven years after the death of Wild Bill Hickok. In compliance with her dying request, she was buried by his side in Mt. Moriah Cemetery in Deadwood.

XXX

THE MURDER OF "PREACHER SMITH"

OF the many tragic incidents that marked the wildest days of '76 in this community, the one in particular by which the people were deeply and visibly affected, and which elicited many expressions of sorrow and regret, was that of the untimely death, by murder, of the Reverend Henry Weston Smith, the pioneer preacher of the Black Hills.

This pioneer preacher of the Gospel came to Custer, in the southern part of the Black Hills, early in the spring of 1876, and worked at mining and other jobs before coming to Deadwood. Capt. C. V. Gardner relates that Smith joined one of his freight trains at Custer and came to Deadwood in May, 1876. Here he found employment with many others in the construction of the Boulder Ditch, a huge mushroom enterprise, that was vigorously pushed through to the finish of almost everybody and everything connected with the concern, except the ditch itself, which is yet unfinished and stands today as a monument to folly. It is not known whether or not Preacher Smith received any compensation for his labor. It is known, however, that many others on the job did not.

My first contact with the Reverend Smith was on a Sunday shortly before his death. As I walked down Main Street I noticed a large gathering of men on the square at the end of Gold Street and heard someone speaking in a loud voice. Thinking only of auctioneers and street fakirs, I walked close to the speaker before I realized that I was in the presence of a minister of the Gospel, who was speaking in an easy, unaffected manner as though he might be at home addressing the members of his congregation. A score or two had hats off, listening intently to his discourse, while the great mass moved about restlessly, apparently paying but little attention to the speaker's remarks. However, no words were spoken to interrupt or embarrass him. Although I did not get his text, if he had given out any, I listened for a while to his sermon and was very favorably impressed by his manner and speech and unmistakable sincerity. I thought but little about the occurrence until after his murder, when I learned something of this man who had been toiling six days a week and traveling twenty miles on foot and preaching two sermons on the Sabbath. It was then that I realized, as I believe many others did, that the people of Deadwood had lost a man such as no community could afford to lose. I have since pictured the man who spoke to the multitude of people in the valley here, as a true disciple and an earnest follower in the footsteps of the Master who preached on the Mount nearly two thousand years before.

On Sunday, the 20th day of August, 1876, he delivered a sermon in the forenoon on Main Street, to the people of Deadwood; after which he started on foot and alone on his way to the town of Crook City for the purpose of preaching a sermon to the people later on the same day, as had been his custom for several Sundays. While on his way, traveling through timber at a point near the edge of Centennial Valley, and about five miles out from Deadwood, he was shot and killed. His body was discovered lying on the trail shortly afterwards by a man on horseback, who passed the body on his way to Crook City, where he made a report of the discovery.

A small party of men composed of Edmond Wolfe and others, immediately went to the place where the body lay. At that time Joseph Armstrong drove by with a hay wagon partly loaded with green hay. The body of the unfortunate preacher was placed on the hay and brought to Deadwood by Armstrong and given into the care of some friends and acquaintances, one of whom was C. E. Hawley, a highly respected churchman. He took charge of the remains, had them prepared for burial, and also conducted the funeral services at the grave, when all that was mortal of the good man was laid to rest in the new cemetery, which is now a residence portion of the Fourth Ward of Deadwood. His body, with nearly all others buried there, was removed some years later to a cemetery higher up on the mountain side, now known as Mount Moriah.

On the same day that the Reverend Smith was murdered, I was standing, in the afternoon, on Main Street between Gold and Wall streets in a group of men who were witnessing some amusing performances, when two horsemen came up the street on a gallop. I noticed something flapping against the shoulders of one of the horses and when they stopped within a few feet of where I stood, I saw that it was the head of an Indian tied to the horn of the saddle, either by the long hair or by a strap. It was not being dragged at the end of a rope as has been asserted by some and believed by many.

While the man who brought it was untying the head that bloodied the shoulder of the horse, he was asked the question, "Where did you get that thing?" He answered, "I killed him down the road." The next question was, "What are you going to do with it?" The answer came in a loud voice from someone on the outside, "Sell it at auction." This plan was agreed upon and one man mounted a platform that stood against the building and cried the sale. The first bid was low, but kept increasing until it reached twenty-five dollars and was knocked down at that bid. The "lucky man" who secured the gruesome prize was Dan Dority, general manager of that famous and unsavory institution known as the "Gem Theatre." If there was any money paid over I failed to see it, and I am certain that I witnessed the whole transaction. The parties to it went away down the street. I never afterwards saw the man who brought in the head. The statement was made by someone that he was a Mexican; this is generally believed, but I don't share in that belief. I stood close to the man and heard his words, which were few, and I detected no Mexican accent, nor did I think of a Mexican at that time. He was rather low in stature, having black hair, eyes, and beard. Apparently his age was about thirty. I afterwards learned that he was known as "Tex."

The head of the Indian sold at auction was kept for a time in a saloon until it ceased to be an object of curiosity or a wholesome ornament. It then was buried under the floor where it remained for about three years when it was exhumed while repairs to the building were being made. It was given to Louis Schoenfeld, who had had experience as an undertaker, and who roomed in my cabin. Louis dressed and polished the skull and hung it on the wall, where it kept vigil over us for many moons before he sent it by express to his former employer at Louisville, Kentucky. I could have kept it had I wished to do so.

On that same day a man by the name of Charles Mason was killed by an Indian at a point in the Whitewood Valley below Crook City. It was reported at the time, and the report afterwards was confirmed, that Mason had killed an Indian that same day before he himself was killed. The head of that Indian was brought into Deadwood that day by the impostor who claimed for himself the honor of killing the Indian.

A report of the confused affairs of that fatal day, which gained currency in later years, was that the body of Mason was brought to Deadwood and buried at the same time and in the same grave with that of Preacher Smith; and that afterwards both were removed and interred in the same grave on Mount Moriah. I was not present at the first burial, and am unable to vouch for the story. Although it was accepted as true by others, I gave the story little credence. However, I have never heard any other account of the burial of Mason.

Who killed the Rev. Henry Weston Smith? Practically all writers have charged the crime to Indians, and that has been the general belief.

No one saw the act committed. While first reports naturally attributed the killing to the Indians, no definite evidence was ever developed to support such belief. It is yet, and always will be, a matter of conjecture.

While this writer does not seek to controvert or change the fixed belief of those who accept the Indian theory, I long ago formed the opinion that it was done by a white man, for some unknown motive. In support of such belief may be cited that there is nothing in evidence that Indians were in that immediate vicinity that day, and the fact that the body was not scalped as was the invariable practice of the Indians of that day.

In 1891, a life-size statue was placed over Preacher Smith's grave in Mt. Moriah Cemetery. It was sculptured from red sandstone by J. B. Riordan, a New York sculptor who was in Deadwood temporarily at that time. It was sponsored by the local

Methodist Church and was paid for by popular subscription. The sandstone being soft, the statue was badly chipped by relic hunters and defaced by weather, ere being enclosed.

In 1914 a monument was erected in honor of this pioneer preacher of the Gospel, on the Deadwood-Spearfish highway, about three miles from Deadwood. This is about two miles from the spot where he was killed, as was located by Edmond Wolfe, one of the men who picked up the body. Wolfe came to Deadwood from Wisconsin for that purpose in 1926, his expenses being paid by subscriptions from a number of citizens. He was accompanied on this locating trip by Mayor W. E. Adams, Editor E. L. Senn, Editor Earl Morford, this writer, and others.

The Smith Monument has become a shrine for Methodism. Every year since 1924 memorial services have been held there on a Sunday closely preceding or following the "Days of '76" celebration.

When the murdered martyr's body was searched after being brought to Deadwood, there was found in his pocket, scribbled on scraps of paper, outlines of the sermon he intended to preach at Crook City. They were sent, with other belongings, to his mother in Ohio. From these notes, the sermon was constructed as it would naturally have been delivered from the outline. A copy of this was obtained by Mrs. Frank Ickes of Deadwood from relatives, and was first read to the public on Main Street, Deadwood, during the "Days of '76" celebration in 1924 by Rev. W. E. Prewitt, pastor of the Deadwood Baptist Church, who impersonated the Reverend Smith. The undelivered sermon reads as follows:

Text: Romans 1:5.

"The Apostle, next to Christ, may be considered as the most proper pattern for imitation by Christians of the present day.

"Of all the disciples of the Lord, none seem to unite more of the graces of the Spirit of Paul.

"Peter was zealous and impetuous, a son of thunder.

"James was called 'The Just.'

"John was full of gentleness and love.

"Apollos was an eloquent speaker and Barnabas was a son of consolation.

"But it was Paul alone who was able to become all things to

[124]

all men. Among the excellencies of his character, none appear more prominent than his self-sacrificing spirit and his devotion to the Gospel of Christ.

"At the time of writing the language of the text he had already suffered severely in defense of the doctrines of Jesus of Nazareth; but still, while contemplating his journey to the very center of idolatry, to a city of luxury and pride, for the purpose of preaching the gospel of purity, temperance, and humility, and although he knew that he should, in all probability, be called to pass through as great trials as he already had perhaps to suffer death, he was still willing to serve God in any way at any time or place, and under any circumstances whatsoever, and declared 'so as much as in me lies, I am ready to preach the gospel to you that are at Rome.'

"Now while we endeavor to gain instruction from the example of Paul, let us consider:

"1. Why he was willing to do this.

"2. Some of the ways in which we all may engage in this great work.

"Why Was He Willing To Do This?

"Answer, he loved God.

"Before he embraced the religion of Jesus Christ, he was zealous toward God, and zealous of the honor of his religion. He believed that Christ was overthrowing the work of God, and he persecuted this way unto death. But when his mind was illuminated by the Holy Ghost, he saw that the honor of the gospel was the cause of God; he saw that this was the way in which God had determined to display the glories of His character. Paul saw in Christ the brightness of the Father's glory and the express image of His person. Him, of whom Moses and the prophets did write: 'the chief among ten thousand, and altogether lovely.' He saw displayed, in characters of fire, the holiness of God's law which had declared, 'The soul that sinneth it shall die.' Also His glorious justice, which sternly demanded the blood of the sinner and declared, 'Without shedding of blood there is no remission.'

"He saw the glory of His wisdom in devising a plan by which He might be just and justify the sinner that believeth. He beheld the wonders of redeeming grace and undying love which led the Father to give His only begotten Son as a propitiation for our

[125]

sins. He saw, indeed, the Divinity of Jesus Christ, in that depth of love which caused Him to leave the glory which He had with the Father, before the world was, and to take upon Himself of the seed of Abraham, to humble Himself and become obedient to death.

"Being thus convinced that the glory of God and Christ was one, Paul gave himself to the work of spreading the news of Salvation in spite of bonds and afflictions, declaring 'None of these things move me, neither count I my life dear unto myself, so that I might finish my course with joy and the ministry that I have received of the Lord Jesus, to testify the gospel of the grace of God.'

"Paul Loved His Fellow Men. He saw himself with all mankind ruined by sin and depravity, totally unable to regain the favor of God without the intervention of an Almighty Savior.

"Here, in the gospel of the grace of God, was found the needed Savior—one able to save to the uttermost.

"This was the reason he was not ashamed of the Gospel of Christ. He saw men in a state of spiritual death; if in Christ, life.

"While the wrath was out against the sinner, He was made to sin for us who knew no sin. Mercy was free. Did the sinner find himself far from God by wicked works, he might be brought nigh by the blood of Christ; were he in darkness, Christ was light; were he sick of sin, Christ was a physician; would he return to God, Christ was the way; did he need gracious influences to lift him from the horrible pit of miry clay, Christ had promised that whatsoever he should ask in His name it should be given. 'If ye then being evil, etc.'

"Although Paul verily once thought that he ought to do many things contrary to the will of Jesus of Nazareth, and while he was hating men and women and persecuting them, he verily thought he was doing God service; yet when he found that there was no other name given under heaven whereby we might be saved, and that through Him men might have everlasting life, Paul could say to all, 'Would to God that not only thou, but all that hear me this day were such as I am except these bonds.' And sometimes he did so long for the salvation of men that he could most wish himself accursed of Christ, cut off from all the blessings of the Gospel, if that would secure their salvation.

"That men might take the blessings of the Gospel, He endured hunger and thirst, and cold and nakedness, stripes and buffetings.

"Some Of The Ways In Which We May All Engage In The Great Work Of Preaching.

"When our Savior said, 'Go ye into all the world,' He evidently intended the use of all means by which men may be brought to a knowledge of the truth. All men are not called to stand up and preach as professed ministers of the Word. There are many ways for a Christian to follow Paul as he followed Christ; many ways in which we may assist in spreading abroad the story of the Cross.

"First. Without money: Christ sent His disciples forth without purse or scrip, but He did not intend that they should live without food.

"Second. By sustaining the social needs of Grace.

"All can do something here, and are required to do something, every man according to his ability.

"Third. The Sabbath school.

"Fourth. By personal efforts to lead men to the Savior.

"Fifth. By holding up the life of a consistent God as a guide to our own lives."

The widespread interest in the life and martyrdom of this heroic preacher led Editor Senn of the *Deadwood Daily Telegram* to gather what he could of his life story prior to coming to Deadwood. This biographical sketch, as published in the *Telegram* on August 18, 1924, was as follows:

"Rev. Henry Weston Smith was born in Ellington, Conn., January 10, 1827.

"He was six feet tall, dark complexioned, black hair and eyes, full beard and mustache.

"As a youth he was an earnest Christian. At the age of 23 he was licensed as an 'exhorter' by the Methodist Church. Later he was ordained as a minister, and held pastorates at several places in Connecticut.

"On Oct. 3, 1847, he married Ruth Yeomans of Franklin, Conn. She lived one year after marriage and she and her infant son were buried in the same grave.

"In 1857, he married Lydia Ann Joslin of Tolland, Conn. She

[127]

and three children survived the tragic death of the husband and father.

"In 1861, Mr. Smith enlisted in Company H, 52d Massachusetts Infantry. He was in a number of engagements, and after nine months' service was mustered out.

"In 1867, he was admitted to the practice of medicine.

"In 1867, the family moved to Louisville, Ky. In the meantime he had resumed work as a preacher of the gospel.

"Hearing a call to do religious work in the new west, he left in March, 1876, for Cheyenne. After being there a short time he came to the Black Hills, first to Custer City, then to Deadwood. He worked as a miner for a livelihood and preached on the streets. He was held in esteem by many for his self-sacrifice and unpretentious demeanor and upright conduct.

"On the morning of August 20, 1876, he preached in Deadwood, then left a note pinned to his cabin door, 'Gone to Crook City, back at 2 P.M.' On the way there he was murdered supposedly by Indians. His body was found later in the day and brought to Deadwood.

"Interment was made in Mount Moriah Cemetery, Deadwood, and a life-size statue of sandstone erected over his grave. This was crumbled badly, being of soft stone. Several years ago an imposing monument was erected on the Deadwood-Spearfish road, near the place of his death.

"He had intended bringing his family to Deadwood a few months after arrival. Two years after his death they moved to Texas. In 1882 they returned to Kentucky and in 1885 moved back to Massachusetts, residing in Worcester."

XXXI

"DEADWOOD DICK"

Possibly there are elements of truth contained in the trite saying, which is generally credited to the great showman, Barnum, that the people like to be fooled. While this trait in people is generally recognized, it cannot be accepted as evidence that most people, when seeking information on matters of historical importance, prefer fiction to truth. With such belief this writer will endeavor to make true answers to two questions that have repeatedly been submitted to him, orally and in writing, as an early-day pioneer of the Black Hills. Undoubtedly the same questions have been asked of other pioneers.

One question is: "Was there really, in the early days of the Black Hills settlement, any such character as has been pictured in stories of fiction as a notorious stage robber, having the name of 'Deadwood Dick'?" This question is answered in the negative. There was no such character.

The other question is, "What do you know about Deadwood Dick?" The following is what I know of four different persons, each of whom has been spoken of, by his associates, as "Deadwood Dick."

The first of these, had he remained in the Black Hills, probably would have retained the soubriquet against all comers. This was Dick Brown, a large and handsome man, having a dark mustache and a goatee to match. He was a proficient banjo performer, an excellent baritone singer, and a versatile actor. He came from Cheyenne, Wyoming, to the southern Black Hills during the fall of 1875. After witnessing a few successful "clean-ups" of placer gold, he became enthusiastic and made a hasty return to Cheyenne, avowedly for the purpose of obtaining money to buy a gold mine. On meeting the Brennan, Stokes and Harney party he expressed the opinion that the Black Hills was the greatest gold mining country in the world, and averred that he had seen a miner with a buckskin breeches leg filled with gold dust; such was his exaggerated description of a small buckskin purse of ten to twenty ounces of gold dust capacity.

It appeared, however, that Dick failed to find available money to carry out his plans. He did, however, make a discovery which no doubt made a stronger appeal to his tastes than mere money would have done, at Laramie, Wyoming. This discovery was the person of one Fannie Garrettson, an attractive woman and also a fine musician. Dick's good looks and winning ways proved sufficient to entice Fanny away from her lover, one Ed Shaunnessy. So together the new pair came to the southern Hills and on to Deadwood in the spring of '76. Here, as a musical attraction, second to none of the many that were performing on Main Street at the time, they secured an engagement at the "Melodeon," a saloon and gambling hall on the corner of Main and Wall streets, where the Fairmont Hotel now stands. Here for many weeks they played to a packed hall and a crowded street in front of it. Fannie at the piano and Dick with his banjo and his strong, clear, musical voice, held their audiences up to the midnight hour. Dick's repertoire of ballads consisted of practically all popular western songs from '49 to '76. Into these songs he would fit the names of the Black Hills and Deadwood in ways so appropriate as to win for himself the appellation "Deadwood Dick." Undoubtedly the appellation had inception in a casual remark by some one who had heard and enjoyed his fine singing. Notwithstanding the popularity gained by these versatile entertainers, their jubilee days in Deadwood were abruptly brought to a close by the appearance of Fannie's erstwhile lower, Shaunnessy, who had followed her with the expressed hope of winning her back.

In this effort he was sorely disappointed, as he was again spurned by Fannie; and on being informed that Fannie and Dick were married, he gave up all hope and became reckless. One night when he strolled into the Gem Theatre he discovered Fannie and Dick together upon the stage. Not being able to restrain himself any longer, he advanced and threw something at them. Whatever it was no one seemed to know, as the object was quickly put out of sight. Some people who witnessed the performance said that it appeared to be a bunch of paper. Dick said that it was an ax. Assuming that the insult was a sufficient provocation to justify him in doing away with his dangerous rival, Dick drew a revolver and killed Shaunnessy on the spot. Then Dick and Fannie left Deadwood for another part of the territory soon afterwards. It was reported that Dick was apprehended and stood trial for murder; but, as there was no evidence produced to convict him, he was set free, and so far as the writer knows he was never again heard of by Deadwood people.

The foregoing circumstances all transpired prior to the advent of the first stage line into the northern Black Hills. The first line was inaugurated in September, 1876, to be followed by other lines in 1877, and also by a goodly number of enterprising individuals known as "road agents." This industrious and menacing element was busily engaged in plying its nefarious occupation on all stage lines running into Deadwood during the summer of 1877, and stage hold-ups were of frequent occurrence.

This condition was sufficient to provide inspiration and ample material to a famous writer of "wild west" stories. He wrote and put into circulation thrilling works of fiction. In his stories of stage hold-ups, he gave his leading character, who was a leader of road agents, the name of "Deadwood Dick." Although this lawless and dangerous bandit was depicted as being absolutely fearless, and a merciless killer of men who evinced an inclination to hesitate in meeting his terms of settlement, he was, nevertheless, endowed by nature with a sympathetic feeling and would, at times, yield to the importunities of women and boys, by returning to the women their purses with a small amount of change, and to boys their "Peter Funk" watches.

It appeared that these thrilling stories of fiction gained wide circulation. Consequently in a very short time after its publication practically every one in this section had heard of "Deadwood Dick." There were many who showed an inclination to emulate that notorious bandit of fiction, and several who sought to appropriate the cognomen.

The second person to be called "Deadwood Dick," for a brief period by his friends and acquaintances, was Richard Cole or "Little Dick Cole" as he was known. He was a stage driver, the one who brought the first stagecoach from Rapid City to Crook City and Deadwood. He had some highly exciting and unpleasant experiences in stage hold-ups. He manifested a desire to be known as "Deadwood Dick." His friends took the matter seriously and for a time he was spoken of by that name. However, as he was not generally known and had not been much in evidence in the northern Hills, his name and fame apparently faded from the public mind, and the field was left open to the next eligible claimant to that much coveted soubriquet.

Some two or three years later a third "Richard" stepped into the breach as the only legitimate claimant to the honor and notoriety that was supposed to be conveyed in the name of "Deadwood Dick." This was Dick Bullock, a resident of Lead City, a gentleman highly respected by all who knew him. He was regarded as a courageous and fearless stagecoach messenger, having served in that capacity for several years, and as one of the guards of the gold bullion while it was in transit to the railroad. Whether Dick himself, or his friends, conceived the plan to push him into publicity, is a question. He appeared to be pleased and highly honored by the plan. However, his claim to the title did not gain the prestige that was hoped for and expected by his many friends. His aspirations were not supported by any credentials, and the general public failed to respond. He departed from the Hills soon after the long stage lines were abandoned, and went to Los Angeles, Calif., where he died some years later.

Notwithstanding his failure to qualify for the coveted name "Deadwood Dick," he was accorded a glowing tribute by a Los Angeles paper as an Indian fighter and stage messenger and veteran of many heroic encounters. So passed from the stage of action Deadwood Dick No. 3.

After the lapse of many years following the failure of the foregoing to obtain permanent title to the title of "Deadwood Dick," and after the appellation and character were presumed to have become universally known as fiction, there arose from the shades of obscurity, garbed in the buckskin habiliments of an Indian fighter, a new claimant for the honors. This eleventh hour arrival was a necessity in the "Days of '76" annual celebration, so he was found and exhibited to tourists as "the real Deadwood Dick." To those who were informed on Black Hills history, he was known to be Richard Clark, an old time resident and worthy citizen of Whitewood, a town ten miles distant from Deadwood, who had been but little known or heard of outside his home town. Investigation of the career of this Deadwood Dick failed to disclose any substantial basis or tangible evidence to justify giving him the appellation. By newspaper correspondents, who sought interesting "copy" rather than truth, he has been pictured as an early day Indian fighter, a scout for General Custer, a dispatch carrier, a pony express rider, a stagecoach messenger, and a treasury guard. This fiction, fostered for commercial purposes to give color to the annual "Days of '76," was carried out even in his death and final resting place.

The following is, so far as could be learned, the true and uneventful history of Deadwood Dick No. 4.

Born in 1848 and reared at Waterford, Ireland, he came to America some time prior to the Black Hills gold excitement of 1876. He joined in the big rush to the Hills in April, coming over the Bismarck route with a large party of men known as the Ward party, because of two Ward brothers starting for the Black Hills with a small herd of cattle. Some place north of the Belle Fourche River the party was fired into by a band of Indians. One of the Wards and a man named Sam Wells were severely wounded, and the cattle were run off by the Indians. The party of men came on to Crook City, the only town at the time in the northern foothills.

There a number of the party, including Richard Clark, settled, and there Clark spent the entire summer and the winter that followed in a cabin with a well known engineer who is still living in this part of the county. Clark continued to live in Crook City until the inhabitants abandoned it and moved to the new town of Whitewood. Here Clark married, reared a family, and entered into the employ of the Northwestern Railroad Company. He lived there and at Lead up to and after the placing upon him of the mantle of "Deadwood Dick." The foregoing is presented to leave to posterity a statement of facts as the writer knows them to be, and to prevent so far as it is possible, the incorporating of pure fiction in the annals of the history of South Dakota.

If the foregoing comes to attention of anyone who takes exception to the statements contained therein, such person is advised to visit and interview any one or all of the Black Hills Pioneers of the seventies. None will be found who will state that he knew, or ever heard, of Richard Clark being known as "Deadwood Dick," until a dozen years ago, or as an Indian fighter, or a scout with Custer, or a pony express rider, or a stagecoach messenger or guard. He was never at any time a resident of Deadwood, and does not enter into the comprehensive annals of the Black Hills, as set forth by many writers of history, until after the birth of the "Days of '76" annual celebration in 1924. Why he permitted himself to be a party to this fiction, and falsely exploited, is beyond comprehension of pioneers who know the facts, and are jealous of the truth in pioneer history.

CUSTER'S TRAIN TO THE BLACK HILLS, 1874

MEN OF THE GORDON PARTY

From left to right, top row: Tommy Quinner, David Aken, Angus McDonald, Lyman Lamb,
Red Dan McDonald, and John Boyle
Lower row: Jim Dempster, Dempster McDonald, R. R. Whitney and B. B. Logan

THE GORDON STOCKADE ON FRENCH CREEK NEAR CUSTER AS IT APPEARED IN THE VERY EARLY DAYS AT BLACK HILLS SETTLEMENT

U. S. ARMY HEADQUARTERS

When the U. S. troops under Captain Pollock arrested and expelled the members of the Gordon party in April, 1875, he left Lieut. Williams in charge. His first action was erection of the above cabin to serve as headquarters for the U. S. troops in the Black Hills

WILD BILL

"Calamity Jane"

Mrs. Henry Weston Smith Rev Henry Weston Smith
Killed Aug. 20 1876

PLACER MINING—DEADWOOD GULCH, 1876.

DAKOTA TERRITORY WAS DIVIDED INTO TWO STATES, NORTH AND SOUTH DAKOTA, IN 1889

At that time the Black Hills were separated from Pierre, the State Capital, by 150 miles of Indian reservations, with no railroad connection short of 1000 miles roundabout. The above photo shows members of the first state legislature and federal judges leaving for Pierre shortly before the legislature convened in January, 1890

THE DEADWOOD-SPEARFISH STAGECOACH WITH HARVEY FELLOWS, DRIVER. OPERATED BY J. S. McCLINTOCK FOR OVER TWENTY-FIVE YEARS

MAIN STREET, DEADWOOD, AUGUST, 1877

DEADWOOD AFTER THE GREAT FIRE
SEPT. 26TH 1879

Crook City, 1876

EARLIEST PICTURE OF PLACER MINING IN DEADWOOD GULCH

Showing claim "21 below Discovery" taken in 1876. Site is about one block up Main Street from present public school building

EARLIEST PICTURE OF HOMESTAKE MINE SURFACE WORKS

Taken about 1887. Subsequently a large portion of the hills shown were milled and the site is now a big hole known as "the open cut"

PROSPECTORS IN DEADWOOD GULCH, 1876

XXXII

TWO KILLED BY AN INDIAN IN CENTENNIAL
VALLEY

DURING the spring and summer months of '76 the atmosphere in and around Deadwood was kept highly charged with flying reports and rumors of Indian depredations and outrages occurring along the highways leading to the Hills, and in the valleys adjacent thereto. So many of these reports were found to be untrue that they hardly created a ripple of excitement, and people had almost ceased to pay any attention to them. Nevertheless, some of these reports proved to be only too true.

On one occasion, which I remember very distinctly, when such a report was readily accepted at face value, a trio of horsemen came racing neck and neck into town one afternoon, with hats off and hair pompadoured. Their story was that they had come dangerously near running into a large band of Indians. I have forgotten the exact number, but it was large. These reported Indians were in Centennial Valley and were stampeding a bunch of horses from the Burton Ranch, which was better known at that time as the "Montana herd."

The report created a furor of excitement. Soon an immense crowd gathered around the informants. Ike Brown and Charles Holland, two bold and enterprising gentlemen, issued a hurry up call for volunteers and assumed the leadership of the party to go after the Reds, to recover if possible the stolen stock, and incidently bag a few Indians. It was open season for big game at the time, with no limit to the catch, and it was optional with the pursuers as to the number of scalps or heads they might choose to bring in.

Of the three thousand or more floaters strolling in and about

[135]

town at that time, it was reasonable to expect that a few hundred of them at least would make quick response to the call, especially those who had spent many hours of their school days in dreaming of the time when they would go West and seek just such opportunities as the one now within their grasp. Such extravagant expectations fell short when the party was ready for the start. Only thirty saddles were filled. However, a large majority of the inhabitants were without horses, and therefore found good reason for not participating in the Big Sioux round up.

As for myself, I was also on foot, having but a few days prior to that lost my horse in the Centennial herd near Crook City. While that was fresh in mind, and I was yet sore over it, I was unable to recall of having lost any Indians, so decided to stay with the majority and await the report of the conquering heroes.

All the party, with the exception of Brown and Holland, made safe return to Deadwood about dark the same evening, and submitted their report, which in substance was as follows: They had taken up the trail of the Indians at False Bottom Creek about fourteen miles from Deadwood, and followed over the first divide where they discovered a lone Indian running on foot over the next divide and toward Spring Creek. They now had good reason to suspect that this Indian had purposely fallen behind the others, to have the white men give chase over the crest of the hill and into a trap for a general massacre.

So the pursuing party left their horses behind and crawled up close to the divide and there paused to reconnoiter. Ike Brown, the most impulsive and daring of the party, raised carefully above the weeds and grass, but what discovery he made was never told, as he fell back to earth with a large hole through his body and died instantly.

It was now getting near dusk and the situation had reached a critical stage. They were in a quandary as to the next move. While they were discussing the matter, Charley Holland settled it by rising out of the weeds for a peep over the hill. He also failed to report. However, a report was made by the Indian's needle-gun and Holland fell dead beside his partner.

No orders were issued or required for the next move, and the leadership of the party fell to the man who was the first to reach his mount. Their brave, but incautious, leaders were left where they fell and the pursuing party made time in getting back to town.

The following morning a formidable body of men was organized and returned to the scene of the evening before. They found the bodies of the two leaders where they fell. They had been stripped of clothing but neither of them had been scalped. This oversight caused some speculation as to the reason, as the hostile Sioux seldom passed up an opportunity for securing such valuable tokens. Doubtless there was a reason but it was not revealed.

On going over the divide from where the shots that killed the two leaders came, they found to their astonishment, that a lone Indian had engaged them the evening before. He had taken up his position behind a scrub oak, where he had evidently made the best use possible of the time by digging in with his knife. Doubtless he was expecting to be overtaken and was preparing to sell his life as dearly as possible. So it seemed that both the pursued and pursuers were ignorant of the plans of the other, and the lone Indian whom I shall designate as "Hide Behind The Stump" escaped, as did also the band that had taken the stock.

I was informed some years ago by Jack McKenzie, an old friend of mine, that he had followed the Reds at a safe distance for several miles, shooting at them with his Winchester rifle, and that one shot had caused a commotion in their ranks; but no evidence of their having sustained any loss was found.

The bodies of Brown and Holland were brought to Deadwood by J. T. Spaulding (Buckskin Johnny), and prepared for burial. Holland's was shipped back to his home at or near Sioux City. He had the appearance of a perfect gentleman. The remains of Brown, I think, were sent away for interment, but I am not certain as to where he was buried.

Brown and Holland were the only two of the party that I knew. Others yet living may have participated in the unfortunate affair.

XXXIII

THE WHITE ROCKS TRAGEDY

TOWERING one mile above sea level, overshadowing on the east the historic city of Deadwood, and keeping silent vigil over the twin cities of the dead, Mount Moriah and Burnham Hill, stands majestically four square to the winds a giant handiwork of nature, known as the "White Rocks." It is not known from whom this colossal structure received its appellation.

A revelation of the scenes witnessed by this towering giant would disclose interesting chapters in a history of the Black Hills. Long have the White Rocks held sway as a trysting place for lovers, table grounds for festivities of church, school and family gatherings, and offering to tourists a delightful view point for making a general survey of the surrounding country; but in such a glowing chapter on the White Rocks would have to be recorded one dark page in its history, a page telling of foul murder committed at its base.

During Deadwood's early days, when hundreds of people were flocking into the Hills from the East, there came two bright appearing young men, scarcely out of their "teens." They were known as Lee and Bill. They were unknown, and probably unnoticed by most people excepting those employed where they roomed and took their meals. It was noticed that Lee had money and settled the bills. As this was nothing unusual little was thought of it at the time. It was later recalled when it was developed that Lee was the son of wealthy parents and was supplied with a fine gold watch, and several hundred dollars in currency. Bill, doubtless, was well aware of this and never left the company of his friend while waiting his opportunity to get possession of the coveted treasure.

This opportunity was afforded during a trip of the pair to White Rocks at a time when there was no one else there. When they passed around to the opposite side from town, Bill's chance came. He fired a shot through Lee's head and rifled his pockets taking everything of value. He did not make any effort to cover his tracks, which he might have done by carrying the body but a short distance into the thick brush. He didn't have the time to spare for any such work as that, so he left the body where it fell and hastened back to town with the intention of breaking a faro bank and getting out of the country with as much money as he could conveniently carry.

The faro bank was not so easily broken as he had anticipated that it would be. When he was making a renewed effort which might have put it into the hands of a receiver, an officer tapped him on the shoulder.

Some person had gone up to White Rocks the day after the murder, discovered the body and brought the news immediately. Bill was easily apprehended. Although he denied committing the murder, claiming to be the rightful owner of the watch and money, the case against him was plain. He was tried, convicted of second degree murder (as I remember the verdict), and sent to the penitentiary for a number of years.

XXXIV

DEADWOOD'S FIRST CITY ADMINISTRATION

DURING the first six months of its existence the city of Deadwood was under the restrictions of no legal authority whatever, and it was generally understood that each person was accorded the privilege of being a law unto himself, in so far as his own personal rights and habits were concerned; provided, however, that such rights and habits were not unduly exercised, or extended too far beyond the limits of the common moral law with which all were presumed to be familiar, and would not infringe upon the rights of others. This code of ethics was so thoroughly understood by the great majority of people who came into the city in 1876, that it proved to be practically sufficient in preserving order in a general way, so far as the masses were concerned. However, those equal rights principles were wholly insufficient in the prevention or suppression of difficulties of a personal nature, such as quarrels, fist fights, and occasional gun fights in the meeting face to face of bitter enemies, and other occurrences of a like nature. Such occurrences even the strictest civil or military authorities would have been unable to prevent. Both of these subsequently proved to be inadequate in suppressing high crimes and in bringing to justice defiant criminals, both after the organization of a provisional city government in Deadwood, and during the Bullock "carpet bag regime." One instance was the willful murder of Cephus Tuttle described in another chapter.

It may be said that, in view of the large percentage of those who flocked into Deadwood in '76 who were criminally inclined, and the wild confusion that followed the big rush, the city fared very well; however, it was plain to be seen that without a legal form of government of some kind, with laws to be administered

[140]

and made enforcible by a majority of its better class of citizens, that the city of Deadwood would soon fall under control of a lawless element, which, while they were strangers one to another, worked in singles and doubles while carrying on their nefarious occupations. That class was not slow in recognizing their relationship to each other, and their mutual welfare, and were soon working together in organized bands against the peace, dignity, and safety of the honest and law abiding citizens of Deadwood.

With this menacing condition confronting them in the rising tide of lawlessness, not alone in Deadwood but elsewhere in the Black Hills, the situation became unbearable, having reached a danger point that was giving the better class of people much concern. It was realized that the conditions could no longer be ignored, but must be brought under control in a legal way.

In September, 1876, a meeting of the citizens was held, in which a resolution was passed, declaring it to be essential and imperative that, for the future peace and safety of its citizens, the city of Deadwood should be organized under a provisional city government. This proposal was approved and consummated by electing as mayor Judge E. B. Farnum and a full set of councilmen.

The new city organization proceeded immediately to function. About the same time a "vigilance committee" was organized in Deadwood under the leadership of one Talbut. It held several meetings in a small room on Siever Street but failed to function effectively, as there were several persons connected with it who were known to be reckless and dangerous, if not criminally inclined. For the good of the community it was soon disbanded. However, it was said to have had a deterrent effect in curtailing the operations of some of the most active members of the law defying element, thereby performing greater service to the community by creating fear in the hearts of the criminal element, of drastic action, than could have been done by the taking of such action.

It is not the intent of this writer, sixty years later, to find fault or to criticize further than what is set forth in a true statement of the official acts of those duly elected municipal officers into whose hands were placed all affairs pertaining to the newly organized city government. Empowered they were to administer and enforce the ordinances as made for the purpose of relieving the people from continuance of the increasing menace of outlawry and for the betterment and general welfare to its citizens. It is here conceded that their administration was conducted in a way which was a deterrent to crime in general, and a check upon the open operations of the lawless element. It was instrumental in effecting a change from the chaotic conditions which had so long prevailed to at least a semblance of law and order.

However, the salutary effects upon society in a general way of the acts of this august body of city solons for which they deserved and received the commendation of law abiding citizens, was lessened by their failure to take action in any way, or to even take up for consideration, the licentiousness and gross immorality, basis for many criminalities, which were rampant in the city at the time of their inauguration and during their tenure of office. Such failure to give those conditions proper consideration, together with their own conduct along the same line, justified the indignation of all citizens who were desirous of having a general city cleaning.

The very first official act of portly Mayor Farnum failed to redound his credit or that of those who gave their sanction, by confirming the appointment to the position of city marshal one Con Stapleton, a "tin horn gambler," who had drifted in from Montana. Just what prompted Mayor Farnum to inaugurate the establishment of law and order and a clean city government by going into the underworld to make this selection of a peace officer, was never disclosed. It may be inferred that he was in sympathy with that element and made his selection accordingly. Or he may have had knowledge of Con's record in Montana which appealed to him. Be that as it may, the appointment was confirmed by the city council and Con entered upon his new duties.

Now this new official, who had been designated as the chief factor to bring order out of chaos and establish a clean government for Deadwood, although he had not long been a resident of Deadwood, had already made a fair start in establishing a record. He had been one of the party who sat at the poker table in Saloon No. 10, with "Wild Bill" and Captain Massie, a few weeks previous, when the former was killed and the latter was wounded by Jack McCall, and who gracefully withdrew from the table without receiving a scratch. Other affairs could be cited not to his credit. I will relate one episode in which Con was a star actor, and without having the benefit of a rehearsal, enacted his role without a hitch in the proceedings.

The affair came about in this way: Another one of his class, D. Tom Smith by name, proprietor of a saloon and gambling resort, after having made a selection from the flock of "soiled doves," had gone to the trouble and expense of procuring a furnished apartment on the second floor of the Chamber C. Davis building on upper Main Street. Here he and his "ownest-own" were apparently living in peace until Con, who was not a bad looking fellow, put in his appearance at the apartment at such times as D. Tom was busily engaged in mixing cocktails at his place of business. D. Tom soon became aware of Con's intrusion upon his possessive rights and for some reason disapproved of it. One day while he was in a bad humor about something, he took a shot at Con. Due to his being a poor wing shot and Con being a good sprinter and an artful dodger, the shot went wild and lodged in the skull of Henry Lundt, a good citizen. He survived for about two years but finally succumbed to the injury.

This deplorable affair, with loss to the community of a much better citizen, came as a direct result of Con's refusing to stay hitched. While this was conceded, there was no one so unjust as to censure Con for side stepping the main issue in this momentous affair.

Without further citations in proof of Con's fitness for being a reform peace officer, it can be said that he plunged into his official duties in the most approved style of landing suckers and letting the big fish slip off the hook. The big fish, the high class gamblers who did most of their sleeping during the day time and who kept their business affairs running full blast through the greater part of the night, were not robbers in the exact sense of the term. They were not accused of taking money from any man until after he had put it down on a gambling table or wheel, using his own judgment in endeavors to increase his capital, and lost. No less than ninety per cent of the sucker element lost out on their own judgment. However, their judgment was, in most cases, materially weakened and their desires accentuated, by the drinks of whiskey which had been employed to jolly and lure them into the games.

As a result of having lost their money in the games of chance, the unfortunate suckers would usually be thrown into a state of high excitement. Many of them became so angered and hostile in the belief that they had not been given a square deal, but had been robbed, that they would, in the heat of passion and under the influence of liquor, unwisely make accusations in such vituperative and abusive language that the accused party, being not only a high class gambler but also a trained slugger, would proceed to knock him down, give him a few vigorous kicks and then call the marshal or other officer to take charge of him. The unfortunate victim would be hustled away to the "cooler" to sleep off his troubles and perchance to dream of facing "his honor" on the following morning, a matter of business which invariably followed and in which he would be required to make a liberal contribution to the city treasury. In default of such contribution he would be permitted to rest for a term in the cooler.

Such was the fate of the suckers who furnished most of the lubricant which kept the machinery of the new city in good running order. The higher class of gamblers, of whom the city marshal himself was an active member, were permitted to continue luring into their nets suckers, winning their money, and slugging them with impunity. A large majority of those whom I have here designated as high class gamblers, as well as some of the ablest lawyers, together with not a few of the business fraternity of the city, were cohabiting openly and shamelessly with prostitutes picked from the underworld. Such were the grossly immoral and shameful conditions which prevailed in the new city of Deadwood before, during, and long after the organization of the provisional city government. These deplorably corrupt social conditions had become so deeply seated and so firmly fixed in the business and social affairs of the city that it required many years of earnest endeavor on the part of ministers of the gospel and reformers, with the assistance of decent citizens, to effect changes for the better and liberate the city from domination of that abominable system of debauchery and corruption. Especially notable among efforts to free the city from the dominance of vice, was the fight made by E. L. Senn. For sixteen years, from 1909 to 1925, with his *Deadwood Daily Telegram*, he waged a relentless fight on all kinds of lawlessness. His business was boycotted by the business elements then controlling the city, causing loss of many thousands of dollars. He was twice beaten up on the streets by men who took exception to his exposé of conditions. His office was set afire during the night on one occasion, and on another was entered and the machinery wrecked. Nevertheless, he "stayed on the job," and when he was appointed to a federal law enforcing position in 1925, he had the satisfaction of knowing that Deadwood was then as free of vice and lawlessness as any city of its size in the state.

XXXV

THE SECOND KNOWN PREACHER IN THE BLACK HILLS

PROBABLY there could have been found in that great civilian army of occupation of the Black Hills of Dakota in 1876 a considerable number of members of the various denominations of the Christian faith, and possibly a number of ordained ministers of the gospel; but if so, preachers were inconspicuous and but little in evidence on the crowded streets of Deadwood during the summer of that year. Only two of such ministers, both of the Methodist denomination, were known to deliver a sermon on the streets or elsewhere in Deadwood. The first of these Godly men was the martyred Rev. Henry Weston Smith who took a stand on Main Street on Sunday mornings and delivered his sermons to the crowds of people who surrounded him, and of whom much has been written.

The other minister of the gospel, though not a voluntary speaker, was selected from the great aggregation of people by a committee of men, who had been informed, probably by his associates, that he was an ordained minister of the Methodist Church. His name was W. L. Rumney (not certain as to initials). The committee had previously obtained the consent of Bill Nuthall, one of the "vilest of the vile," that they might have a sermon preached in his spacious dance hall. So this fine looking and intelligent appearing man of military bearing was requested to deliver a sermon, with assurances that he would not be interrupted during his discourse. He evinced surprise at this unexpected request. He told the committee that preaching the gospel had been for many years his chosen profession and it mattered little to him when or where he was called to speak "The Word." So all gambling paraphernalia in the infamous "Bella Union" ceased operations and for more than half an hour this minister of God occupied the floor. His clearly spoken words resounded through the crowded hall and not a voice was heard to embarrass him. Evidently he had many times before delivered sermons to thousands of soldiers, as it was learned that he had been an officer in a Georgia regiment during the Civil War. After closing his address and thanking his audience for their kind attention he started out, but was halted while a good sized purse of money was collected and presented to him, for which he thanked them and again mingled with the people on the street. Many who heard his sermon and expressed themselves declared that they had never heard a better one. Probably there were men in that hall who never before had heard a sermon preached.

This good man soon afterwards departed for the southern Hills. He had contracted a severe cold which developed into pneumonia, which caused his death, and he was buried under pines a long way from his native soil.

XXXVI

THE WOLF MOUNTAIN STAMPEDE

In relation of the adventures of the early-day pioneers and trail blazers of Black Hills, a great deal has been written with much stress upon the dangers, hardships, and privations encountered and endured by these first comers. This phase of our early history appears to have been greatly overdrawn. While it is true, as regards a comparatively small percentage of the great mass of immigrants who flocked into the Black Hills at that early day, it may be said that, with but few exceptions, only those who had forgotten or who had blindly ignored the well known maxim that discretion is the better part of valor in their excessive desire to be the first to reach the grounds in order to secure for themselves or their absent friends a first choice of gold mining properties, paid the penalty for their rashness and indiscretion by suffering hardships, and in a number of instances with their lives. Starting out as they did, at their imminent peril, in small groups, even single families, in foolish attempts to pass over hundreds of miles of barren bad lands, in forbidden territory swarming with hostile savages, it was inevitable that they suffer for their folly.

Aside from the great difficulties encountered by such reckless and unfortunate people, but little trouble was experienced in making the first trip to the Black Hills. While it is true that a great majority of the people who came in at the time were poorly equipped with effective weapons for making successful stands against formidable bodies of hostile savages, they very wisely took the precaution to unite in numbers sufficiently strong to assure them against attacks by Indians, and also to equip themselves with all requisites for making extensive and hazardous journeys. Therefore, aside from the unfavorable weather conditions met with, and the momentous thrills incident to such trips, they experienced but little trouble in reaching their destination.

To many of this latter class who had withstood the dangers, hardships and struggles of the great Civil War, this first trip to the Black Hills came as something in the nature of a spring or summer outing. Yet a considerable number of this favored class, who so luckily escaped the trials and dangers to which their less fortunate brothers were subjected, suffered at a later season of the same year some decidedly bitter experiences in roughing it, such as invariably attend all gold mining stampedes in cold climates.

The Wolf Mountain stampede occurred in the month of November, 1876. It was an outgrowth of fraudulent business enterprise which, it was said and was never controverted, had its origin in the office of a large livery barn which was situated on lower Main Street in Deadwood. This was owned and operated at the time by one "Red Clark," a man who undoubtedly had had former experience in mining enterprises and "salted mines," as he certainly exhibited extraordinary skill in launching and engineering this gigantic humbug as a mining enterprise.

In order to deceive the people, the scheme which had been so deliberately planned had to be handled with diplomacy. Clark was the man for the job and the one who put it through with a degree of success which no doubt exceeded his wildest expectations as a money maker for himself, but which spelled disaster to hundreds of that gullible element who comprise a large part of all mining communities.

Conditions which gave birth to this nefarious enterprise were an overstock of saddle horses and pack animals which had been utilized in various lines of business throughout the spring and summer months, but which, owing to the impossibility of procuring hay for their winter's feed had become practically valueless. As the first touch of winter came upon Deadwood, their owners disposed of their stock, chiefly to livery men, at very low prices, if at any price whatever above their feed bills of a few days standing. Consequently while other livery men were sending out their surplus stock of animals to the range to be cared for during the coming winter, this cool calculator on lower Main Street was filling his stables and corrals to capacity. The number of head, I was informed, was 65.

In view of the well known fact that there was at the time but very little horse feed available while this man Clark was holding and increasing his stock of animals, people living in his vicinity were commenting on his lack of judgment and shortsightedness. Some even expressed doubts as to his sanity. At the same time the emissaries of this conscienceless schemer were putting into effective operation a plan through which not only those Doubting Thomases but hundreds of other unsuspecting persons were easily entrapped.

As an introduction to this heartless scheme, two horsemen leading a pack animal rode up Main Street one evening at dusk, at a time when the street was thronged with people, halted in front of a grocery store, walked in and purchased a liberal supply of groceries. While making payment for them they carelessly displayed a large buckskin purse apparently well filled with gold dust which quickly caught the eyes of many persons who were in and about the store at the time. While the two strangers were carefully arranging the pack on the back of their animal they were accosted by a third man from the crowd with something like this:

"Hello, Billy, where in the Sam Hill have you been keeping yourself all this time? I thought you had left the Hills long ago. Been off prospecting?"

"Yes, part of the time."

"What luck?"

"Oh, not so bad. Come over here, Jim. I am glad I've met you."

After a few words spoken in undertones the two men parted with a "now keep this to yourself." "You bet you," and the two mystery men mounted their horses and disappeared in the darkness, leaving a crowd of people whose curiosity had been so thoroughly aroused that a repetition of this farcical performance was wholly unnecessary. The astounding news was broadcasted and spread like wild fire. In less than 48 hours thereafter almost any man to be met with on the streets could give one some inside information regarding the great discovery of placer gold which had just been made in the Wolf Mountains some 300 miles to the westward. Men were seen scurrying hither and thither in frantic endeavors to procure saddle horses and pack animals. Those who had horses out in the valley herd were off in the night after them. Others who had no horses were early business callers at Clark's and other livery stables. I, like many other westerners, had had some costly and discouraging experiences in Idaho and Montana. Therefore, I decided to take it easy and await further developments and more authentic information. However, I was far from being immune from this contagious gold fever which now struck so forcibly that I was not long in deciding that even a mere chance in any good thing was preferable to no chance at all. As an eleventh hour caller at the Clark stables I was shown their remaining animal, a fine looking pony indeed, but with only three serviceable legs. I was assured that the animal would travel all right after being warmed up. In view of its being their last horse, to close the stock the price would be put down to bed rock, only $65.

As I was not making donations, this generous offer was rejected. I then found two men each of whom had a team and a wagon, who were intensely excited and anxious to start for the new mines at the earliest moment possible. They were then endeavoring to make up a party of men with a sufficient amount of freight to haul to defray their expenses for the trip. With my assistance they soon had other men enlisted for the trip and we were not long in getting our supplies and luggage in readiness for an early start on the following morning. The teamsters agreed to deliver our goods at the new mines for six dollars per hundred weight, regardless of the distance or road conditions.

While I had no intention at the time of returning to Deadwood during the winter, mines or no mines, and was stocking up with an ample supply of flour and bacon to carry me well through the winter, I noticed that some of our party made ready to start out on that long and perilous journey with less than a month's supply of provisions and apparently with as little concern as though they were expecting to get back to their homes in Iowa at hog killing time. They may have been intending to depend on their rifles and their prowess as hunters for wild meat to put them through the winter. This nonchalance on their part was no concern of mine and no comments were made, as it was their company for the trip, and not their future, in which I was directly interested.

While we were making preparations for the start, C. C. Higby, a well known grocery merchant came to me and, bemoaning his inability to join our expedition, presented me with a map which purported to outline the entire route from Deadwood to the Wolf Mountain mines. This map he informed me had just reached him together with a letter from an old friend, who advised him to pull up stakes and start at once if it were physically possible for him to do so and stating that he had just received a letter from an old California partner of his who had been on the ground and who had sent him a full description of the new district and gold fields and assuring him that it was beyond doubt the richest discovery of placer gold that had ever been made, unequaled even by the famous discoveries made in the Paramint district of California.

This unexpected revelation was all that was necessary in making assurance doubly sure. This wonderful map, evidently the work of an expert draftsman, showed a route from Deadwood to Spearfish, to Rifle Pits along the Montana Trail, to Sundance Mountains, over said mountains and on to Miller's Grave, thence on to Crazy Woman's Creek, thence along the south or west fork of said creek to a range of mountains, thence down through an expansive valley, and so on all the way, by easy stages, to the new Wolf Mountain mines only 280 miles. So all that was necessary in reaching our destination would be to follow this visionary map line to its western terminus. I accepted the map for what it was worth and placed it in my pocket for future reference.

Notwithstanding the fact that it was supposed that adequate preparations had been made by our belated party for its part in that never to be forgotten exploration, our trip from start to finish was wholly devoid of means of comfort and pleasure. While this disagreeable fact was of minor importance in that colossal movement, I will describe our bitter experience somewhat in detail to show in some degree the trials, privations and sufferings of scores of other deluded mortals who, under much less favorable conditions, had earlier joined in that frenzied scramble for wealth and remained away longer than did our party.

Our plan for an early start was frustrated somewhat by the weather. The evening and night before there was heavy snowfall of about two feet which was accompanied and followed by a strong drifting wind, approaching a blizzard. Regardless of this timely warning, we failed to profit by it although our wagons were delayed thereby until the noon hour. Our party of men, who had been tramping the streets with the loss of one night's rest, was further delayed until four o'clock that afternoon. Then, with spirits at concert pitch, we shouldered our rifles and bidding farewell to Deadwood started out on foot over the roundabout Crook City Trail for Spearfish, reaching the Jones Ranch at dusk with only the light from the snow to guide us.

The high winds which were still blowing had not only covered up all trails and wagon tracks, but had completely filled all gulches and gullies even with their banks, with drifts of snow. This impeded our progress to such an extent that it was with much difficulty that we were enabled to make any headway at all. After floundering through the drifts of snow for a time it became clearly apparent that much dissatisfaction was being manifested in the ranks of the party. The high spirits of a few hours before had fallen to zero and a disruption of the party was only averted by the fact that our worldly belongings were ahead of us at Spearfish and there was nothing for which to turn back.

A better feeling was soon restored by a Captain Brown, one of the men of the "Sixties." He agreed with me to alternate in breaking a trail for the others to follow. We did this nearly all of the way to Spearfish, a distance of twelve miles, which we reached about midnight, so completely exhausted that we were all glad to roll up in our blankets, boots and all, and lie down where one place was as good as another.

The weather having moderated during the night and our party feeling much refreshed the next morning after partaking of a warm breakfast, all again were in good spirits and ready to resume our westward march. Very good time was made that day considering the road conditions and also the condition of our teams which had not fully recuperated from the effects of their hard drive through the deep drifts of snow on the previous day. Wading in the creeks at that season of the year was one of the unpleasant features of the trip which had not been taken into consideration when our plans for the trip were being made. However, no complaint on that score was heard. Every man was ready to wade through even though the water should reach above the tops and fill his boots with ice water.

On the second day out from Spearfish we overtook and passed

a herd of about 200 head of cattle owned by John Deffenbach, who afterwards was murdered by Indians. The herd had been started to the new mines and was being driven by its owner and two of his herders.

If there had been any doubt concerning the authenticity of our information regarding the existence of the new Wolf Mountain mines, it would then have taken flight. Here were two different parties acting upon information obtained from entirely different sources. The situation at this time was intensely inspiring. So after promising to mark the trail for the cattlemen to follow, with renewed confidence and in high spirits, we pressed onward.

The morale of our intrepid little party of adventurers had now reached its highest point. All were ready to battle with Indians, road agents or any and every opposition which might be met with. Even the fury of the wintry elements held no terror. Every one was thrilled with enthusiasm and animated by the greatest expectations. One evening darkness overtook and forced us into camp upon a high open limestone plain, where the biting zero winds could and did flank us from every quarter. Here was the beginning of the end of our ill-advised expedition. The unexpected and unhappy disruption came, not from any adverse report from the new gold fields, but from the fact that most of our party had started out from Deadwood without making suitable preparations for such a wintry trip. Here we found that wood and water were at a long distance from our camp and not available in the darkness, and our solitary lantern was out of commission. It was with great difficulty and discomfort that we were enabled, with the little water that was brought along and no light, to prepare our supper which consisted of raw and burnt flapjacks and bacon served in darkness.

After finishing our supper all of the party, excepting our teamsters, were soon rolled in blankets, lying on the limestone rocks, not to sleep, but to shift at short intervals from one hummock to another in trying to adjust our weary and shivering frames to conform to the topography of the land, or rather the rocks, and await the coming of day. Our two teamsters, after having tied their horses securely to their wagons to prevent them being drifted away by the fierce winds, went to the wagon in which they slept upon a smooth surface, fully protected from the winds. They proceeded to prepare themselves with rattlesnake antidote, the one item with which they were amply supplied. While they were lost to the world and dreaming of gold mines and money bags, the hungry and shivering animals were industriously engaged in effecting an entrance for their heads at the rear end of a wagon containing oats. Succeeding in their efforts, they proceeded to satiate themselves with a real Thanksgiving feast. They continued their destructive operations by dragging out and trampling the contents in the snow.

Such was the deplorable situation we found the next morning, and it was viewed with alarm. The drowsy, half drunken teamsters were aroused and were soon wide awake to the situation. Then came the question "What are we to do now?" This was quickly answered by both teamsters. "We will have to turn back as we will be unable to proceed further without horse feed." To this I entered protest, advising the scraping up of the scattered oats and putting them with what we had in the other wagon and continuing on our journey westward. To this they objected, but agreed to decide the question by a majority vote. This was taken resulting in eight votes to turn back and a less number against. I protested more vigorously and insisted on pushing ahead, pointing out to them that by turning back at that stage, after having nearly reached our goal, would be a waste of efforts and the sacrificing of the chances of a life time. By pressing forward, I argued, even at a great disadvantage, and being amongst the first to reach the new mining district, the possibilities of locating or otherwise obtaining some of the best and most valuable mineral locations in the district, was surely a matter to be seriously considered. I also called attention of the two teamsters to the fact that I had paid them $25 for which they had obligated themselves to deliver my goods at the new mines, and that I did not consider their reason for turning back at this point a valid one. Their answer to this was that their animals had already failed and that it would be impossible to finish the trip.

Now with the exception of a few, the field was against me. While some of the men gave no reason for voting to turn back, and had but little to say, others, especially those who had so unconcernedly started out as though they were off on a rabbit hunt, had a great deal to say about the matter at issue. Without attempting to make answer to my argument for continuing the trip to the mines, they presented some very strong, unanswerable as well as unprintable reasons why we should turn back. They carried their point by sheer force of numbers, and the slogan "back to Deadwood" was raised with a whoop. The way they bawled me out with the able assistance of the funny man might have put to shame a like number of Comanche Indians.

In this predicament, with not so much as a three legged pack horse even if I had had a kingdom at my disposal, I would have been unable to procure a pack in that barren region. There was no alternative except to turn back with the crowd. This I did with much reluctance, but with a determination to fall in with Deffenbach and drive cattle to the mines. However, we failed to meet the cattleman, but overtook him further back returning to the Black Hills. He informed us that a party of three men, returning to the Hills, had struck the trail ahead of him and had advised him for his own good to turn back at once, stating that they had traveled all through the country ahead of him, had been everywhere and gotten nowhere. They had failed to find any mines or to hear of any, and were half frozen and nearly starved, and had come to the conclusion that the whole business was a fake.

By this unexpected information our speed back to the Hills was accelerated to the limit of the endurance of our jaded animals. Sleet and snow was the weather program on the Sundance Mountains as we passed over them. Spearfish was reached late one afternoon where all of the party excepting myself and one other man went into camp for the night. We struck out straight through the timber for Deadwood arriving there late in the night after having the time of our lives in struggling through gulches, ravines, snowdrifts, fallen timber and underbrush, in the darkness. The wagons arrived the following day bringing in our luggage. Whether the bulk of our party continued to the eastward I never knew, as I saw only two of them afterwards.

Thus ended my unpleasant and unprofitable participation in that widespread delusion. The enormous bubble had burst and its fountain source was revealed. The perpetrator of that stupendous fraud was bitterly denounced by his deluded victims who were pouring back into Deadwood from different directions for several weeks. Many of those who had so impulsively rushed out into the storms were suffering intensely from frosted faces, hands and feet. Many were undoubtedly marked for life. One poor fellow, with feet so badly frozen as to necessitate amputation, was sent away to his home by sympathizing friends. Many had pitiful stories to relate. They told of meeting others who were lost on the prairies traveling in opposite directions from each other, all searching for trails which they hoped would lead them to a place of refuge from the blinding snow storms and biting zero weather.

It was never known whether or not all who rushed out from the Hills in that mad scramble, ever returned here or to other settlements. It is not unreasonable to presume that many of them never did and that they perished in the blinding storms which were raging on the prairies of Wyoming and Montana. This presumption is supported by the fact that many inquiries came to Deadwood in the years following, from relatives and friends, for persons who were last heard of in Deadwood in 1876. When I came to realize what had been the experience and suffering of other victims of that delusion, who had strayed farther away from their cozy winter quarters than I had in chasing the golden will o' the wisp over bleak and barren wastes, I felt truly thankful to Providence and the agencies which had intervened in saving me from a like fate.

The originator, and, so far as I could learn, the chief beneficiary of that unparalleled confidence scheme, who was directly responsible for all the human and animal suffering it entailed, very soon afterwards disposed of his Deadwood property holdings to the Northwestern Stage and Transportation Company, and with well filled purse went on his way.

XXXVII

FIRST CHURCH ORGANIZATION IN THE BLACK HILLS

THE first church organization in the Black Hills was organized by Rev. Lanson P. Norcross in January, 1877. Mr. Norcross, a graduate of Chicago Theological Seminary, was sent to Deadwood from Colorado by the American Home Missionary Society, representing the Congregational denomination, and arrived upon the ground in November, 1876. He announced service for the following Sabbath morning in what was then known as the Centennial Hotel, under the management of Mr. Morgan, and situated on premises next to a store later occupied by Adams Bros.

Services were held in this room for two or three Sundays, and next in a vacant room in the Interocean Hotel. A good sized box stove was purchased by subscription for heating this room. The first service was held December 3d, 1876.

When services began six persons were present but at the close about 35 were in attendance. The same day the Congregational Sunday school was organized. The day was exceedingly cold. Nevertheless, some forty children became members at that time. This school was maintained continuously for many years increasing in membership to about 150. At the time of its organization, W. H. Baccus, first superintendent, offered free use of his carpenter shop just south of Smith's undertaking rooms located on Sherman Street. Here the church organization was perfected, and services were regularly held for several months. The floor was mother earth covered with sawdust and shavings; for pews, rough boards laid across boxes or carpenter's horses. This room was generally well filled Sunday mornings and evenings, and the Sunday school increased in size and interest. Prayer meeting was held

[158]

regularly every Thursday evening. The Sunday school supplies were furnished for several months by the Congregational Sunday school of Cheyenne, Wyoming.

The church organization was completed on January 15th, 1877. Eleven persons united by letters from home churches—four ladies and seven gentlemen. The last two of the original members of the organization, C. E. Hawley and E. C. Bent passed on to their reward some years ago.

The pastor labored faithfully at a time when Christian work and efforts were received with the utmost indifference and almost opposition. Sunday was the busiest day of seven: gambling rooms on every hand, street auctions, theaters and dance halls, crowded saloons without number. Miners and strangers flocked into town upon the Lord's day as the most opportune time to dispose of their dust, meet friends, "buck the tiger," or purchase supplies for the coming week. A number were faithful and the little church plodded on. A few from Central City and Lead worshipped with this organization at that time.

It was one Sunday evening in the early spring of 1877, when an alarm of fire was sounded, and a black volume of smoke was discovered emanating from the roof of the "Senate" saloon on Main Street, then owned by and operated under the management of Mann and Manning. There was no fire department, with a street of pitch pine buildings. Merchants began rushing their wares into their underground fireproofs. Great confusion followed, a bucket brigade was formed, men went to work, and it is doubtful if men ever worked harder. Soon the fire was extinguished although it was a close call for Main Street.

It was time for church services when the fire was extinguished. The little audience room was nearly full, waiting for the preacher. Presently Mr. Norcross came, dressed in a miner's suit, with disheveled appearance. He had been one of the hardest workers at the fire. He did not expect to hold service, but it was voted that he should, and his audience gave good attention.

As time went on, immigration increased, attendance at church and Sunday school grew larger and the necessity for more comfortable and commodious quarters was apparent. Committees were appointed and money borrowed at the bank to buy a lot. Desirable locations were held at fabulous prices. The present site of the Congregational Church building on the extreme point of McGovern Hill, near the conjunction of Deadwood and White-wood creeks, was finally selected and purchased. Considerable grading was done to prepare the location. The building and soliciting committee consisted of C. E. Hawley, A. W. Hastie and E. C. Bent. They raised about $800 by subscription.

The ladies conceived the idea of a church festival and regardless of church relationship or beliefs, believers and unbelievers, Catholics and Protestants, went to work and arranged for this enterprise, the first of its kind to be held in Deadwood. The ladies participating were, as remembered, Mesdames Stebbins, Dawson, Higgins, Graves, Sheldon, Fay, Scott, Durban, Beary, Preble, Shoudy, Miller, McCutchen (nee Fisher), Geary, Langdon, Morgan, Rockefellow, Ammerman, Manning (nee Scott), Giddings (nee Travis), and the Misses Harrington, Rucker, Bolson, Wagner, Higgins, Travis, McCutchen, and many others whose names cannot now be recalled. It was conducted two evenings in June, 1877, in a new building being fitted up by Mr. Strauss for a dry goods store on Main Street. This gathering was a very pleasant affair and was devoid of anything like games of chance and raffles. The net proceeds of the festival, including money contributed to the ladies fund, were nearly $700.00. The expenses were light as nearly everything was donated.

The people worshipped for a few Sabbaths without pews, rough boards being used for seats, but it was a luxury to have a church home, though humble and plain. The new church building was first used in June, 1877. The dimensions were 25 feet by 35 feet and would seat from 125 to 250 people.

Capt. W. A. Beard, of New Bedford, Mass., at that time residing and conducting a grocery store in Deadwood, had promised a bell for the new church when completed. He fulfilled his promise by donating the one used thereafter for over 50 years. It was the first one brought to the Hills and can now be seen in the Adams Memorial Hall in Deadwood. This bell was given free transportation to Sioux City, and from that point was brought to Deadwood, free of cost, by the late Fred. T. Evans.

A great deal of the pastoral and other Christian work devolved upon Mr. Norcross, he being the only protestant minister in the Black Hills, excepting the Rev. D. Ames who subsequently officiated occasionally at the Congregational Church, until a Methodist Church organization was formed in 1878.

No minister residing in the Hills since Mr. Norcross' experience of '76 and '77 has performed more arduous duties or labored more earnestly in the service of his Master than he did.

Resigning his pastorate in the summer of 1878 he returned to Wisconsin, then to Illinois, and later to Nebraska, where he was called to a pastorate when last heard from by Deadwood friends.

On one occasion in 1878, when the incoming stagecoach with its lone passenger reached the much dreaded Cheyenne crossing, it was held up as usual by road agents. The lone passenger was Rev. J. W. Rickett, a graduate of New York, who had been appointed general missionary for the Black Hills, representing the Congregational denomination. This solitary passenger was greeted with the order, "Hold up your hands, or I will blow your brains out." "Poor luck tonight, gentlemen," said Mr. Rickett, "only a poor preacher aboard." "Never mind," retorted the gentleman. "Get down from that box." He alighted at once, saying, "I never carried a firearm in my life, you can search me. Here is my baggage, only a small valise." He was then ordered to get in and throw out the mail sacks, all of which were cut open and searched, the registered packages being riddled.

The first church building of the Congregational organization was swept away by the big flood of 1883. Undaunted members and friends, with assistance of the general public, soon raised means for a new building which was used by the church until its last services were held in 1923. For a considerable number of years the church suffered such losses in membership and financial support, as were inevitable while the population of Deadwood was being reduced from almost 7,500 at the peak to 2,300 in the 1920 census. By 1923 the membership and attendance was so reduced that a pastor could no longer be supported, and services were discontinued indefinitely. The organization was never officially or legally disbanded. It has been in a state of suspended animation. Whether it will ever be revived remains to be seen.

The church building was sold by the Congregational Conference of South Dakota to the Salvation Army in 1935. It is now in use of that organization, which was given use of it for several years prior to purchase for a small amount.

XXXVIII

ORGANIZATION OF LAWRENCE COUNTY

DURING the year 1877, following closely upon the heels of the peace treaty between the United States and the Sioux Indians, organization of the first three counties in the Black Hills, namely Lawrence, Custer and Pennington, was effected. Governor Pennington was, at his own request, empowered by the territorial legislature of Dakota to take the initial steps in organizing these three counties and to supervise and consummate the organization in a way that would be to his satisfaction. He named one county after himself, one after General Custer and one after his intimate political associate, John Lawrence. The Governor then sent out from Yankton, then the territorial capital, one county commissioner for each of the three counties; the other two he selected from the two most populous towns in each of the counties.

This story will relate only what occurred in Lawrence County. The two commissioners were selected, one from Deadwood and the other from Crook City. The choice for county seat was to be determined by a majority vote of the three duly appointed commissioners. They held a meeting, cast a vote and to the great surprise and disappointment of a big majority of the citizens of the county, Crook City was declared the winner. This glaringly unjust choice met with tremendous protest as it was well known to all that Deadwood had a population of at least five to one over Crook City. So the accusation of bribe taking was for the first time heard and repeated in Deadwood.

Vigorous disapproval of the decision of this trio of newly created officials quickly brought results. As remembered, one session of the Board was held in Crook City. However, it scarcely had time to function before an order came from some source for its immediate removal to Deadwood and it went.

[162]

The Board found suitable room space in the Bonanza Hall on Lee Street, as did also the first Territorial District Court held in Lawrence County, Judge Granville G. Bennett presiding. Two or three sessions of the court were held in the hall, at which both Judges Bennett and Barnes presided.

In the meantime a more suitable court room was found on Main Street. The Board of Commissioners, with Gates in the chair, effected a lease with Cuthbertson and Young, shipping merchants and wholesale dealers in food stuffs, for the second floor in a building which was suitable for all court purposes. Judge Gideon C. Moody who succeeded Judge Bennett, held court in this hall several sessions, and up to the time of the great Deadwood fire of September 26, 1879. During that period many highly important mining cases were either settled or put into shape for certification to a higher court. The writer served as a juryman in a number of these cases.

The county lease on the hall was drawing to a close when a new lease was drawn up and duly signed by both parties to the contract. Almost immediately subsequent to this transaction the disastrous fire occurred and the building with its entire contents, including all of the official records of Lawrence County, went up in smoke.

The dilemma into which the county commissioners, the court and all other public officials of Lawrence County were thrown by the loss of the court room and county records, brought immediately to the front the subject of a temporary court room, which quickly became the chief topic of conversation. The commissioners, being unable to find a more suitable court room, effected a lease with Jacob Werthheimer for a box house on upper Main Street. Jacob Anthony had a new and commodious frame building on upper Main Street which he was endeavoring to sell to the county. Cuthbertson and Young came forward and reminded the Board of Commissioners that they were holding a contract to furnish the county just what they had furnished it on a previous lease and that the second lease was still in force and effect. It was true, they said, that the structure had been destroyed, but they were intending to build another equally as good or better, and the work was being started and would be put through to a finish just as quickly as it would be possible for labor and means to do this. The *Daily Times* took up their proposal with the statement that the Board could not rightfully ignore the Cuthbertson and Young contract. The *Times* asked, "Can one party legally ignore or cancel a lease or contract without the consent of the other party?" and answering its own question said, "We say not."

However, the Board had apparently been sitting tight, and turned a deaf ear to all proposals. They had had, in the meantime, a wire from Fred T. Evans, to the effect that he was starting from Sioux City for the Hills with plans and specifications for a Court House. His proposal was to erect a court house on the corner of Sherman and Pine streets. The Board, as well as every one else who knew him, knew that "Big Fred" was a man of action, especially where money matters were involved. They evidently had decided to make no selection of a court house lot pending the arrival of Fred Evans.

Although there were numerous ash lots easily available for their purpose, the fight for a suitable location for the erection of a Court House was now on and was vigorously pushed by three different parties. The *Daily Times,* on entering the conflict, dignified the three contestants as "Rings" and, as remembered, gave vent to something like this, "Whenever the public crib is to be tapped it invariably brings to the front one or more rings of patriotic and public spirited citizens in the locality where the crib is to be tapped. The erection of a Court House for Lawrence County has developed several of these organizations. The Bullock, Nye, Graham, Ludwig, Damon, and Swearengen ring want the Court House on lower Main Street. The McLaughlin, Cuthbertson, Burns, McHugh and Keithley ring want it near the corner of Main and Lee streets. The McKinnis, Evans, Kirkendall, Tallent and Scriber ring want the Court House on the corner of Sherman and Pine streets. Last but not least, the Jake Anthony ring not only wants, but has secured, the Court House for upper Main Street, as Jake had organized himself into a circumference of hugh diameter and got away with the baggage. The county, through the enterprise, taste and liberality of one of Lawrence County's old and best citizens, is provided with a court room without one cent of expense to the county."

So Jake's extremely liberal proposition, just what it was is not now recalled, proved to be acceptable to the Board, and all court proceedings were thereafter transacted in the new building pending the settlement of location of the new court house. The trouble was settled when Fred Evans stated that he proposed to build and complete the structure on the corner of Sherman and Pine streets for the sum of $12,000. Whether the lot, which at that time was of little value, was included in that sum, is not now remembered.

Captain West, a mining engineer and contractor, was immediately put on the job of superintending the work. Scarcely had the work begun when the citizens of Sherman Street and other streets became aware of the fact that Charley McKinnis, one of the most active of those patriotic citizens, was having his lot on upper Sherman Street brought up to grade at the expense of the county. From that time and for many years thereafter, recriminations were rife.

XXXIX

SETH BULLOCK—FIRST SHERIFF

In this recital of early-day activities in the Black Hills, it is fitting to mention the names and official positions of some of the first legally authorized officials. They were selected from the numerous body of applicants by his Excellency, Governor Pennington, for the purpose of bringing order out of chaos, and the establishment of a civil government in the first three duly organized counties within the borders of the Black Hills, Lawrence, Custer, and Pennington. One of the most active of the time in which I write, was Seth Bullock, the first sheriff of Lawrence County.

He was, like the majority of early day westerners, of limited education, although of distinguished appearance and unassuming manners. He had had former experience in this same line of duty as an under sheriff in Lewis and Clark County, Montana Territory. That experience apparently had fitted him for the strenuous duties which devolved upon him by a regime of lawlessness. It is doubtful if the Governor could have made a more appropriate selection.

Seth Bullock proved himself to be an officer of good judgment, endowed with the rare faculty of keeping his own counsel. Being also a good judge of human nature he seems to have known just how far it was advisable to go, and when and where to halt in the performance of his duties. He was a man of good moral character, in accordance with which his deputies evidently were selected. Truly may it be said that during the brief term of his official service the turbulent, lawless and grossly immoral conditions which were prevailing throughout the county, and more especially in Deadwood where the semblance of a city government existed, were greatly ameliorated.

This gradual transition from a lawless to a more healthful and law respecting status was due largely to a change in the people, who very quickly recognized that they were now living under and subject to a legal form of government, and that their actions would be judged in accordance with the newly established laws of the land. Sheriff Bullock, in assuming the strenuous duties devolving upon him, very wisely adopted a workable hands-off policy to be used in extreme cases instead of using the more drastic measures with which he had been empowered. To this policy he strictly adhered throughout his official career as sheriff and subsequently as United States Marshal.

XL

ACCIDENTAL TRAGEDIES

IT is well known to the first pioneers in the Black Hills that during the first few years there were many disastrous and deplorable accidental casualties. A great majority of the fatalities were easily avoidable. Many serious accidents which occurred in those pioneer days resulted from sheer carelessness on the part of managers or foremen, by beginning with inadequate facilities for safe performance of such work as sinking shafts or driving tunnels.

Every old time miner to be found today can tell instances in which he barely escaped death from loosely thrown together frameworks at the top of the shaft, or rickety windlass and half-wornout bucket ropes used in hoisting tubs of five hundred pounds of earth. The writer recalls one such instance of a tub falling squarely on the man below; another, of the dropping of a ladder in a 45-foot shaft; and other instances of a like nature.

Worst of all was the amateur powder manipulator who knew as little of the nature of dynamite as he did of filling a prescription in a drug store. However, he had to learn, and he and others with him had to pay the cost of experience. This writer was one time lowered into a mine at Terraville, following an explosion of 200 pounds of giant powder, which had torn to shreds a man named Rosevere, and two other miners, one Philip Weyman. I was informed by a miner who was in another compartment, that he had passed the man who was preparing the charge with his pipe in his mouth, and had said to him, "Cut that pipe." Five minutes later the explosion occurred.

Another instance equal in its dire results, though under different circumstances, produced a profound impression on the mind of the writer, for two good reasons. One might be ascribed to "luck" by those who believe in chance, that I escaped being a victim of an awful catastrophe which snuffed out the lives of three good men. The other reason is that I happened to be a close eye witness and, so far as I know, the only witness to that tragedy.

I was starting on foot from Terraville to Deadwood. For some unknown reason I took the main traveled road around by Central City. Had I taken the half mile cut-off by Gayville, as I usually did, it would have put me right at the building where I would have stopped at the time the explosion occurred. Just as I reached the nearest point on the Central Road to a building opposite on the east side of Bob Tail, situated on the mining location known as the High Lode, which was being used at that time as a blacksmith shop, the most terrific and deafening sound that I have ever heard pierced my ears. Facing the building I saw it and apparently everything connected with it shot upwards and spread out in all directions, many of the timbers reaching a height of several hundred feet.

A few minutes later, after the debris had fallen and the space was clear, I took a survey of the country around. Not a living creature could be seen, and with no thought of there having been human beings in that vortex of destruction, thinking that some one had left a fire in a condition to cause the explosion, I proceeded on my way to Deadwood. It was not until several hours later that I learned the tragic results of what I had witnessed. In that mass of wreckage were human bodies to be picked up in gruesome bits and prepared for burial by many sympathetic hands.

Three lives were sacrificed due to criminal negligence of some one who should have been, but never was, apprehended and held accountable for that crime of storing dynamite in a blacksmith shop. One of the men killed was Professor Willis P. Bower, principal of the Terraville School, with whom I was quite intimately acquainted, and whom I regarded as a young man of much promise, a friend to all who knew him.

Just what amount of high explosives was stored in that building, or by what means it was exploded, will ever remain a matter for conjecture.

XLI

BILL GAY, THE GAYVILLE MURDERER

ONE of the first parties of white men to enter the northern Black Hills during the fall of 1875 was known as the Gay party. This small party arrived in Deadwood Gulch in September of that year. By being among the first to reach the new gold fields the members all secured choice placer claims. Two of the party, Bill and Al Gay (brothers), came from the Spotted Tail Indian Agency, where they had spent most of their worthless lives. Both of the men had married squaws and were rearing Indian families, at the expense of the United States government. When the gold rush which followed General Custer's expedition through the Black Hills started these two worthies deserted their Indian families and hastened to the new gold fields. Here, for several years following their arrival, they were exceedingly prosperous in business affairs, and apparently both had banished from their memories all thoughts of care of squaws and papooses.

They secured numbers Four and Five above the Discovery in Deadwood Gulch, two of the richest placer claims in that gulch. Upon these claims they opened up a saloon and started the town of Gayville, which very quickly developed into one of the wildest and wickedest towns in the Black Hills. However, it proved to be of short life. Al Gay took charge of the saloon and for a time he conducted a wonderfully profitable business while his brother Bill gave his attention to placer mining. From these claims he cleaned up approximately one hundred thousand dollars. A large portion of this money was squandered in gambling, drunkenness and riotous living. A lesser part of it was utilized in constructing and furnishing, on one side of his mining claim, a neat and comfortable residence. Here Bill lived for a considerable period, apparently in peace with the world, cohabiting with an exceptionally good looking young woman whom he had selected from a number of painted beauties, and, because of his lavish display of wealth, was easily procured from one of the numerous brothels in Deadwood. So far as was generally known, there was never an open break between Bill and his "wife" as he was pleased to call the woman. However, it developed later that he frequently called her to account for reasons of his own, whether well founded or not, because he was suspicious and madly jealous of her.

While it was clearly evident that the woman cared nothing for Bill Gay, nor any one else in particular, she was by no means desirous of severing her relations with him, and leaving her luxurious surroundings so long as his gold sack maintained its plethoric condition. So she devised a scheme whereby she could convince her jealous mate beyond a doubt of her loyalty to him, and was abiding an opportunity to put the scheme into effect. This desired opportunity was soon afforded through a change in mining industry.

During the spring of 1877 and after the great excitement over the placer mining industry had subsided, many prospectors, especially those who had had practical experience in quartz mining, turned their attention to that branch of the business. During the winter of '76 and '77, they made a number of discoveries. The great Homestake and several other mines of lesser importance were yielding their precious ores in abundance. The excitement over quartz mining became so intensified that not only the miners and prospectors, but practically all other residents, were led into the belief that every hill and ledge of quartz formation adjacent to, or anywhere in the vicinity of the Homestake mine, was a veritable bonanza. This excitement over quartz mines was by no means confined to the Black Hills country, but spread far and wide as did the excitement of the previous year over placer mines.

Although the influx of people to the Black Hills in 1877 was much less than in 1876, it was in a more orderly and business like way, and the amount of capital brought in for investment in mining property was much greater than the first year. Many among the well-to-do classes of people of the eastern states became so deeply interested in the mining situation in the Black Hills that they turned their property holdings into cash and brought it to the Hills to be invested in mining speculation. One of these deluded victims

[171]

of that gold quartz craze, was a man named Forbes. He came from New York bringing with him a large sum of money and limited business acumen. In a very short time after his arrival in Deadwood Gulch, Forbes became the proud possesser of a worthless quartz location on the mountain side, above and adjoining Bill Gay's claim. Whether the location was made by Gay, or some other party, is unknown. Whoever it was, found no trouble in convincing Forbes that a treasure of great value had been touched in the tunnel, and was awaiting a small amount of capital for its development into a paying proposition equal to the best yet discovered in that locality. Without further assurance, the deal was consummated and for a short period both the beguiler and the beguiled were equally exultant over the deal. Now that a great gold quartz mine had so fortunately been secured by the investor Forbes, a quartz mill for reducing the ores from the mine was next in order.

Plans for construction of one of the latest and most approved patterns of quartz mills were called for. It was to be capable of treating not only the ores from the Forbes mine, but those of the other mines in that vicinity. In a remarkably short space of time plans and specifications for the required plant were at hand, were approved by the promoter, and the plant was promptly constructed, by competent millwrights, at a cost of several thousand dollars. In the meantime, while the construction work on the plant was in progress, Forbes had an up-to-date and well furnished residence erected on the hill side near his mine, and also near the residence of Bill Gay. When completed this residence was occupied by the Forbes family which consisted of Mr. and Mrs. Forbes and one son, Charles, who was about eighteen years of age. This boy, coming fresh from an eastern college, where he probably had been closely confined to his studies, and very little in society, apparently was fancy free, and not until his advent into the Black Hills had come in contact with, or fallen under the entrancing influence of a female charmer. It was here that he came into daily contact with the gay and bewitching Mrs. Gay who, with a profusion of smiles, and sinister designs, very quickly ensnared the heart of young Charles. He fell for her and fell hard, becoming desperately infatuated with his charmer.

He felt that he must find a way of expressing his feelings. She must get the story from his own lips. They must meet clandestinely. So he penned a missive to his enchantress which ran like this: "Meet me this evening, my darling, by moonlight at 8:00 o'clock, at the corner of the big barn." Next he must find a way of getting the note into her hands without being detected. He hunted up a colored man known as "Nigger General," who specialized in such secret service, gave him the missive with instructions and a liberal reward for his services, and awaited the result which was immediately forthcoming. The missive was promptly delivered into the hands of Mrs. Gay. Just what she said to "Nigger General" was not disclosed, nor were her thoughts. She probably thought: "That fool; now I have just what I have been waiting for, a chance to show my drunken, jealous-hearted husband that he has nothing to howl about. Just wait until he comes home, I will give him a surprise." So when the besotted husband came home he was met at the door by his tearful spouse and the delicate missive was shoved into his hand. He was informed between sobs, that the bearer of the message was a colored man. The irate husband waited for nothing further but mounted his saddle horse, put spurs and was soon in Deadwood. There he found "Nigger General," and questioned him as to who employed him to deliver the note.

"Nigger General" was exceedingly reticent when touched upon any subject having connection with his special line of business. So when the question was put to him by Gay he feigned a lapse of memory. This momentary lapse, however, was speedily overcome with Bill's forty-four coming out of its scabbard, and the name of young Mr. Forbes was blurted out. Without waiting for further information Bill remounted his horse and made a flying return to Gayville. This writer was just leaving that town when Gay entered it, whipping his horse with his hat and yelling at the top of his voice. He was followed by two companions who were also whipping their steeds without mercy, in their endeavors to keep up with their leader. Without exchanging words with the writer or anyone else, Gay rushed up to the Forbes residence, dismounted, ran in and shoved the fatal missive into the face of young Forbes who, it was said by a witness, denied its authorship. Without waiting for further remarks, Gay shoved the muzzle of his revolver so close to Forbes that it burned his face with powder, as Gay pulled the trigger and scattered his victim's brains over the room.

After the perpetration of this brutal murder, Bill Gay returned to Deadwood and surrendered himself to Sheriff John Manning. Judge Bennett, the presiding District Judge, ordered the empaneling of a Grand Jury. This was done and after all facts in the case were obtained, the Jury returned a true bill of first degree murder against Bill Gay. When the case was brought up in the District Court for trial, Bill had for his defense the ablest legal talent that money could obtain. Notwithstanding that he was tried before an honest and upright judge, and by twelve supposedly honest and unprejudiced jurymen, the nearest approach to justice obtained by the state was a ten-year sentence to the penitentiary. Even this travesty on justice was too much for Bill's numerous chums. After expenditure of what was said to be forty thousand dollars of Bill's available cash, these friends succeeded in having his sentence commuted to three years. After serving his short term he returned to Deadwood, and to what was yet to be the most disgraceful feature of that shameful affair. This Indian agency loafer, Indian wife deserted, and red handed murderer, was met at the outskirts of the city by a brass band.

Bill Gay next opened up a saloon in the town of Spearfish. It was there, in his saloon, that one of the most inexcusable murders that ever disgraced a Black Hill's town, was concocted by a number of so-called vigilantes, in which Gay was implicated, namely, the hanging of the wounded and dying man, Harry Tuthill, who was not known to have been accused of a dishonorable act.

Gay next went to Montana where he murdered another man, and no longer having the money to purchase immunity, he was promptly hanged for this, his last crime.

XLII

HANGING OF AN INNOCENT BOY AT RAPID CITY

ONE of the most outrageous deeds of violence which blacken the pages of early Black Hills history, was perpetrated by a mob of self-constituted "law and order" regulators, composed of less than a dozen usurpers of the right to speak and act for the hundreds of good citizens of Rapid City, who were desirous of having their municipal government established and maintained upon a basis of justice to all, and to have the laws of the new city administered in conformity with the laws of the territory of Dakota. Here is the story of the willful crime of murdering an innocent boy who was not guilty of violating any law. The story was related to this writer by the late John Jennack, for many years a citizen of Deadwood, whose veracity has been unquestioned.

He was employed as assistant stock tender for the stage company in Rapid City during the summer of 1877, at a time when the Indians were killing many white people, and everyone was on the lookout for a raid. One day when Dave Marble, Howard Worth, and others were on the hill north of town, cutting logs for building purposes, they discovered a party of men with a number of horses in a bunch of timber northwest of the town. They believed them to be Indians preparing for a raid on the town so they hurried in and so reported. In a very short time the entire town was up in arms. A party of men made for the supposed Indian rendezvous and quietly surrounded it. They found three white men who, when aroused, found themselves prisoners. One of them was a boy, who, Jennack said, was about his own age and size, which was at that time 16 years. He was designated by this "necktie party" as "Kid Hall." His true name was Mansfield and his father was a reputable citizen, a hotel proprietor of Austin, Minnesota. The two men,

Louis Curry, known as "Red Curry," A. J. Allen, known as "Doc." Allen, two horse thieves, and this youth, who had not been known nor heard of in that vicinity until that day, June 20, 1877, were given a preliminary hearing before justice of the peace, Robert Burleigh, charged with horse stealing. Both Allen and Curry, seeing no chance for escape, admitted their guilt.

The kid pleaded not guilty. Both Allen and Curry assured the justice that the boy was not guilty and that they had never seen him until that day when they overtook him trudging along the road and offered him a ride on one of the horses, which he gladly accepted. Nevertheless, all three were bound over to the next term of the circuit court and were put in a log cabin for the night with a guard placed over them. However, but a short time elapsed before a party of masked men appeared, seized the three, and departed with their prisoners for a big pine tree south of town. The story of a "masked" party was given out by friends of the mob. Jennack never spoke of the masks but stated that he and another boy about his age, named Nelson, followed the crowd and sat under some bushes between the big rocks and the tree and witnessed the whole sickening performance. Jennack gave me the names of four active members of the mob, whom he knew very well. Small ropes about the size of clothes lines were put around the necks of the prisoners. Jennack said that an old man named Wright had followed the party, begging them not to murder the boy because he was innocent. The two thieves also pleaded strongly for the boy, saying, "Do as you will with us but spare him for he is absolutely innocent."

The hangmen threw the ropes over a limb of the tree after standing the men on the rocks and tightened the ropes. They were uncertain as to what was best to do with the boy and asked the question, which was answered by the ringleader of the mob, who was a "leading citizen" of the town. He vociferously shouted, "hang him, hang him, dead men tell no tales." So the innocent lad was swung up, the rocks kicked out from under him and the two men, and the crowd dispersed.

The following morning the justice of the peace went up to the hill to hold an inquest over the bodies. He found that the ropes had slackened letting the feet of the victims touch the ground, and as their hands were tied behind them they had just wriggled around until they were strangled to death, which gave the name to Rapid City, "Strangle Town."

All action concerning the affair might have ended then had not old man Wright kept up his fight for justice. He was joined by other citizens of the town and the fight for a grand jury investigation was kept up for two years or longer until one was selected and Mr. Wright started looking up witnesses in the case. Jennack came to Deadwood soon after witnessing the tragedy and was employed as a hack driver by this writer. He remained with me until he married. He then moved to a ranch on Hay Creek, twenty-five miles north of Deadwood.

Mr. Wright came up from Rapid City to look for him and went out to the ranch and asked Jennack if he would testify to the facts in the hanging case. Jennack assured him that he would go if his expenses were paid, so arrangements were made for his attendance before the grand jury at Rapid City. It appeared that Wright was not short of money. He seemed to have plenty to spend in bringing the guilty parties to justice. But the guilty parties, in collusion with their friends, decreed that it should not be done.

According to a statement made by one of the grand jurymen, a brother of one of the mob of stranglers, whose statement was published in a Rapid City newspaper in recent years, the strategy which they agreed upon, and which was successfully consummated, was that all who deemed it inadvisable to have this outrage aired in the courts and given out to the world, should unite in circulating the report that in their opinion old man Wright had become demented and should be removed to the insane asylum at Yankton. Then it followed, instead of having a legally constituted board of insanity to inquire into the sanity of this Mr. Wright, they made arrangements with a well known doctor of Rochford to, in some way not divulged, induce the old man to accompany him to Yankton, where he was taken over by the superintendent of the institution as an insane person. The old man afterwards became ill and died. Nothing further was done and the perpetrators of that crime were left free to spend the rest of their lives in wrestling with the skeletons in their private closets.

XLIII

MURDER OF THE WAGNER FAMILY

OF the many horrifying scenes to which the eyes of early day pioneers became accustomed, none was more revolting than the sight they beheld when they discovered the Wagner family murdered and mutilated, about fifteen miles northwest of Crook City and north of the Bear Butte country, on July 17, 1877.

The Wagner family, of foreign nativity, was composed of two brothers and a young woman, the wife of one of the boys. The three had left their home in Minnesota and arrived in the Black Hills during the rush of 1876. They arrived safely in an ordinary farm wagon loaded with household goods and drawn by a strong ox team.

It was probably their intention to engage in farming as they spent their time in a valley near Crook City. For some reason, probably because of the increasing Indian menace, they became dissatisfied and decided to return to their former home.

They loaded their wagon with their possessions, hitched up the oxen and started on the long homeward trail. They were trying to overtake Pete Osland, a freighter and a countryman of theirs.

They had reached a point north of Spring Creek when they were fired on by a band of savages. John Frederick, an acquaintance of the family, claimed to have witnessed a part of the tragedy, but as he was putting himself out of sight he saw little of it. He saw the Indians and heard the first shot that was fired but was unable to furnish the details on the butchery.

The Bismarck stage arrived on the scene shortly afterwards while the bodies were still warm. The stage halted for a few minutes to enable the passengers to view the situation, and then hurried to Crook City and gave the alarm.

[178]

MURDER OF THE WAGNER FAMILY

W. J. Thornby, a reporter for the *Deadwood Pioneer*, organized a party, procured a wagon and team and brought the mutilated bodies to Crook City where they were buried.

The party found that the oxen were both shot down in their tracks. One was dead and the other was in a dying condition. The two men had succeeded in getting a short distance along the road and were about twenty paces apart before being shot down. They were stripped of all clothing but were not scalped as their hair was cut short.

The body of the woman was found near the other bodies. She, too, was denuded and her body badly mutilated. The demons had thrust an ox goad through her abdomen. She had long, beautiful hair which was taken with her scalp.

The contents of the wagon, which consisted of household goods and supplies for the trip, were partly taken by the murderous reds, and the rest of the goods were scattered in all directions.

XLIV

VIGILANTES TAKE ACTION

ONE of the get-rich-quick enterprises of Deadwood during the summer of 1876 was the traffic in horses. Many animals changed hands in a brief period of time. The better class sold here had been driven in by the immigrants and freighters from Iowa and Missouri. An inferior grade was brought in as saddle and pack horses, from the surrounding country. Many of this class were picked up by the "rustlers" on the range around the outskirts of the Hills, where they had been turned out to graze by their owners.

One of several parties who were known to be engaged in this precarious business, and with whom I had some acquaintance, having purchased a horse from him in December of that year, was known as "Beans Davis." Most of the time he stayed out in the valleys, but was seen frequently on the street in Deadwood, and at Central City, where he had a partner named George Keating, who was at that time owner of or an interested party in a butcher shop business.

The butchers in the Hills towns would go out on the range and purchase cattle and drive them in to slaughter pens to prepare for market. No one suspected that Keating was procuring his supply of meat in a different manner. But it was developed in the summer of 1877 that he, in connection with Davis, who had shifted from horse stealing to the more profitable business of cattle rustling, were picking up their supply on the range without permission or paying therefor. These animals were driven, in small lots, into the timber where they were prepared for the meat market. While the owners of these stolen critters were missing their cattle, they were unable to determine whether they were being rustled or had strayed. However, their suspicions were aroused and the following interesting incident resulted:

Keating, or his partner Davis, having more beef than they needed for their own shop, sold part of a load to another butcher. Just after payment was made by the purchaser, a stranger stepped in the front door. Keating, or Davis, glanced at him and made a hasty exit through the back door. This occasioned surprise among those who witnessed it and aroused suspicion. It inspired the editor of the *Central City Enterprise* (Bartholomew was his name, I think), to report the affair under the heading, "The wicked fleeth when no man pursueth." It is presumed that the stranger was recognized as one of the ranchers whose cattle had been rustled.

From that time on the Vigilantes of Spearfish Valley, under the leadership of "Who was Who," engaged in finding the rendezvous of these two enterprising young business men. It was located and one night the Vigilantes descended upon them while at their cache, which was located at a spring at the foot of Lookout Mountain, about two miles east of Spearfish. They were aroused from slumber, taken under pine trees and swung up from earth. The bodies were left swinging to be found the next day, cut down and buried.

XLV

A FATAL QUARREL

THERE probably are a number of people yet living in this section who remember the gun battle which took place in Central City in the summer of 1877, between John Bryant and William Adams, in which they were both shot to death. The trouble between these men arose from the act of Adams in posting notice of claim to a mill site on a Placer Claim (No. 13, I believe) above Discovery Claim on Deadwood Gulch, upon which a part of Central City is located, and which was owned at the time by John Bryant.

The right of Adams to make this location was disputed by Bryant. Whether these parties had any quarrel over the matter at the time the notice was posted is not known. However, on the following morning, Adams, who at the time was in partnership with Gus Oberg in the restaurant business, remarked, after eating his breakfast, that he was going down to take possession of his mill site. He was advised by his partner and other friends to be careful and not get into trouble. He persisted and walked down past the Bryant cabin with his belt strapped around him and his revolver in plain sight.

Bryant also with a belt and a six shooter in plain view, was standing near his cabin. A conversation was started and hot words ensued. According to two witnesses, each man was keeping an eye on the gun of his adversary as though he was expecting a quick movement. Adams, who had evidently planned a ruse, whipped out another pistol from his pocket and shot Bryant through the body. He then turned and ran, but had made only a rod or two, when he was overtaken by a bullet from Bryant's pistol, which caught him in the hip and felled him as he was crossing a small stream. In falling he turned his face to Bryant, who was following, threw up his hands and his head back, just as Bryant fired the second bullet which entered his mouth and up through his head, killing him instantly. Bryant then walked back into his cabin where he lingered in great pain for a day or two and died.

Bryant was a native of Illinois and was a brother of the late Frank Bryant, a well-known and highly respected mining man. Adams was employed for a time in a grocery store in Deadwood and was considered to be honest. I never knew where he came from but presumed that it was Salt Lake City as he was, at the time of his death, reporter for the *Salt Lake Tribune*.

XLVI

MURDER OF HOFFMANN BY ED DURHAM

OF a small party of gold seekers who came into the Black Hills in February, 1876, three of the members were the fortunate locators of the mining claims which embraced the principal portion of the Deadwood City townsite, while several others of the party grasped the opportunity of securing the most desirous city lots ere they had been surveyed and platted. One of those who held a first choice was Ed Durham who selected a piece of ground which, after being platted, became the lot which adjoins the site of First National Bank on the west side of Main Street.

Here Ed erected a two story frame building of rough lumber, with glass doors and windows. In this building he opened and successfully operated a saloon for a year or more, up to the time in 1877 when the great scramble for quartz mining locations was at its height. Ed was prospering and had made many friends as he was regarded as an exceptionally square dealer, even though he was engaged in a precarious and discreditable vocation. While apparently he had struck the high road to prosperity, he failed to escape the lure of gold quartz and became dissatisfied with his occupation. He found a ready, though not a cash buyer, named Hoffmann, a pretentious German who was holding a card up his sleeve to be played when opportunity presented.

Durham disposed of his stock of liquors and bar fixtures. The building and lot he sold to Hoffmann; the price, as I recall, was $1,400, $200 cash down and $100 to be paid in monthly installments. Ed, after paying for his mining location and a good supply of equipment, pitched into a hard rock proposition. Although the prospect was encouraging, development was extremely slow and highly expensive. Ed's ready cash was soon dissipated. Up to that

[184]

time his spirits were kept up to concert pitch. But they dropped to zero when he went down to collect his first $100. Hoffmann stood him off from week to week, compelling him to suspend work on his mine.

Then the second $100 became due. While Hoffmann was obtaining high rent, he still failed to make a payment. Durham, though not a whisky addict, took on a supply for the occasion, and came down with "blood in his eye" and demanded his money. Hoffmann had rented the rear end of the hall to the Girard brothers, barbers, and was sitting in one of their chairs when Ed came in. Hoffmann then told him he did not consider him a legal owner, as it was government property when he appropriated it, and gave him to understand that he would make no further payments.

Durham made reply with his forty-four caliber revolver and Hoffmann crumpled to the floor in death. This writer was at the time standing just outside, leaning against the narrow space between the door and window, when the first shot, which went wild, was fired and crashed through the window, treating me to a shower of broken glass. The second shot, which quickly followed, was of deadly aim.

Durham hastily passed out by me. Although we were acquainted, he spoke not a word, but turned, with his smoking revolver in hand, and went up the Lee Street stairs. By this time a crowd had gathered, some following him. One, Pat M'Hugh, a saloon keeper with a shot gun, followed him to Williams Street, ordering him to halt. Durham kept going until Pat sent a charge of shot into his hips and legs. He then gave up his gun and was taken to jail and held to trial on a charge of first degree murder. He was later brought to trial, and though public sentiment was largely in his favor, he was convicted of second degree murder and sentenced to fourteen years in federal penitentiary. So far as is known, he was never again heard of in Deadwood.

XLVII

A FATHER AND TWO SONS

IN contemplating early day events the writer recalls one of the many tragical occurrences which comprised largely the history of those stirring times. Possibly there are others yet living, who remember the coming to Deadwood from Indianapolis, of a tall, straight, elegantly dressed and dignified old gentleman of about seventy years, by the name of Andrew Wallace.

This man was particularly conspicuous because of the extraordinary style of his hat. It had been constructed along entirely different lines from any of the many styles of hats seen on the streets at that time, which were built, strictly in accordance with the flat formations of our mineral deposits, while Mr. Wallace's hat was a two-story silk structure, built on the vertical plan. The old gentleman was accompanied by his two sons, Joseph and "Sank." Besides being college graduates, these two young men were talented musicians. The elder Wallace was reputed to be quite wealthy but he was desirous of increasing his wealth through possession of a rich gold mine.

Looking over the gold belt of the Black Hills, he very quickly found something which appealed to his judgment, and purchased a gold quartz location on the southwest slope of the mountain which protrudes down into Deadwood Gulch midway between the towns of Deadwood and Central City. This location lay along the side of, and later may have become a part of, what is now known as the North Homestake Extension.

It was here, fresh from their college studies, those two young Hoosiers, thoroughly equipped with all known mining implements and other essentials for cutting into that mountain, doffed their elegant tailor made suits, put on overalls and plunged into the

[186]

work with determination. But after a siege of several months their enthusiasm cooled, and they weakened and finally abandoned the project.

While the two brothers were chasing the golden will-o'-the-wisp on their side of the hill, there were men on the opposite side, which faced down the gulch, who had been for months endeavoring to tap the same body of ore which was supposed to spread out from the center. These men, as one of them remarked, had become thoroughly disgusted with the showings made, and were preparing to pull up stakes and abandon their claim; but they decided to defer their vacation.

They had noticed that the old gentleman with the silk tile, while passing over to his side of the mountain, had stopped and examined the specimens from their mine. They conceived a ruse to catch him. They went to the DeSmet-Cheyenne Mine and obtained, by some means, a lot of fine specimens and placed them on their latest output of worthless rock. They watched and waited a return of the old man who appeared again the next day, examined the specimens and departed to return the next day to pay them a visit. Up to that day he had not spoken to them.

He inquired as to how they were getting along. "Very poorly," answered one. "We believe that we have the makings of a valuable mine but we are going to lay off for the present as we are short of funds and have no credit."

"Have you thought of selling it?" he asked.

"No, but we would, if we could get back what we have expended on it, which is six hundred dollars."

Right then and there their mine changed ownership. A new force of men was put on at once, and work on the hill was vigorously prosecuted for several weeks following, but without obtaining satisfactory results. In a short time work on both sides of the mountain was indefinitely discontinued.

This big mountain, of inviting possibilities, has subsequently been made the target for tremendous onslaughts of high power explosives, by which it is somewhat pitted and scarred. If it has lost any of its pristine grandeur it is not noticeable to a casual observer.

Notwithstanding the old gentleman of the high top tile had been the victim of two mining failures, he exhibited no signs of being a "quitter." In the language of that day he was a real "go-getter." He had the pluck and the money to back his efforts. So he pulled up stakes and went around to the opposite side of the gold belt and there purchased a partially developed mine, which made an excellent showing of becoming a paying proposition. Here the new owner, preparing a comfortable residence for himself and his sons, proceeded at once to have erected a small plant for purpose of treating the output of his latest and best enterprise. Probably this enterprising old gentleman had once more resumed his placid frame of mind and was congratulating himself on having at last attained the goal of his ambition. His son Joe had become physically unable to perform manual labor. Being of a literary inclination he did much writing for newspapers and soon went to Rapid City where he established an abstract office. He was soon after called by death.

"Sank," his brother, who played at times in the Deadwood orchestra of the early days, and who had for quite a while mingled with and been recognized by the best society, unfortunately stumbled into that overflowing stream of contamination of which the "Bad Lands" of Deadwood was the principal source. He went from bad to worse until he became a drunken lunatic. In that condition he went one night to his home, shot down his father and then turned the gun upon himself with fatal effect. The old man, who was badly wounded, was able to get back to his home in the East.

Thus passed from the scene three persons who had been endowed by nature and fitted by culture to keep step in the foremost classes of the social and business world.

XLVIII

THE BIG HORN EXPEDITION OF 1877

OF the many thousands of immigrants who came to the Black Hills during 1876 and 1877, especially those who flocked into Whitewood and Deadwood gulches, there were apparently three different classes, each of them being imbued with different aspirations.

One class was the impulsive, haphazard element, who apparently came with no fixed purpose, and with little expectation or hope of engaging in any line of business. They depended largely upon their chances of finding employment in working for others more fortunate than themselves. Many of that class, after dissipating the few dollars brought with them, returned to their homes with returning freight teams, at little, if any expense.

Another class of fortune seekers, more self-reliant and fairly well provided with funds, came apparently with fixed determination to assume a part in the developing of the various resources of the Hills either by location or purchase of mining properties, or by entering into some of the many other lines of industry which were speedily being established. To this class, with bold initiative, earnest endeavor and indomitable spirit, and others of like characteristics who came later, is due the many wonderful industrial developments which followed.

The third class, of which there were many, apparently were adequately provided with sufficient capital for embarking in business enterprises; but after making a survey of the business situation, becoming convinced that there was no chance of acquiring a gold mine of any promise at a reasonable figure, and finding that commercial business of every kind was greatly overdone, decided either to return to their homes in the states, or to go farther west in quest of golden opportunities. There were many of these disappointed pioneers, as well as many old westerners, who arrived in the Black Hills too late to obtain any mining properties worth consideration, who were ready to give full credence to and act upon the glittering allurements so convincingly spread before them by some of the longhaired, bewhiskered, and buckskinned element of agency society, who posed as border scouts, but who probably had spent the major part of their time hanging around Indian agencies, living the lives of that race. Such worthies, and a few old, down and out prospectors who were desirous of procuring grubstakes, were conspicuously in evidence, relating their long and varied experience as hunters, trappers, and prospectors in the Rockies and Big Horn mountains. They told of rich gold placer discoveries made when they were unable to undertake their development, but would, if furnished means to procure an outfit, lead any party of prospectors who might wish to explore the Big Horn mountains, northwest of the Black Hills, in Wyoming.

Information leaked out from inside sources that several of these knowing ones had definite knowledge as to the exact location of the long lost Log Cabin gold mine. This had the effect of causing many unbelievers in fireside stories to prick up their ears in anticipation of further information.

At just what period the supposed discoverer of the long lost Log Cabin gold mine lived, the writer will not venture to say. However, I am certain that, if any credence is placed in statements then made and supported by considerable evidence, there does exist a long lost and wonderfully rich Log Cabin gold mine. Many in Deadwood believed this. The question arose as to where this long lost mine could be found. The answer then given was, "Big Horn Mountains."

In the month of July, 1877, after the story had been revamped and widely circulated, a large, though unorganized, party of about one hundred go-getters, led by a motley crew of go-showers, were in the saddle and headed for the new land of Ophir, followed by wagons and a number of scrub ponies and burros as packs. Herman Bischoff, a Deadwood pioneer merchant, who resided in Deadwood until his death in 1931, had large part in this movement, and kept in his diary detailed account of the expedition.

They left behind a host of well wishers and susceptibles to

that contagious malady known as "gold fever," who decided to wait and be prepared to lead in the rush for the ground floor of opportunities if results should warrant such action. This expedition to the Big Horn Mountains has usually been spoken of as a "stampede"; in fact it was not a stampede, except for the encouragement given all departing for new regions in mining sections, as those who are left behind are interested in the outcome.

This movement was inaugurated primarily as an exploration and mineral research expedition, and was therefore a perfectly legitimate and common sense undertaking; but owing to inadequate preparations for such a large undertaking, and other handicaps, among which were the lack of competent leadership and the small percentage of practical miners and prospectors in the party, it resulted in a lamentable failure. Fortunately, after having gone west for more than a hundred miles over the Montana trail, they turned to the southwest without encountering a band of Indians who were at the time closing in towards the Hills from the northwest.

On reaching its first objective, the Big Horn Mountains, the party found itself without a leader who knew anything whatever as to the feasible approaches to the mountains. The impostors who had boasted of having traversed the country, and claimed to be familiar with every bull trail and every mountain sheep trail, were unable to determine their location. Under such discouraging conditions the party split up into small sections, going in different directions.

The largest party, it was reported, skirted the east range of the mountains and circled around to the Cheyenne River. So far as was known, all made safe return to such parts as they sought to go. Possibly some of the smaller parties entered and passed over the ranges, but if any prospecting for minerals was done it was not generally known.

The long lost Log Cabin gold mine is still around the corner and some lucky miner may yet make his fortune by discovering it.

XLIX

THE MURDER OF CEPHAS TUTTLE

Of the many disgraceful crimes which marked the coming of civilization in the Black Hills region, and which darkened its early history, I recall no other which was actuated by motives more beastly, or with less regard for the life of a human being, or which merited and received more universal and bitter condemnation of this community, than the cowardly murder of Cephas Tuttle by one of a party of five or more conspirators. This occurred in Hidden Treasure Gulch, near Central City, in the month of August, 1877.

It was a case without a parallel which will ever stand in a class of its own in the records of Black Hills criminality, for the reason that, in the commission of this crime, it was clearly shown that the murder had been premeditated, and the method of its execution so carefully planned by the conspirators, that, although the crime was committed in broad daylight, with a number of miners at work at the time in that vicinity, no evidence could be obtained by which the guilt could be fastened upon those who, according to general report and belief, committed the murder.

Without presuming to present now a wholly authentic statement of the facts of this affair, the purported facts as they were freely circulated throughout this section at the time, and were generally accepted as true, were to this effect:

Of the several rich gold quartz claims discovered and located in Hidden Treasure Gulch, one was known as the "Keets Mine." Adjoining this was the Aurora Mine, which was owned by Cephas Tuttle and a man named Johnson, who were developing their claim. The Keets Mine manager, it was said, had obtained permission to run a tunnel through a portion of the Aurora ground, which, it was found, would pass through a rich ore streak in the Aurora. The tunnel was constructed to run close to the Aurora shaft, so close that it would, and did, break through the side wall of that shaft, which afforded the Keets Mine an air shaft. This advantage was objected to by the Aurora Mine management. Tuttle also accused the Keets miners of stealing rich ore from the walls of the tunnel where it passed through his claim, and they were ordered to cease their operations. This order was ignored. Tuttle then threatened to ignite a box of glycerine at the bottom of his shaft and destroy the lineament for a distance. This threat was also ignored, and the Keets miners continued to work.

Tuttle then prepared the charge, and after the miners went off shift he fired it, completely destroying the Keets tunnel. Tuttle evidently did not realize that he was antagonizing men who were not easily thwarted in their plans and determination. When Tuttle went down his shaft he was shot dead by one of the five men who were seen immediately afterwards running from the cabin on the Keets Mine.

A hack driver made the statement that the owner of the Keets Mine came to the hack stand in Central City, boarded his hack and ordered him to drive to Deadwood where he immediately called at the sheriff's office.

The sheriff and his deputies went to the ground and arrested the men who were employed in the Keets Mine. All of course denied knowing anything about the murder.

I understood that the men were arrested and brought to trial but no witness could be found who could or would give any information concerning it. The case was dropped.

L

A ROBBER RUSE WHICH FAILED

DURING the summer of 1877 some very rich placer claims were discovered and developed in both Bear Gulch and Potato Gulch, twenty miles west of Deadwood. One of the fortunate discoveries was made by a man named Myers, who succeeded in cleaning up $16,000 as his summer's work. In the fall he decided to return to his home. Instead of sending his gold dust by Wells-Fargo Express, and having it insured, he preferred to take it with him. He readily found four of his friends who were anxious to leave the Hills and return to their homes, and were glad of the chance to go along with him as guards. So he and the five others, including his son, known as "Kid" Myers, all well armed, started for Cheyenne, Wyoming, with two wagons.

Their first day out was without incident. They probably were feeling safe and were not expecting trouble, when ready to camp for dinner on the Cheyenne road about twenty miles south of Custer City. They stacked their guns against a tree within easy reach of their spread for dinner, and after they had taken their places they saw three men riding at some distance on the road. These men dismounted and one of them casually came up to them, apparently as though he was seeking information regarding the road. When close to the diners, he made a leap for their guns, grabbing a shotgun. He shouted, "Up with your hands!" Of course all hands went up instantly. The "Kid" was apart from the others of the party and sneaked around to where his father's gold sack was hidden. He had his shotgun and like a flash he turned it loose on the would-be robber, killing him instantly. The others jumped for their guns. The "Kid" was the first to grab a rifle, which he fired at the two dismounted men as they fled into the brush, leaving their horses. They were never seen nor heard of afterwards.

The party resumed their journey after sending an account of the affair back to the sheriff of Pennington County, who, with a party of three men went to the scene of the attempted holdup. Upon examination of the body they found that he was Bob Costello, a border outlaw, as his name was tattooed on his arm. After holding an informal inquest over his body, a ditch was dug and, with his shirt placed over his face, he was covered with dirt and left for disposal of his remains the night that followed, by a pack of ravenous wolves. After unearthing the body and regaling themselves, they scattered the bones in all directions.

It was afterwards learned that Costello was at the time out on bonds, which he had forfeited, for shooting his own father in Bismarck, North Dakota. The late George A. Clark shared in the proceeds derived from the sale of the equipment of those three bandits.

LI

THE FATE OF BEN FIDDLER

ONE of the unveiled mysteries which surrounded the fate of many Black Hillers during the first years of settlement, was the tragic death of one of its honored and useful citizens, named Ben Fiddler.

Sometime in 1876 or 1877, this young man, a blacksmith by trade, arrived in Deadwood from Fairfield, Iowa. He acquired a frame building which was situated on a corner lot on Williams and Denver streets, now the site of the Gillmore Hotel. There he opened a shop and for two or three years did a profitable business.

The year following his advent in business, there came from Pennsylvania a cousin, Jack Geisler, who was a German, although born and raised in this country. He was also a blacksmith and was employed as helper by Fiddler. It was not long before Geisler disclosed a fiery and ungovernable temper. At times when irons failed to weld to suit him, he threw them with all his force against the side of the building. He would beat and abuse horses that refused to stand quietly while being shod. He was finally discharged by Fiddler and took his departure for Arizona.

Fiddler later decided to return to Iowa, and being an inventive genius, built a tricycle. There were two large wheels behind. It was guided with a chain and propelled by arm power. While it was easily propelled on a level surface, it required the full strength of even a burly blacksmith to propel it up an incline.

Ben disposed of his holdings in Deadwood, mounted his "go-devil," and took his departure. He finally arrived in Fort Pierre where he opened a shop and worked for a time. He then returned to Deadwood and later filed on a tract of land near Fort Meade.

He finally disposed of this property and entered upon a venture which proved to be his last.

In the meantime, while Fiddler was on his Fort Meade ranch, Jack Geisler returned to Deadwood accompanied by a slender, smooth faced, swarthy young man whom he introduced to me as Bill McCarthy, but dubbed him "Billy the Kid." They brought with them three ponies whose aggregate value could not have exceeded $100. The horses were placed in my care and the young men slept in my stables.

Jack gambled quite a bit and was frequently under the influence of liquor, but Billy was never seen gambling or taking a drink. Billy was quiet and had little to say to anyone.

When Fiddler disposed of his ranch he joined Geisler and Billy. They assembled a complete hunting outfit, including wagon, teams and supplies, for the purpose of hunting buffalo, bringing the hides and meat into Deadwood for sale. Their hunting trips finally led them to a fine location on Little Powder River, Montana. There they built a cabin and were soon prepared for hunting on a large scale.

Not long thereafter Jack and Billy appeared in Deadwood with the astounding information that Ben had accidentally shot himself.

The story, as related by Jack, was that he and Billy had gone out for game, leaving Ben at the camp engaged in making a grindstone, and when they returned they found him lying on the stone dead. They were unable, they said, to tell until the next morning just how his death occurred.

At daylight on the day following the death they rode three miles to a horse ranch and brought back with them three men who made an examination. They decided that in stooping over the stone with his revolver in its holster, the gun had fallen on the stone and was discharged, shooting Fiddler through the body.

They secured lumber, had a coffin built and buried Ben where he fell. When they arrived in Deadwood they turned Ben's gun over to me and I sent it to his parents in Fairfield with a letter telling of Ben's death.

It later developed that Jack had written his uncle before returning to Deadwood, trying to explain things which had aroused some suspicion. A sister, Kate, responded with a direct accusation of foul play in Ben's death, as she had known of some of Geisler's previous misdeeds and did not place credence in his statements. She also inquired as to the disposition of Ben's property. Jack responded by saying that the wagon was worthless and the horses had been sold to pay funeral expenses, and other bills. Since the only expense was for lumber in making a casket, the statement was an apparent falsehood.

As the death occurred two hundred miles from a settlement and the two witnesses were probably involved, no court action was ever taken in the matter; but it was the firm conviction of those acquainted with the men that Geisler had shot Fiddler in a fit of anger and then appropriated all available property belonging to him.

LII

BATTLE AT THE RIFLE PITS
(By Minnie P. Massie)

READING of the death recently of J. T. Spaulding, "Buckskin Johnnie," pioneer, noted scout and plainsman, at his home in Yountville, California, calls to mind an episode of early days in what was then Dakota Territory and Wyoming. Buckskin Johnnie figured in the episode as one of the rescuers of a party of immigrants that was for three days corraled by Sioux Indians.

It was a small caravan of Kansas people in 1877, farmers mostly, who had for three years in succession been impoverished by grasshoppers. It had left them almost hopeless of a livelihood, so learning of the new field to which people were flocking, they loaded their household goods and their families into farm wagons, hitched up teams of horses and oxen, even yoking their milk cows, using them for beasts of burden, and started for Dakota Territory.

After being three months on the long trail, much of it scarcely a wagon track, upon reaching the little stockade of Spearfish they had the disappointment of finding the country so dry and sere that they decided at once to push farther on to the Big Horn country in Wyoming. They even added a few new recruits from the stockade to their numbers, so there were some 12 or 15 wagons containing about 35 or 40 men, women and children. The men were armed with good guns and ammunition, warned that it was a dangerous proposition to go on into the intervening territory with women and children in the party. The late Charles W. Pettigrew, himself a plainsman and big game hunter, was again chosen leader of the caravan. With all due caution they had made a journey of 20 miles and had come to a little stream since known as Sand Creek. Camp was pitched for the night. On the way they had passed three haymakers working diligently at harvesting the native grass for the purpose of selling it to men with teams in the Black Hills mining camp of Deadwood. The men stopped their work long enough to add their note of warning as to Indians, saying, "It is reported that there are 300 on the war-path since the Custer massacre."

In the early hours of the morning, as the guards were pacing back and forth keeping watch over the sleeping camp, an alarm suddenly rent the air—the cry of "Indians, wake up, Indians are on your trail!" It was one of the haymakers they had passed on the way. "They have killed my two partners and they nearly got me. We were so dead tired after the day's work we just got careless and all went to sleep and didn't stand guard. They're headed this way an' you'd better get ready for 'em."

Although the camp had been made near the stream, the leader ordered the teams harnessed and the wagons drawn just as close to the bank of the stream as possible. "Just leave room for rifle pits to be dug outside the circle of wagons and draw each one close up behind the one in front," he said. As fast as they were in place, men were set to work with pick and shovel to dig the pits. A larger, round pit in the center of the corral was dug to shelter the women and children.

Bread was baked in the Dutch ovens and several of the women, instructed by the leader, added to the supply of ammunition by melting lead and molding more bullets. By daylight, which came early as it was midsummer, everything was done that could be for a possible siege, and on looking through the field-glasses feathered heads were discovered peering from behind the round, red hillocks beyond the creek bank.

All day the redskins lurked there, but seemed inclined to keep their distance, occasionally sending a shot toward the camp, only one of which struck the wagon box against which Mose Pettigrew, eldest son of Charles Pettigrew, and another man were leaning.

The heat of the July sun was intense. To the 19 women and children packed like sardines in a box in the small central pit, it grew unbearable. A tent was stretched over the pit, the sides rolled up allowing the breeze, when there was any, to circulate across the pit.

The long day and the night wore away without special inci-

[200]

dent, but as the animals up to that time had been kept close in, now they must be allowed to graze. As they worked their way slowly out from the camp, much anxiety was felt by their owners. About noon a group of 18 or 20 painted savages dashed out on their ponies in an effort to stampede the stock. However, they were still tired from the long journey across the plains, as there had been a rest of only three or four days at the stockade, so the gentle farm animals were not easily excited even by such a sight and noise as was made. A volley of shots from the rifle pits had a tendency to halt the savages. Bullets were sent in return, for the Indians were well equipped with Uncle Sam's guns and ammunition. Nearly all fell short of camp, although one struck the rifle barrel of a Dutchman in the party.

So steady a fusillade was sent out from the camp that it was not long until the redskins beat a hasty retreat. It was then that those of the caravan felt sure the number of them had been overestimated. However, after three days of such siege, although the caravan succeeded in withstanding the attempt to drive off the livestock, it was decided to send back couriers to the stockade for reinforcements. On the evening of the third day under cover of the darkness it was done, the men carrying tools with them and stopping to bury the two unfortunate haymakers who had been killed.

LIII

FIRST DIRECTORY OF DEADWOOD

CHARLES COLLINS, organizer of the Collins-Russell Expedition
to the Black Hills in 1874, also known as the "Gordon party," as
related elsewhere in this volume, became the first postmaster at
Central City, two miles from Deadwood, in 1877, and publisher of
the *Daily Telegraph*. In 1878, he published the first directory of
Deadwood and adjacent mining camps. A copy of this rare volume
is in the Adams Memorial Museum in Deadwood. It is the original
source of much authentic information of those days.

There were then in the Black Hills, forty-four quartz mills,
having 790 stamps possessing an average daily capacity of crushing
1,120 tons of quartz. He estimated the average value of all ore
crushed at ten dollars a ton. The average cost of mining, hauling,
handling and milling the ore then he fixed at five dollars a ton.
He gives a complete list of the mills, their location, ounces produced, number of stamps and production capacity.

The population of Deadwood at that time is given as 4,000,
not including some suburbs which were subsequently merged with
the city. Central City's population is given as 2,000. Lead's population was about 1,500. Other adjacent mining camps were Elizabethtown, Gayville, South Bend, Golden Gate and Anchor City.
Business interests of Crook City, Galena, Pactola, Rockerville, Hill
City, Sheridan, Custer City, Rapid City, Spearfish, and Victoria
are also included in the directory.

Over 1,000 names, chiefly business men, are listed in the Deadwood directory. The "Business Directory" included the following,
with their locations:

Forwarding agents: Cuthbertson & Young.

Assayers: C. C. Davis, George N. Hewitt, J. F. Sanders, J.

Rosenthal and Co., Sander & Engelshirchen, Ed Sieber, S. A. Wheeler.

Attorneys: A. Allen, Atwood & Frank, Charles E. Barker, Bennett & Wilson, E. C. Bearley, J. H. Burns, Caulfield & Carly, W. H. Claggett, Gaffey & Frazier, Henry Frawley, F. Gantt, Gooding and Graham, R. W. Hamilton, Harney & Watson, Hayden & Bennett, F. W. Knight, W. C. Kingsley, W. L. Kuykendall, Mose Liverman, J. H. McCutcheon, Miller & Hastie, Morgan & Corson, D. T. Potter, Parker and Storly, Ed A. Westmore, B. C. Wheeler, Williams & Simonton, J. M. Young.

Auctioneers: W. L. Travis, Leimer & Co., M. N. Levy, Sam Soyster.

Bakeries: Charles Elsner, George Eggert, R. M. Johnson, J. A. Wilson, J. M. Stephens.

Banks: Brown & Thum, Miller & McPherson, First National.

Barbers: A. Bauman, Girard Bros., Thomas Smith, E. R. Simms, John Worth.

Bath Rooms: Frank Welch.

Billiards: Taylor & Riddle.

Blacksmiths: Samuel Ickes, Joseph M. Richel, T. B. Tarpy, E. C. Tual, F. C. Thulen, Walsh & Landon.

Boarding: Idaho Boarding House, Wentworth House.

Boots and Shoes: D. P. Burnham, Hamilton & Co., Charles Karcher, J. Losekamp, J. D. Sears, Fred Zipp.

Breweries: Black Hills Brewery, Mrs. E. A. Brown, Fred Heim, Rosenbaum & Decker, Parkhurst & Conk, Downer & Co.

Builders and Carpenters: M. H. Brown, Kidd & Benn, John Foster, W. Shaw, Stewart & Martin, S. P. Wyman.

Butchers: Butterfield Bros., N. Frank, R. H. Geary, Steve Geis, Rosenbaum & Co., William Sauer, Jake Shoudy, Smith, Coad & Farber.

Candy Manufacturer: George Eggert.

Chandeliers: Gayle & Dion.

Clothing and Furnishings: Sol Bloom, I. W. Chase, Chambers & Cohen, Dan Holzman, I. M. Monash & Co., Munsta & Lilienthal, Sol Rosenthal, Strans & Whitehead, M. J. Werthheimer, Welf & McDonald.

Commission Merchants: Daugherty, Kelly & Co., Leimer & Co., Matheissen & Goldberg, William McHugh, Waiten & Castner.

Commercial Agency: Hooper & Wilkil.

U. S. Commissioner: A. R. Z. Dawson.

Confectioners: Cella & Hall, H. Gilman & Co., Hillary & Co.

Corrals: Buffalo Corral, R. L. McGuigan, J. Simpson, D. H. Spear.

Dentists: J. J. Clach, R. R. Buchanan.

Dressmaking: Mrs. R. A. Clark, Mrs. E. H. Slossen.

Drugs: Bent & Deetken, F. P. Hogue, Hulburt Bros., Spooner & Co., H. Stein.

Dry Goods: F. Poznansky, Strans & Whitehead, Welf & McDonald, Sol Rosenthal, M. Werthheimer.

Firearms: McAusland Bros., Gaston & Shankland, Sam Soyster.

Freight: Pratt & Ferris, H. L. Dickinson, Agent.

Freighters: Daugherty & Co.

Fruits: Niche Curcio, Cella & Hall.

Furniture: Braves & Curtis, F. A. Kriegar, Mankato Furniture Co., Star & Bullock.

Grocers: Hildebrand & Harding, Mathiessen & Goldberg, T. S. Martin & Co., Deffenbach & Hollenback, Miller & McPherson, Wardner & Bittinger, Adams Bros., W. A. Beard, Browning & Wringrose, Chew & Co., T. T. Cornforth, Ben Holstein, R. D. Kelly, C. H. Lewis, Vaughn & Decker, J. M. Robinson, W. L. Zink, Rodenhouse & Bros., J. A. Meeker, S. J. Scriber, Thomas Whittaker.

Gunsmiths: McAusland Bros., Theo. Roche.

Hardware: Jensen, Bliss & Co., R. C. Lake, C. R. Leroy, Star & Bullock.

Harness: Peter Meyers.

Hotels: C. V. Andersen; Marie Bernard; "Overland," Pichler & Bartels; "I. X. L.," Jim Vandanacher; "Sherman House," Warner & Borman; "Welch House," Welch & Farley; "Merchants," Jacob Werthheimer.

Jewelers: S. T. Butler, E. M. Gillette & Co., C. B. Jacqemin, S. Rosenblott, H. Seffer.

Ladies' Furnishings: Welf & McDonald.

U. S. Land Office: A. S. Stewart, Register, F. McKenna, Receiver.

Lumber: A. D. Steward.

Wholesale Liquors: Bishop & Johnson, Big Horn Store, Ben

Baer, Chambers & Cohen, Hermann & Treber, Ben Holstein, Wm. McHughes, Partridge & Co., Gottstein, Idleman & Co., Hugh McCaffrey.

Livery: Patton & Flaherty, H. Place, W. M. Wilson.

Machinists: G. Chandelfosse, Theo. Roche.

Meat Market: G. L. Barnard.

Millinery: Mrs. R. A. Clark, Miss Annie Dunne, Mrs. E. H. Slosson, Mrs. M. J. Smith.

Mining Broker: H. H. Folk & Co.

Mining Engineers: McIntyre & Foote, Kelly & Bruce, Rohleder & Smith.

News Depot: Burnham & Co., C. T. Clippenger.

Newspapers: Daily Enterprise; Times, Porter Warner, publisher; *Pioneer,* A. W. Merrick, publisher.

Notary Public: M. Liverman, J. F. Watson.

Painters: John Banks, G. W. Beals, G. C. Eldridge, W. Cornell, W. D. Robinson.

Photographer: Albert Pollock.

Physicians: L. F. Babcock, Joseph Fortier, Z. S. McKown, C. W. Myers, M. Rogers, H. Stein.

Queensware: Graves & Curtis, Star & Bullock.

Real Estate: C. G. Ankeny & Co., L. C. Miller.

Restaurants: C. V. Anderson, George Eggert, J. C. Czechert, Gregory & King, R. S. Hukill, J. R. Gandolfo, G. A. Roberts.

Rooms: J. L. Bowman, A. O. Kimball, Mrs. L. E. Lynch.

Saloons: "Bella Union," J. B. Billings, J. L. Bowman, Wm. Brennicke, G. D. Billings, J. D. Coleman, J. Conway, D. W. Dougherty, H. C. Dunning, "Eureka Hall," Fitzgerald, Healy & Bruce, Al Swearengen, R. A. Goodyear, "Grand Central," Harlow & Co., C. Haserodt, J. Hayes, "Hazen House," "I. X. L.," T. Hanley, "Little Bonanza," W. F. Johnson, Mahen & Connor, H. Maillard, Paul & Wall, O'Neill & Orton, James Ryan, "Red Bird," J. Rosebraugh & Co., L. C. Richards, G. G. R. Sangiovanne, Sigel & Vanocker, George Taylor, J. D. Russell, Wardner & Ryan, Thomas Weaver, Williams & Meskil, Mullen & McReavy.

Sash, Doors, and Blinds: R. B. Horrie, Miller, Silkenson & Co.

Second Hand Stores: Joseph T. Bliss, Sam Deubre, Gaston & Shankland, S. J. Scriber, Sam Soyster, Geib, Stone & Co.

Sewing Machines: P. H. Fisher.

Ship Carpenter: (Prairie Schooners) James Burling.

Stages: Cheyenne, N. W. Ex. Stage & Transportation Co., Sidney.

Stationery: Hamilton & Co.

Storage: Cuthbertson & Young, Forbes & Co., J. F. Carl.

Surveyors: Blackstone & Parshall, McIntyre & Foote, Rohleder & Smith, T. N. White.

Tailors: H. N. Hartendorf, Held & Co., Osburn & McLary.

Theaters: Arcade, Bella Union, Gem, Langrishe, Graves & Martin.

Tinware: H. A. Piper.

Tobacco and Cigars: H. J. Brendlingen, Wm. Brown, M. Fishel & Co., Hughes & McNary, Hamilton & Co.

Undertaker: B. P. Smith.

Watchmaker: M. Roath.

LIV

OVERLAND STAGE BUSINESS AND HOLDUPS

IT is not the intent of the writer to go further at this time than
to touch upon the high points of this subject, much less to undertake writing its full history or to expatiate to any great length upon
the different phases of that one time important industry, which
took the lead of all industries inaugurated in the Black Hills during
the first years of their settlement by the white people. I could give
a complete and accurate history of that one time paramount industry, and possibly it should be done, that generations to come may
know and appreciate the importance of this factor in the opening
to civilization of the Black Hills. It served its purpose and passed
on never to return.

That business was indeed the chief factor, and did more than
any other agency, in the tremendously dangerous undertaking of
wresting this land of enchantment from the clutches of savagery
and placing it upon a high plane of civilization, where it proudly
stands today, the admiration of the world. Though it was the primary industry of early days in the Black Hills, it was not because
of the magnitude of the enterprise, nor the capital invested therein
and the dividends derived therefrom, nor the princely salaries paid
to its employees. It was paramount because of the position it assumed and maintained at the forefront in the line of duty, the great
work that it performed, the dangers that it encountered and the
responsibilities under which it was operated from which there were
no avenues of escape.

A superficial view of that most essential of all industries which
pioneered the way and opened up the Black Hills for settlement
by the white people and developed its vast resources, might mislead
one into a mistaken belief that it was one of the roughest of occu-

pations, to be operated in a careless and indifferent manner. In truth it was just the opposite, requiring great care, inasmuch as its operators were at all times responsible for the safety of its patrons. Every person taken aboard a stage coach for transportation from one point to another on the line, held legally and morally against the stage company a guarantee of safe delivery, from the moment they entered the coach until their destinations were reached, excepting from accidents or "holdups" for which the company was not legally responsible. Of the countless number who were transported over those pioneer stage lines, whose lives were intrusted to the care of the companies' employees, not a life was lost and no accident of a serious nature occurred which was attributable to the carelessness of those employees or for which the company was in any manner responsible. Nor did we hear of a complaint being made by any of the many thousand wayfarers who passed over those lines, of an insult or ill treatment by any of those employees. There appeared to be, at all times, not only a unity of purpose, but also a kindly fellow feeling pervading the entire transportation system, ranging from the general manager to the underpaid stock tender, and this friendly feeling was freely imparted to the traveling public. It is doubtful if there could have been found amongst that great number of stage companies' employees even one who had not at some time conferred a favor or tendered his services in a way to cause some weary traveler to say to himself or herself, "There's a man."

Although other similar instances could be cited, I will relate just one of which I have knowledge which showed the openheartedness and generosity of those stage men. This was in the case of a young man who was stricken with heart trouble and was suffering so intensely that it was deemed advisable by his friends to send him to his home in the states. He was placed on the Pierre stage and well cared for on the way, arriving at Pierre more dead than alive. There one of the stage messengers, Johnnie Hunter by name, procured a hand sled, placed the sick man on it, hauled him across the river on the ice, carried him to the train and saw that he was made comfortable. The man lived to reach his home. This is not cited as an exceptional instance. There were many like Johnnie Hunter, in fact they were practically all Johnnie Hunters, from the highest to the lowest in the service.

OVERLAND STAGE BUSINESS AND HOLDUPS

John Dillon, a wealthy merchant of Fort Pierre, and John Schwarts, his clerk and general manager, took the initiative in providing passenger transportation into the Black Hills, establishing a passenger service line between Fort Pierre and Rapid City. While there were no regular stage coaches in their equipment, there were a number of strong, serviceable spring wagons capable of carrying six to eight passengers. This line went on the road in the month of April, 1876, and continued up to the latter part of May. Owing to the increasing Indian menace at the time, these stages were compelled to drag along with freight trains. They were unable to make satisfactory time and not long continued. The great want and urgent need of passenger transportation between the Black Hills and the outside world was sorely felt long before the dreams and hopes of the people, both in the Hills and abroad, were realized. Their cries and demands for relief in their enforced isolation were continually sent out, but no relief was forthcoming for several months thereafter.

Capital was willing to relieve the pioneers in their enforced isolation at the opportune time. The capitalists, however, were the judges as to the matter of time, so the people waited and waited. Gilmer and Saulsberry, experienced stage men, had their ears to the ground and heard the cries for communication with the outside world. They were fully advised in the matter and were amply prepared to furnish relief as soon as conditions would warrant it. Having had some unpleasant and unprofitable experiences in that line during the previous year, they were not disposed to make any further move in the matter of passenger transportation until satisfactory plans had been made for taking care of the Indian situation, which at the time was by no means reassuring. They also decided to make ample preparations for meeting and putting out of business white horse thieves by furnishing those troublesome factors a full supply of hot lead and greased hemp rope at such times and places as occasion demanded.

After these and other important preliminary measures had been attended to, they gave attention to the Black Hills situation. On the 25th of September, 1876, the overjoyed populace of Deadwood, who had congregated on the Main Street, realized that their cries had been heard as they beheld for the first time a well equipped and finely provisioned Concord coach and six come swinging around the corner onto Main Street. Salvo after salvo of shouts went up and the valley rang with the echoes as they reverberated between Black Rocks and Forest Hill. "Now," said one, "We will get our letters fresh from home. The last and only one I got had more whiskers than I have and I haven't shaved since I left home."

"Well," said another, "I can't see what good it will do me, there are no brake rods under it to take me out of this darned hole." These and other like pleasantries were freely indulged in at that time.

This Deadwood and Cheyenne stage line was thoroughly equipped with elegant Concord coaches. There were two types of these coaches. The one designated as a passenger and mail coach was intended especially for that service. It was constructed with one door on each side with a drop glass window light, neatly painted wooden sides with leather curtains in front and back of door and leather boots in front and back of the body for carrying mail, baggage and express. The body was swelled, the bottom of it was rounded or belly shaped. This constituted the rocker and rested upon heavy leather straps called leather springs. These were attached at each end to iron knees or braces known as thorough braces.

The other type was constructed in exactly the same way with the exception of having canvas curtains and no glass side doors.

Both types of these stages were employed on that line, but how many I am unable to say; enough however, to maintain a daily service run between the two towns, Deadwood and Cheyenne, Wyoming. This stage service was continued uninterruptedly, with the exception of horse or horse thief troubles, during the entire winter of '76-'77, up to March 25, 1877.

The first attempt at stage robbery in the Black Hills was made in the early morn of that day at a point two miles south of Deadwood, on Whitewood Creek. The stage was being driven by Johnny Slaughter, a young man, resident of Cheyenne, the most popular driver on the line, who, no doubt, was at the time swinging his long whip and touching up his leaders in anticipation of the nice warm breakfast that would be awaiting his passengers and himself on their arrival at Deadwood, when bang! sounded the report of a sawed off shot gun. Simultaneously came a fierce demand to "halt" and John's dreams were cut short as he fell from his elevated seat to arise no more. The spirited animals, probably mistaking the sharp report of the gun for an extra loud crack of Johnny's whip, dashed forward down the road at a terrific rate of speed, over rocks, ruts and stumps giving the passengers a lively shaking up. They ran several hundred yards before B. P. Smith, who sat up by the driver, succeeded in gathering up the lines and bringing the frightened animals to a full stop, after which he drove them into town. The body of Slaughter was brought into Deadwood where it was viewed by the writer and many others. It was prepared for burial and sent back to the home of his father, who was a city magistrate at Cheyenne.

It is asserted by those who claim to know the facts in the case that the perpetrators of that cowardly deed were Joel Collins, Jim Berry, Frank Towle, Sam Bass and one "Reddy." Three of them spent the following summer at Potato Gulch, a mining camp 20 miles west of Deadwood where Joel Collins became a partner of the late Anse Tippie in a grocery and saloon business. There, in the back room of the saloon, the plot to rob the express train on the Union Pacific Railroad was concocted. I received this information from Mr. Tippie.

The express train robbery was successfully put across that fall and the amount of gold coin obtained by the robbers was $80,000. Nevertheless, after all of their plottings, troubles and risks in putting it through, the affair ended disastrously for nearly all of those who were engaged in it as, with two exceptions, they gave up not only the loot but also their lives with it.

During the summer of '77 holdups on the Cheyenne stage road were of frequent occurrence. However, few murders were committed nor was any considerable amount of loot obtained by the robbers.

"Dune" Blackburn and John Wall, two of the most active and desperate characters on the road, led in most of these failures. They were both captured, convicted and served time in the penitentiary. As most of their stunts were bloodless affairs, no stiffer sentences could be given them.

In the fall of '78, a gang of "would be" stage robbers held up the stage at a point on Hat Creek known as "Robbers Roost," in the southern part of the Hills. On the stage at the time, besides Scott Davis, the messenger, and John Denny, the driver, were three soldiers who had been sent along as guards. These guards failed to halt with the stage and fled precipitately into the brush. Denny also very quickly decided to leave the job of standing off the robbers to Davis who was shot in the hip and disabled. The holdups, after getting rid of the entire posse of guards, took fright themselves over some imaginary danger and fled into the brush. The coach was left untouched.

A bold but foolish attempt at robbery by amateurs, though not strictly a stage holdup, was made on the Homestake narrow gauge road at Brownesville, a wood camp, 12 miles south of Deadwood. It was known that a large amount of money was being taken out that day to pay off the timbermen. The train was in charge of Captain Blackstone, civil engineer, and the treasure box, a handbag, was in charge of Wm. A. Remer, paymaster. The holdups were in the thick brush when the order to halt came. The train stopped and Blackstone attempted to fire a shot into the brush but his rifle jammed. Remer was more successful. Poking his shot gun out in the direction from whence the order came, he fired, putting enough shot into the gang to convince them that they had mistaken the number and had tackled the Lead train, so they decamped without leaving their future addresses. This gang, with one or two exceptions, were caught, tried, convicted, served time in the pen and came out thoroughly reformed and useful citizens.

The most heartless, as well as the bloodiest, stage robbery ever perpetrated in the Black Hills, occurred on the 28th of September, 1878, at Canyon Springs station on the Cheyenne road, 40 miles south of Deadwood. In this bloody affair at least six men were implicated. Four of these men were well known to this writer, three of them favorably. Their names were Charles Carey, Doug Goodale, Frank McBride and one known as "Red Cloud" as he came from the agency. There were two others said to be "Big Nose George" and Al Speer. These latter I did not know, at least by those names. Many of that class were well supplied with names having one for each move or occasion. Four of them were young men who came to Deadwood and vicinity. For two and a half years, during which they located a number of gold quartz claims in Sheeptail Gulch, two miles west of Deadwood, where they erected a large log cabin and made their general headquarters, the three supposedly honest, hardworking boys were opening up what appeared to be a promising proposition. Then the tempter, outlaw Carey, with whom they were acquainted, came to their camp and it was changed into a veritable robbers' roost where the heinous crime was concocted.

Carey followed the vocation of taxidermist and moved about to different places, lastly to Deadwood where he occupied a log cabin across the street from where the writer was living. I had several conversations with him and listened to his boasting war stories, as he claimed to have been a soldier. While his stories failed to impress me in his favor, I had no suspicion of his being a hardened criminal, as I now have no doubt he was.

One day in September, 1878, I left my house for a short time leaving the door unlocked. When I returned I missed my fine, new Winchester rifle. It was gone and so was Carey. I was determined to recover my gun if it were possible to do so, and I believed that it was. I thought that Carey had stolen it, but was not absolutely certain. So I waited until I learned that Carey had again taken up his abode in Sheeptail Gulch. I then hunted up John Manning, the sheriff of Lawrence county, told him my story, proposed to swear out a search warrant and that he and I should go and search the cabin. "No," said Johnny. "I think that you are mistaken. Anyway you may be and I don't want to go and stir up the boys just on suspicion." I insisted that we should go but he flatly refused. So I was unable to push the matter further.

In less than two weeks thereafter, the bloody scene at Canyon Springs was enacted. Their plan of operation, which they successfully put through so far as the holdup went, was that the entire gang, with the exception of Red Cloud, who was to be left behind, should go in a spring wagon to Canyon Springs station and wait. Red Cloud was to remain in Deadwood until the treasure coach, Old Ironsides, was ready to start south with its precious cargo, then steal the fine pacing horse owned by Blanche White (a woman of the town), ride in advance of the stage and notify the gang of its coming. Red Cloud carried out his part as agreed and when the stage coach rolled up to the station it was met by a galling fire from the log building. Their first move was to capture "Stuttering Dick" Wright, the big stock tender, tie him up by the hands as high as he could reach, to the rafter in the station. Gagging Dick was unnecessary, as it would have taken him quite awhile to have sounded an alarm, however it was done. They then knocked chinks from the cracks and prepared for action. Carey in poking his gun (my gun) through the crack broke off the nice silver front sight that I had put on the gun and this caused him to make use of a few choice invectives and it may have caused him to do some bad shooting. It was at the time, and is yet, my belief that both Doug Goodale and Frank McBride were averse to doing more killing than was found to be necessary in putting across the holdup; and that Carey, a hardened criminal, did most of the shooting.

Their first volley felled Hugh Campbell, a telegraph operator, from the seat by the driver, Gene Barnett. Campbell was killed outright. Gail Hill, one of the messengers, was shot squarely through the body, but was not killed and was able to crawl behind the stable and lie down, where he raised up and shot down one of the robbers. Scott Davis, another of the messengers, was untouched and made quick time in getting behind a large pine tree where he could give them as good or as bad as they sent. The robbers, finding themselves unable to dislodge Scott by shooting at the tree, one of them, Carey, carried out a ruse that worked successfully. This was to push Gene Barnett in front of himself towards the tree. Scott, not wishing to kill or wound Gene, left the tree and made his escape in the brush. The robbers then turned their attention to the iron safe containing the gold bricks, said to be worth $40,000, put it into a spring wagon and left the bloody field, taking their wounded comrade, Frank McBride, and leaving their dead man, Big Nosed George. The old spring wagon proved to be too rickety to carry the load and broke down before they reached a place of safety. This trouble, and their handicap of having to care for their wounded comrade, so completely demoralized the gang that they were forced to hide the gold bricks, or at least a part of them, and scatter, as the agents of both the express and stage companies were soon hot on their trails. As I remember the outcome of that affair, the robbers were all run down and captured, with the exception of Carey, the one in whom I was most deeply interested. The gold bricks, as I recall, were all located and recovered. William Ward, an agent for the stage company, it was said, related a great cock and bull story about following Doug Goodale to Atlantic, Iowa, who took with him two large gold bricks which he placed in the show window of his father's bank. Ward

said he recovered the bricks and captured Doug and started back
to the Hills with him and that he jumped off the train and made
his escape. Ward may have found the bricks where they had been
hidden, but the rest of his story was incredible. I knew Doug
Goodale too well to classify him as an arrant fool. If any of the
gang had taken bricks out of the country, it certainly would have
been Charley Carey.

Red Cloud evidently kept out of the holdup but rode his stolen
pacer on to Pierre, where he found an officer awaiting to take care
of him and also his mount. He was tried, was easily convicted of
grand larceny, and served two years in the pen.

The passenger, express and general business increased so rapidly
and to such an enormous extent during the summer and fall of '76,
that Gilmer and Saulsberry realized that it would be impossible
to handle the increasing business. They decided to discontinue a
stage line which they were operating at the time in Utah, and
transfer its equipment to Sidney, Nebraska. This was done by
bringing 87 fine stage horses and other appurtenances to supply and
maintain a daily passenger service between Sidney, Nebraska and
Rapid City, Dakota Territory. This line was established in March,
1877. Two years later, the Cheyenne line was discontinued and all
of its business transferred to the Sidney-Rapid City line along
with all other coaches. The treasure coach, Old Ironsides, was then
put on that route which was extended to Deadwood. Ironsides was
escorted to and from Deadwood and Sidney by eight of the most
fearless and reliable men to be found as guards. These men were
at all times heavily armed with rifles, revolvers and sawed off shot
guns. They were ever on the alert for business in their line, which
was to shoot down, on sight, any outsider who might so far forget
himself as to order a halt, if there were any of them alive to perform that service should the outsiders take the initiative and fire
the first volley, as was too often the case with the impulsive,
amateur road agents. While only eight of those messengers were
on duty at any one time, there were many others who served in
that capacity.

Of those fearless men, the writer remembers: Jesse Brown, Scott
Davis, Jim Brown, Gail Hill, Billy Sample, Ross Davis, Hunter,
Boone May, Johnny Cockran, Bill Lynn, Jean Decker, Bill May,
Norm Seebolt, Joe Goss, Joe Satterley. I remember also a few of

the many stage drivers who held the reins and applied the lash, who were equally subjected to all dangers and hardships with the messengers and more so to bad weather conditions. Among the drivers who served on the various lines were Gene Barnett, Red Raymond, Jim Brown, Dick Cole, Russ Hawley, Ralph Hawley, Bob Pugh, Locke Wescott, Billy Court, George Dean, Sam Ridgeway, Hank Monk, Harvey Fellows, Jim Sample, Kid Ellis, J. W. Smith and Dan Lilley.

There were very few successful stage holdups pulled off on the Deadwood-Sidney line during the long service it had as a carrier line. The last attempt occurred in Pennington County, which resulted in a hemp stretching exhibition by one "Lame Johnny" after a futile attempt had been made by himself and others in a tryout for quick returns. It may be said that they were in a way successful, at least so far as Johnny was concerned.

One of the biggest propositions in the get-rich-quick undertakings of those stirring times, though not exactly a stage holdup, was so closely related that it may properly be given here.

This bold venture occurred at the express office at Sidney, Nebraska, on the seventh of March, 1882. On that day, owing to the heavy roads, Old Ironsides was an hour or two behind schedule time in reaching Sidney. Just twenty-five minutes before the train was to pull out, the express shipment of gold, valued at $300,000 was handed by the messenger to Chet Allen, the agent, to put on the outgoing train. Although the conductor had special orders to wait thirty minutes any time that it was found to be necessary to do so, Allen claimed that he hadn't sufficient time to make the transfer and refused to do so, preferring to wait until the next day. This was done, and the next morning the express was missing. After a furore of excitement among express messengers, the gold bars were found in the same building in the middle of a large pile of coal, where Allen and his associates had placed it, with the hope of its being overlooked. While there was little doubt that Allen was guilty, there was no evidence to convict him. Others were convicted and punished.

This Sidney stage line was continued without interruption, or at least without loss of life or any further serious mishaps, as I recall, up to the time that the F. E. & M. V. railroad reached Chadron, Nebraska. Then all the long line stage business was taken over by the Northwestern Stage, Express and Transportation Company, a St. Paul corporation. This company was incorporated in 1877 and established a stage line between Deadwood and Bismarck on the Northern Pacific Railroad. Captain Blakely was president of the company and Colonel C. W. Carpenter and others well known in the Black Hills were interested in and identified with the company's affairs. This stage line was thoroughly and handsomely equipped with an elegant array of stages and new stage coaches. These coaches had been made to order and were constructed expressly for and adapted to, the transportation of passengers, heavy express and dead freight shipments. These stages were constructed with flat bottom bodies longer and much more commodious than those of the Concord thoroughbraced types. The rockers were made separate from the bodies, were rounded at the bottom, and were securely attached to the body by upright braces. The rockers rested upon heavy leathern straps the same as were those of the Concord coaches. The leather springs instead of being attached to the upright thoroughbraces, were attached to the stirrups forward of the front axle and back of the rear axle, and passed over other stirrups which were fastened directly over the axles. These coaches were therefore much stronger and better adapted to rough usage and standing the strains of heavy shipments of both passengers and freight than were the Concord thoroughbrace type. A full line of these stages was kept on the Deadwood-Bismarck route through the years that the company operated that line, and were afterwards transferred to the Deadwood-Pierre route when the company abandoned the Bismarck route.

The Northwestern Stage, Express and Transportation Company continued its operations on the Bismarck stage line for several years, during which time it transported to and from the Northern Pacific Railroad many thousands of passengers and thousands of tons of mail, freight and express. All this, too, in the face of continuous handicaps of snow, blizzards, high waters and, what was worst of all, the almost impassable gumbo roads. In many places, and for many miles at certain times in the year, one turn of the wheel would almost double its weight with sticky mud. This would adhere so tightly to the wheels and other parts of the coach that it had to be chopped and spaded off. This great handicap to transportation was by no means confined to the Bismarck route. It was encountered on all other routes leading into the Black Hills. There may be seen to this day, along the old stage routes, mounds of earth resembling huge ant hills, the mud that was chiselled off the stage coaches fifty years ago.

This last named stage line, the last of all long route stage companies to operate in the Black Hills country, ceased to operate on the Bismarck route on the advent of the Northwestern Railway into Pierre, and transferred all its stage line equipment to the Deadwood-Pierre route where it operated in connection with that railroad. It continued business on that line until the Northwestern Railroad reached Rapid City, via Nebraska in 1886. It then abandoned the Pierre route and practically went out of business. It shipped out or sold most of its equipment, retaining however, two of its big coaches, and kept them plying daily on the Deadwood-Rapid City route until the Northwestern extended its line to Whitewood in 1887. The two coaches kept on the Deadwood and Rapid City line were the one owned now by the City of Deadwood, and its exact counterpart. The one in Deadwood was driven to the final wind-up by Billy Court, and the other was driven, not only to the end of the company's stage business but also to the finish of the big stage, by Bob Pugh, another of the Company's old and trusted drivers. While rounding out his faithful services, he lost control of the heavy craft in descending a steep, icy hill west of the old fair ground near Deadwood, where the stage and team slid over a steep embankment, crippling some of the horses, smashing the coach beyond repair and injuring, but not severely, the lone passenger, J. C. Ryan, a Spearfish merchant. The coach was later picked up in pieces. The company went out of business when the railroad trains were run into Whitewood. So the long route stage business like many of our promising mineral leads, was followed up until it naturally pinched out.

What became of the coaches used on these lines, I do not know, with the exception of three of the lighter and older ones and the larger one known now as the old Deadwood Coach, all of the Northwestern line. Three of these were purchased by this writer. One of them was upset and smashed in a runaway near Buffalo, Wyoming, and left to rot on the prairie. The other two, and the Deadwood-Spearfish stage of which I shall speak later, were retained by the writer until 1923. The large one is now the property of the city, the small one, I still own.

Another of these long distance stage lines, inaugurated in 1879, was put in operation between Deadwood and Medora on the Great Northern Railroad and was known as the Deadwood-Medora stage line. This line was owned, or at least financed, by a French nobleman, Marquis De Mores, a capitalist, who invested heavily in lands in the northern part of Dakota territory, and who established a town on the Northern Pacific and gave it the name of his wife, Medora. The route of this line was from Deadwood via Spearfish, Dakota and Stoneville, Montana to Medora.

This Medora stage line was operated under the management of Rasse Deffenbach, a Deadwood cattleman. The enterprise proved to be a failure and was soon abandoned. Another, a short hack line was established in the seventies, between Spearfish and Sundance, Wyoming, by Tony Gerig, and was kept in operation by different owners, until it was finally put out of business by the automobile.

The last and only real stage line to be operated in this vicinity after all the long route stage lines running into Deadwood had gone out of commission, was the Deadwood-Spearfish stage line. This was inaugurated in the seventies by James Rogers of Spearfish who kept it operating for several years. He then sold the business, with all its stages and equipment to this writer, who with Harvey Fellows as driver, maintained and kept it in operation as a daily, seven days in the week for twenty-five years, carrying passengers, mail, express and all kinds of heavy freight that it was possible to load and transport on a Concord stage coach.

This particular Concord mail and passenger coach, which has heretofore been described, was operated all those years on that line with the exception of such times as it was found to be impossible for four or even six horses to draw the 1800 pound vehicle over the execrable mud line known as the Deadwood-Spearfish wagon road. This so-called wagon road was originally laid out along section lines and was left with little attention given to it by county commissioners or anyone else excepting those who were absolutely compelled to negotiate the trip, until such times as practically all of the bridges and culverts had been washed away by high waters and the road rendered unsafe, even dangerous if not wholly impracticable, to travel. The county commissioners would then get busy and have it placed in travel condition and again leave it until recurrence of the same conditions.

Such is the history of that mud line during the first thirty years of its existence, up to the time the automobile made its advent into this section, and not until then did our county officials awaken to the imperative necessity of opening safe lines of communication between the county seat and the surrounding towns. The old rock and mud road was then changed into a highway second in excellence to few in the state. This was accomplished by the expenditure of more money in its construction in a few weeks time than had been expended on its upkeep during the thirty years that it had been used as a stage road. Although the modern, cushioned wheels of progress were utterly unable to negotiate this mud road in its primitive condition, the resourceful and indomitable stage man, Harvey Fellows, was ever ready with a means to an end, and negotiated it with the old Concord stage and four horses. Many times this was possible only by tearing away wire fences and keeping on high ground by driving obliquely through fields of grain and meadow lands. On more than one occasion did he take from his team one horse, mount it and ford or swim False Bottom Creek to determine whether or not it was feasible to cross the stream with the coach and its load of passengers and mail. During his long services as a stage driver and mail carrier he did not fail to make connections with the outgoing trains, excepting such times as it was physically impossible to do so. On numerous occasions his team would, after dragging its heavy load up the long ascent of mud road, be left standing at a place known as the Rest House and the driver would shoulder the letter sacks and hasten up the mile of incline to the "Tunnel" and there put it on the out-going train. This is being related here as a reminder of the hardships and physical sufferings attendant at times on practically all overland stage service.

During our long service on the Deadwood-Spearfish stage line, we transported, at a conservative estimate, an average of ten passengers per day. A total of 90,000 passengers, together with great amounts of mail, express and freight were transported during those 25 years over that muddy or icy valley and mountain road, but not a single life was lost, with only a few accidents of any considerable moment. Of the hundreds of thousands of dollars carried over the line during our run of nine thousand days, not a dollar was lost. Nor was there a stage holdup, though there were many times when stage robbers missed their opportunity for securing rich hauls of from five to eight thousand dollars. Though this old Concord stage coach escaped the highwaymen and has no bullet holes to exhibit, it was subjected to all other dangers known to overland mountain staging, and has the distinction of having traveled over a greater mileage than any other ever heard of by this writer. It has to its credit at least 300,000 miles, and what is more remarkable, it was engineered over that vast mileage by the one driver, Harvey Fellows. This driver has, beyond the shadow of a doubt, the great distinction of having driven more miles perched upon the hurricane deck of various overland stages than has any other driver, living or dead, having to his record a stage mileage of more than 500,000 miles.

This occupation had its beginning at Denver, Colorado, in 1863, and was kept up practically without interruption for fifty years. The latter half of that time was spent on the driver's seat of the old Deadwood-Spearfish stage coach. Having the physical endurance of an iron man, he steered the old craft safely through long phases of bad weather disturbances, rain, snow, hail, blizzards and hurricanes and over the dangerous, icy, slippery so called mountain wagon roads, many times when the mercury stood twenty to thirty degrees below zero. While the passengers, wrapped in their furs, shut up inside, rubbed their ears and pounded their hands, Harvey would sit up on the hurricane deck of the old coach with his whip in one hand and the icy lines in the other, with the stoicism of a graven image. Ofttimes, at the end of the route someone would ask the question, "Harvey, you found it pretty cold, didn't you?" "Yes, it was pretty chilly," he would reply.

At last, after all those fifty years in battling the elements through storm and stress, this indomitable and ever resourceful stage driver was finally set afoot when the automobile came in and drove out the horse drawn overland stage business. So with his occupation gone, this veteran stage driver, at an advanced age, retired from active service, with an overland stage mileage of 500,000 miles.

Such is the history of the old Deadwood-Spearfish stage coach and its inseparable business partner, Harvey Fellows. After this writer and he gave up the stage business, R. L. Todd stocked the Spearfish line with Ford cars, the best to be obtained at that time. This light equipage, however, was soon found to be insufficient to handle the business as the paved highway and rapid transit so increased it, that in order to meet the increasing demands and properly handle the business, he later improved the service by stocking the line with the most comfortable, as well as the most expensive and up-to-date equipment to be obtained.

This historic stage line again changed ownership in 1925 and became the property of Henry Weare, a man of great wealth, who made other improvements on it under the management of C. B. Craig.

Harvey Fellows, after all his years of dangerous stage driving, succumbed to injuries received at close of a "Days of '76" parade in Deadwood. The old coach, mounted on a truck with Harvey in the box, came to a stop at Amusement Park. Harvey, forgetting that it was mounted on a truck, started to dismount and stepped from the wheel hub as he had been accustomed to do for many years. He fell the remaining distance to the ground injuring his hip. He was given every possible aid, and removed to his home in Spearfish. His injuries were not expected to be as severe as they later proved to be. He grew rapidly worse during the night and early morning hours. He passed away at noon, Friday, August 9, 1929. The coach from which he fell was the one that he had driven for over 20 years.

LV

ROAD AGENTS OF PIONEER DAYS

It was inevitable that, in the big influx of fortune hunters to the Black Hills following the discovery of gold, there should be a very large percentage of disreputable characters who came to get wealth, not by toil, but by filching it in some way from those who toiled for it.

In this class were "road agents" who held up the coaches which were the only means of travel into the Hills in those days, and robbed passengers of their valuables. This necessitated employment of fearless, expert gunmen to guard "treasure coaches" of the express company which carried out gold produced here. But other stages, not so well protected, were easy prey for the "get rich quick" rascals of those days.

One of the express coach messengers or guards of those days was Jesse Brown, a Pioneer of '76, who resided in Sturgis until his death in 1932. Thinking he could tell many tales of the early days which would be interesting to the present generation, he was requested by friends to relate some of his experiences with "road agents" and he responded by telling of one gang in the story which follows. Such tales are interesting, and they should be told by those who have personal knowledge of them, ere they pass in their checks, that there be left for posterity a truthful record and not the fanciful fiction of "dime novels," written by those who never even saw the Black Hills. Mr. Brown related:

"During the years of 1877 and 1878 few coaches into the Black Hills escaped without some experiences with the road agents. This particular gang I refer to had been operating along the line between Jenney's stockade and the Cheyenne River. They held up several passenger coaches at different times and were on the lookout for them.

[223]

"One Sunday morning in Deadwood, in Wes Travis' livery stable, very unexpectedly Archie McLaughlin came walking into the back part of the barn. One of the messengers happened to catch sight of him as he entered the door. He called to his aid one of the bystanders and placed Archie under arrest, taking him to the jail, and turned him over to John Manning, sheriff.

"I met them as they were coming back. Bill May was the messenger, and they told me what they had done and that Archie had told them that Mansfield was in town. So Bill and I went on a search for him. We found him on Sherman street in a house belonging to an actor in Jack Langrishe's theater troupe, I have forgotten the name. We got to the door before he saw us. He was standing at a table drinking a glass of milk. He set the glass down quickly and reached for his gun, but he was covered before he got it. He threw up his hands as commanded and we took him to jail and placed him in a separate cell from Archie. That afternoon we went to the jail and had an interview with each one separately. They both told about the same story in regard to their companions, Smith and Tom Price, and where their camp was.

"The next morning we got saddle horses for Bill and Jim May, Wes Travis, Archie and myself, and went to the place where the camp was supposed to be. There was some smoked dry bread and a small piece of bacon and a few magpies sitting around, nothing more. Archie then told us that this camp was only temporary and the main camp was 10 miles from there, southwest from Lead City. Nothing daunted, we struck out for the camp. After we had traveled about seven miles, we were on a ridge. Open timber, not much underbrush, but to the west of us there was a small valley covered with a dense growth of quakenasp, spruce and willows.

"Archie and I were riding together behind the others when he pointed down to the thicket and said, 'down there is where our saddles are cached.' I called attention of the others to this. We halted for a minute and concluded to go down and see if the saddles were still there. Archie pointed out the exact spot as nearly as he could. We thought that it would be best not to take Archie into the brush and I was delegated to guard him while the two Mays and Travis went to search for the saddles.

"It was only a minute until the whole scene was changed to tragedy. Sure enough, a camp was found, but it was occupied by two desperate men. The first thing I heard was 'throw up your hands.' The command was not obeyed—two guns went up instead. We might say five, because the five of them fired at about the same time. I made Archie sit down on the ground and place his arms around a tree and handcuffed his hands on the opposite side of the tree. Then I ran down to where the battle was going on. I met our three men coming out of the brush and asked if any of them were hurt. They said they were not, but there was one man in the brush who was pretty badly hurt, so far as they could tell, and one had got away. The wounded man was Tom Price.

"After it was all over the Mays and Travis went to the Teeters' ranch where Englewood is now, and got a team and wagon to take Tom Price to town. He was shot through the stomach, the ball coming out close to the spine. After they got back with the team and fixed Price in the wagon on some hay, we let Teeters drive back to his place and we went to the main camp about three miles farther south expecting that Smith might attempt to reach it and get some things that he had there before leaving, but he was not there, and did not come.

"They were well supplied with provisions, blankets, ammunition and everything that went to make up an outlaw's outfit.

"Tom Price got well!"

LVI

FREIGHTING TO THE BLACK HILLS

THE first essential in Deadwood in caring for the freight outfits, was stock corrals for the use of the bullwhackers and their
teams, and for newcomers who wanted a place for their teams.
There were two stock corrals established in the month of May,
1876. In them the stock was placed each night under guard, after
having grazed in the valley during the day, also under guard.

The Montana herd on Centennial Valley was conducted by Mike
Burton and Joe Cook. The Crook City herd was in charge of a
man whose name I do not recall.

The fee for caring for stock was two dollars cash in advance
for each animal. For this sum the stock was taken to the valley
to graze and would be delivered any time within a month when
called for. However, there was no guarantee of such delivery.

One of the stock corrals in Deadwood was substantially built
of hewn logs, fifty by eighty feet and six feet high, on the corner
of Main and Shine streets. It was built and owned by William
Lynn and a partner named Bartlett. Big Bill Lynn, as he was
called, was the tallest man in the Hills, being six feet, eight inches
in height. Although he had an Indian proof corral, it was situated
on a hill and was not easily accessible. Lynn soon sold the lot and
entered the employ of the Wells Fargo Company as a stage messenger. Later he engaged in mining near Galena where he was
killed by a cave-in in April, 1889.

Before coming to Deadwood, Bill had an unpleasant experience
with Indians at Rapid City. One evening he ventured out a short
distance from town to bring in his team of mules and was surprised and fired upon by Indians. Bill kept his scalp but lost his
mules.

[226]

FREIGHTING TO THE BLACK HILLS

The Montana Corral, established at the west end of Gold Street, was owned and operated by Billy Harrier. Billy was popular and by having an ideal location, did practically all of the business in his line. Later he sold his corral to Job Lawrenson and located on a ranch northward in the valley. One day while riding out in a one-horse cart, carrying a scythe, his horse became frightened and ran away. The blade of the scythe entered Billy's thigh, cutting an artery and he soon died from loss of blood.

About the first of June, Wes and Ches Travis, two brothers from Helena, Montana, came to Deadwood and established a livery and sale stable at the west end of Wall Street. They were both experienced livery men, Ches being of a more quiet and affable disposition than his brother. He confined himself principally to the care of the stables, and bookkeeping, while Wes, who was of a wild and boisterous nature, did all of the buying and selling of horses, either at private sale or auction. It is doubtful if there ever lived a more accurate judge of horses than Wes Travis. A walk around a horse would determine the animal's value. He was never known to purchase a horse that he could not sell. One of his favorite stunts in selling was to saddle a broncho, ride wildly up and down the street, the horse pitching and bucking, and then go back to the stable and remark that he had probably made a mistake in horses. Such publicity was usually followed by a sale from the corral. Wes took to drinking, finally to excess, which interfered with his business judgment. He finally succumbed to liquor, deserted his family and departed.

LVII

THE DEADWOOD WATER QUESTION

TURNING back the pages of history to those stirring times so vividly remembered when the people of the Black Hills were actively endeavoring to open their way to civilization, and this young city of Deadwood was battling for social order, I recall no instance other than those of a tragical nature and the great fire and flood visitations, which equalled in far reaching effects upon not only the citizens of Deadwood, but also those of all surrounding communities, as did the vitally important and intricate controversy known as the "Deadwood City Water Question."

This complex problem which greatly stirred the people, figured largely as a determining factor in the great legal battle for supremacy in the control of affairs pertaining to the mining interests of this section, as well as other interests in which the general public shared.

This important and heated legal contest was a matter of issue between the two most powerful mining corporations in the Black Hills, namely the Homestake and the Father DeSmet. It was fought through the courts and skilfully saddled upon the legally qualified voters of Deadwood for final solution.

In order to impart such information as will enable the reader to obtain a clear understanding of this water proposition, it is necessary to go back to its inception and the circumstances from which it evolved.

This issue, which resulted ultimately in the Deadwood City water election, originated in the locations of the two principal and most desirable water rights adjacent to the great gold mineral belt, made and recorded in the spring of 1876. One of the locations was made by one Foster and others on Deadwood creek at the mouth of

Poorman's Gulch, and was known as the Foster water right. A certain amount of water was diverted from the stream and carried along the north side of the gold belt to a point opposite to and above the level of Central City.

The object of the locators of this water right was to furnish water to the placer miners should they need it, and also to supply Deadwood with water for domestic purposes. It appeared, however, that the miners found adequate supply of water in the creek, and the city was receiving an ample supply from another source. Consequently, the Foster ditch, up to the time of the building of the first stamp mill by the Father DeSmet Company, failed as a paying enterprise. That mill was erected directly over the ditch and was being successfully operated with water pumps from a shaft sunk near the creek.

The ditch was offered for sale to A. J. Bowie, superintendent of the DeSmet Company. Bowie, no doubt, was intending to make the purchase, but he was in no hurry to close the deal. Whether he considered the price exorbitant or for other reasons not disclosed, he held the offer under advisement for a time, too long for his own good.

The other water right referred to was located on Whitewood Creek on the opposite side of the mineral belt from the Foster location, at a point about two miles south of and up the gulch from Deadwood City, and was known as the Boulder Ditch water right. This location was made by George Atchison, Ira Myers, and William Hartley. Probably there were several others financially interested in the enterprise. Just what were the investments of each of the three promoters of the company is not known. Hartley gave out his losses at the end as twelve thousand dollars.

This ditch was constructed along the mountain side south and east of Whitewood Creek to the city of Deadwood. A flume four feet in width was constructed around the brow of the hill now known as "Brown Rocks," practically overhanging the city of Deadwood and at an elevation of about two hundred feet above it. The ditch was to be carried along to a point about two miles below the city, which was as far as its promoters intended that it should go, although they gave out as their objective a point known as Boulder Park, an area ten miles distant from their water right location, and barren of valuable minerals.

This Boulder Ditch, with a capacity of five hundred miners' inches of water, was, considering the means of its projectors, a stupendous undertaking. However, it was put through to the point to which it was destined to go. The enterprise was inaugurated at an opportune time when there were about two thousand husky, unemployed laborers in and about Deadwood, and at a time when sow belly and beans were exceedingly scarce.

The construction work was started and vigorously prosecuted to a finish. Trees of all sizes that stood in its course were uprooted and thrown along its creek side to prevent the huge stones, which were being blasted from the ledges, from tumbling down to the road below. It appeared from the many detours made in following up and down the various draws that the company found man power cheaper than lumber, although both timber and saw mills were near at hand. Undoubtedly, the promoters of the scheme, like the Foster ditch company, had in mind the sale of water to both the placer miners and the citizens of Deadwood, and eventually the sale of the ditch to the city.

However, owing to the great depth of the gravel to bed rock and the uniform descent of both Deadwood and Whitewood gulches, with no abrupt falls for gravel and boulder dumpage ground, sluicing was impracticable. Consequently the miners in Whitewood Gulch, like those in Deadwood Gulch, were not in the market for water, nor was the city of Deadwood. So after testing and adjusting the big ditch and finding it in good condition, the owners turned off the water, left the ditch out of use for a time and turned their attention to other matters, hoping, no doubt, that the city would eventually purchase it.

While the Boulder Ditch was under construction Judge Barron, an aged attorney, conceived the plan of locating a water right near the head of City Creek west of Deadwood. This he did and diverted the stream to a water tank or reservoir overlooking the town on the northwest side, and proceeded to furnish a portion of the town with a fairly good quality of water, although there was both a dairy and a slaughter pen in one of the draws above.

From the first year of its existence the city of Deadwood was badly in need of pure water. The two main creeks, Deadwood and Whitewood, were flowing mud from the mills above, while the smaller streams were being badly polluted; yet this deplorable situation caused but little complaint from the residents because there were so many transients in the city at all times and so few who were willing to declare their intention to make Deadwood their future home for any definite length of time. Consequently the water question was seldom brought up for discussion by the people who were using the water from the two small streams, City Creek and Spring Creek, and many so called springs, which were nothing more than holes sunk along the edges of the creeks where the water could seep and filter through the sand and gravel and reach the holes in a fairly clear, if not wholesome condition.

So it was not until the status of quartz mining in the great mineral belt, centering about Lead, was definitely settled and generally understood, that the citizens of Deadwood became thoroughly aroused to the menacing effects of the unsanitary conditions arising from water contamination, and the water question was brought up as a paramount issue to be disposed of. It was the understanding at the time that the Homestake management had made a proposition to the citizens of Deadwood to furnish them with an adequate supply of pure water for all purposes, on condition that certain terms proposed by the company were found to be satisfactory and agreed to by the city of Deadwood. Just what those terms were was not generally known at the time. I have no recollection of their being given out to the public.

It appeared from later developments that superintendents of the two great mining corporations, the Homestake and the Father DeSmet, were so deeply engrossed in forestalling each other in securing every available mining location on the belt, that they overlooked for a time the most important factor in successful mining operations. It was not until nearly all mining locations of any considerable value had fallen into their hands that these two powerful corporations locked horns over the water question.

When the matter of bringing water to the city of Deadwood was brought to their attention, Sam McMaster, superintendent of the Homestake, took the initiative by quietly calling on Foster and purchasing the Foster water right, and other ditches.

Although his company held no interest whatever in that locality at the time, Foster became so elated over the sale that he took on an overdose of liquor and proceeded to express his unfavorable opinion of the superintendent of the Father DeSmet Mine and manager of the Borland interests, in the presence of that august official, A. J. Bowie. Bowie immediately awoke to the alarming situation, and lost no time in finding George Hutchison, president of the Boulder Ditch Company. That gentleman, like Foster, was so anxious to rid himself and his partners of their big "white elephant" that he lost no time in making the transfer to the Borland agent, probably for less than one half of what he might have received had he known what the situation was. So this unexpected move by Bowie gave McMaster something to think about.

The Homestake Company was immediately enjoined from polluting the water of Whitewood Creek, and at the same time the DeSmet Company, in order to put its ditch into effective use as was required by law, made a proposition to the mayor and council of Deadwood to furnish the city with a full supply of pure water needed for all purposes free of charges for one year. In the mean time it would establish a reservoir and a complete water system of sufficient capacity to meet all future requirements. This exceptionally liberal proposition was readily accepted by the council. However, there was no binding contract or agreement of any kind placed on record, if drawn up at all.

It was now up to the management of the Homestake Company to make a move. This was done through its able counsel, who very quickly convinced the city solons that the water question, to be legally decided, must be submitted to the legally qualified voters and settled by a majority vote.

So the tentative agreement made with the DeSmet people was held in abeyance. It was the understanding of many at the time that the DeSmet people believed, as did most of the Deadwood citizens, that it held by far the advantage over its rival. So with no thought of sharp practice being resorted to, they readily assented to the proposal to put the decision up to the legal voters of the city. This was done and the day of election set some weeks distant. During the interim the contending litigants, each with a brilliant array of counsel, were threshing out their differences in court.

The Homestake Company was accused by its opponent of muddying and polluting the water of Whitewood Creek, and the DeSmet people had a small force of miners ground sluicing in a small gulch two miles down the creek below Deadwood. They also claimed to have a few customers for water in Deadwood with the promise of more, to use their water. The Homestake management contended that they were not polluting the water to any detrimental extent, and that the mining operations of its opponent were only a subterfuge resorted to in its endeavor to make a show of using water. The newspapers had now enlisted and were taking sides in the conflict.

The *Deadwood Pioneer* was influenced by the Homestake management, and proceeded to point out to the citizens of Deadwood the superior advantages held by the Homestake Company over its rival for furnishing the city with a full and everlasting supply of pure water; and that if the people erred by voting for the DeSmet proposal, they would regret the mistake to the last day of their lives.

The *Times*, it appeared, had made a commitment, which put it astride the fence and it declined to be jarred loose. The *Press* rallied to the support of the DeSmet, and a convincing line of argument for several weeks flowed from the prolific pen of its able editorial writer, Mayor Snider. He called attention of the citizens to the fact that the same stream of pure water, which was being promised them by the Homestake Company, was already above their heads, and asked why they should sacrifice what was now in their hands for an uncertainty that could, at best, be obtained only after several years waiting; and furthermore, that the City Creek water, which had been taken over by the Homestake to be used as an auxiliary, could never be anything better than a contaminated pool.

These contentions continued during the several weeks preceding the election and reached the polls as a battle royal. The contestants met at the polls, apparently of nearly equal strength, with a seeming advantage in favor of the DeSmet Company. This illusion, however, was quickly dispelled at the opening of the polls.

The Homestake management apparently had not overlooked anything, legal or otherwise, which might tend to be a disadvantage to its cause.

Johnnie Flaherty, a trusted representative of the Homestake Company, attended by a well trained corps of workers, was early at the polls, well supplied with convincing arguments (?). At the appointed hour the polls were thrown open, not alone to the legally qualified voters of Deadwood, but to the world at large. Appearance at the polls was all that was required as proof of eligibility to vote.

This stupendous farce continued without interference from the opening to the closing of the polls. When the votes were counted, it appeared that the "no's" had carried by a large majority, and the Homestake Company was declared the winner. It was a great battle of ballots, but it was a shameful travesty on "the right of suffrage."

LVIII

THE HOMESTAKE MINE

GOLD has been found in many parts of the Black Hills in paying quantities. Many mines have been opened and developed, and are today producing the precious metal. Placer deposits were first operated and as exploration proceeded, veins of ore were discovered. Many of the lodes are free milling, making low grade ore profitable.

The outstanding mine of the Black Hills, the one which has consistently grown in production and value until it has become the greatest low grade ore mine in the world, is the Homestake. It is known to thousands who have no interest in mining. The hazard of mining has been removed so far as it is possible to eliminate hazard in such business. The following are excerpts from a history of the Homestake, written by Bruce C. Yates, for many years superintendent of the mine.

"The history of the discovery and development of the Homestake Mine is but a chapter of the general history of the development of the great west; and is as full of romance as was the great gold rush to California in 1849 or later to the territory of Alaska. Many of the hardy prospectors who came to the Hills in 1875 and 1876 were old campaigners in California, Alaska and other mining fields.

"Moses Manuel was one of those prospectors who had sought nature's wealth in many climes. Upon his return from southeastern Alaska in the fall of 1874, hearing of the wonderful possibilities of the Black Hills through newspaper reports of General Custer's expedition, he made his way alone over the mountains from Portland, Oregon, to Helena, Montana, determined to visit the new El Dorado. He met his brother Fred at Helena and together they started for the Hills, going by the way of Green River, Laramie

[235]

and Cheyenne. They reached Custer some time late in December, 1875, or early in 1876. Not finding anything of promise there, they started for the northern Hills, going by the then traveled route through Hill City, across Box Elder and Elk creeks and then down Spruce Gulch to Whitewood Creek. The account of his trip from Custer and how he came to discover the Homestake Lode of Lead, is best told in his own words:

"We loaded four horses at Custer with provisions, tools and camping outfit. Our first camp was near Hill City, where there was a party of prospectors sinking a shaft on placer ground. The water was bad in the shaft and they wanted assistance. We finally got a shaft to bed rock and found there was not enough gold to justify working it at that time. Fred and I left there and went to Palmer Gulch, near Harney Peak. We started to sink a shaft in the gulch and got down to the water. The next day we saw a large party of men coming up the gulch, locating claims as they came, and we found that there was excitement at the lower end of the gulch. They staked out claims adjoining ours. They were Colorado miners, and fourteen of us went together and sank a shaft to bed rock but didn't find anything to justify working.

"We broke up camp again, and Fred and I left and struck out for what is called Box Elder, camped there and prospected that creek and got fine colors. Had been there a few days when some men came along and reported rich findings a little farther north. We got in with two other men, one by the name of Hank Harney, and went down Spruce Gulch to Whitewood Creek and made camp. The excitement was running high; everybody was reporting rich diggings and new strikes. Finally a little gulch called Bob Tail was struck. We all got a claim apiece on that. My claim was located near what is known as the Golden Terra quartz mine, and Fred and I got hold of two thirds of it. We made camp at the mouth of Bob Tail Gulch. We wanted to locate a number of quartz claims and got placer grounds in the Gold Run, for which we traded the DeSmet Lode Claim. Towards spring, in the latter part of March or April, four of us found some rich quartz. We looked for the Lode, but the snow was deep and we could not find it. When the snow began to melt I wanted to go and hunt for it again, but my three partners wouldn't look for it, as they did not think it was worth anything. I kept looking every day for nearly a week,

[236]

and finally the snow got melted on the hill and the water ran down the draw which crossed the lead, and I saw some quartz in the bottom and the water running over it. I took a pick and tried to get some out and found it very solid, but I got some out and took it to camp and pounded it up and panned it and found it very rich.

"Next day, April 9th, 1876, Hank Harney consented to come and locate what we called the Homestake Mine. We started to dig a discovery shaft on the side of this little draw, and the first chunk of quartz weighed about 200 pounds and was the richest ever taken out. We came over next day and ran an open cut and found we had a large deposit of rich grade ore. We ran a big open cut and saved the best quartz by itself. Afterwards we built an arastra and hauled the ore over. We ran the arastra the following winter and took out $5,000. That spring we sold the Terra to John Bailey of Denver and Durbin Bros. of Cheyenne for $35,000.

"The next work we did was to bond the Homestake to a California company for $40,000 and the Old Abe to Wostom Bros. for $5,000. Brother Fred and Hank Harney took a trip to Chicago and I stayed to work the Homestake alone. I put up a ten stamp mill and bought a half interest in Gwinn's stamp mill. I ran the ore from the Homestake through this mill; all the other mills in the neighborhood were running the Homestake ore at this time. When I had a spare man more than I could work on the Homestake I would put him prospecting on the Old Abe chute of ore. By that time the two bonds had expired and no sale had been made. Fred and Harney came back and we had improved the property so much we concluded it was worth more than the bond and we wouldn't sell for any such figure.

"L. D. Kellogg, the agent of Senator George Hearst, came up one day and wanted to get a bond on the Homestake and we agreed on a bond at $70,000 for thirty days. A few days later Captain Huron came up and wanted to buy the Old Abe, and offered us $45,000 for it which we took. Both bonds were complied with and paid for within the limited time."

Mr. Yates continued:

"The Homestake lode claim purchased about the same time constituted the entire holdings of the Homestake Mining Company at the time of its incorporation, November 5th, 1877.

"At the present time the mineral lands belonging to the company consist of 577 patented mining claims aggregating 3,653 acres. This includes the property of the Father DeSmet, Deadwood Terra, a consolidation of the Deadwood and Golden Terra, Caledonia and Highland, originally operated as independent companies and consolidated with the Homestake about 1901."

LIX

EARLY DAY GRAVES

THE report of finding in Custer County of an unknown grave brought to mind an early day incident. It is probable that few are now living who are familiar with the circumstances connected with it. It is a story of the murder of a young man by Indians, and his burial by his party on the Fort Pierre-Rapid City wagon road in the month of April, 1876. A short time after the occurrence another party of which I was a member, came in over the same road. In passing the grave, which was on the hill a short distance above the road, it appeared to be open. On approaching it we discovered that wolves had been working industriously in their efforts to reach the body it contained, but thus far had been prevented from doing so by loose rocks, which had been placed on the grave, falling back in the hole. However, they were still on the job, as was evidenced by the fresh dirt thrown out.

Our few minutes stay there was employed in gathering and placing in the excavation the few small rocks to be found near by, hoping to give the wolves trouble sufficient to cause them to abandon the work. There was nothing in evidence to show whose remains had been thus left in the lonely, unmarked grave.

A sequel to this story was learned a few years later. While relating our experience at the grave to a party of men, I was informed by a man from Pennsylvania that he was one of the party who buried the murdered man. He said that the man came from a far eastern city and that his name was Hogan; that they came through from Fort Pierre with a freight train, which, being heavily loaded, made slow time. They had reached a camping ground, two days travel from Rapid City, but Hogan was so impatient that he arose early the next morning and declared his intention of going ahead on foot, saying that he could easily save one day's travel. The trainmen and others told him that it would be folly to attempt this and that they should all stay together as they were now in the heart of the danger zone.

Notwithstanding the advice and entreaties of his party, Hogan shouldered his pack and left them. Later that day they came upon his dead body, stripped of pack and apparel. The train was halted for a short time and a shallow grave dug. The body wrapped in a blanket was placed in it, and covered with dirt and a few rocks, as it was found by our party.

LX

BLACK HILLS SCENERY—STATE PARK

No volume concerning the Black Hills, in Sioux Indian language the "Paha Sapa," would be complete without at least brief mention of its wonderful scenic beauties. They are in reality rugged mountains with several peaks, Harney, Custer, and Terry, named from historic, Indian fighting generals, rising to more than 7,000 feet above sea level. Early explorers referred to them as the Black Mountains. In later years the more euphonious "Black Hills" was applied to them. Repeated efforts and suggestions to change this to Black Mountains, or some other variation, more truly descriptive of the area, have been met with strong, almost unanimous protest of residents, and it is probable that they will always be called the Black Hills.

One traveler, who had been the world over, asserted that in rugged scenery these Black Hills are on a par with the Swiss Alps, so the name is frequently amplified as "The Black Hills, the Switzerland of America."

During the past dozen years a number of motion picture companies have come to the Hills to "go on location," for production of movies and talkies based entirely or partly on Black Hills history and legends. One director who spent an entire summer with his company in the Hills, including some well known "stars," said:

"I have shot scenes in the Grand Canyon of the Colorado, in the mammoth forests of California, in the most rugged portions of the Rockies from Canada to Mexico, but nowhere have I found more beautiful scenery than in the Black Hills. Here within a small area I find a variety of scenery which can be found elsewhere only by repeated moving to a number of locations."

Much of the Black Hills area is covered by ponderosa pine

[241]

trees, some of them several hundred years old, attaining a height of seventy-five feet or more. Some sections have been denuded by tornadoes, fires, and in getting necessary timber for mining enterprises. But thanks to the conservation policies inaugurated by President Theodore Roosevelt, denudation was halted before reaching to inner areas, and the greater part of the Hills embraced in forest reserves. Under the watchful care of foresters, fire losses have been reduced to a minimum and denuded areas have been replanted to produce additional forests for coming generations. While lumbering is carried on to a considerable extent, it is under government supervision, and only matured, surplus trees are cut.

Interspersed with the forests of ponderosa pine are many gulches and slopes of spruce; birch, quaking aspen and other small trees are interspersed, with a great profusion of wild flowers.

A quarter of a century ago, South Dakota's foremost citizen for many years, Senator Peter Norbeck, envisioned an entrancing playground, not only for coming generations of South Dakotans, but for the nation as well. Custer State Park in the southern, most rugged part of the Hills, was established. It was zealously fostered during his administration as governor, and hundreds of thousands of dollars were spent in construction of highways to theretofore inaccessible beauties. This fostering was continued during the three terms he served as United States senator until his death in 1936, and the area of the park steadily increased by purchases from private owners and exchange of state lands for federal forest reserve. So well was this work done that in 1927 President Coolidge spent his entire summer vacation in the Hills with headquarters in Custer State Park. In recent years there has been added to the natural attractions of Sylvan Lake, the Needles, the Cathedral spires, and other awe inspiring scenery within confines of the park, the crowning achievement of the world's greatest sculptor in heroic figures, the Mount Rushmore Memorial. There, for thousands of years to come, a continually increasing throng will view the gigantic statues of Washington, Jefferson, Lincoln and Theodore Roosevelt, carved in enduring rock which does not disintegrate more than one inch in sixteen hundred years.

The people of South Dakota owe much to Senator Norbeck for his foresight and persistence in giving Custer State Park to posterity, and it may well be regarded as his monument. Increasing scores of thousands of tourists visit it and the rest of the **Black** Hills, and it is estimated by those informed on such traffic that not less than 100,000 came during the tourist season of 1938.

LXI

PIONEER CITIES

EVERYONE who visits Custer can understand why the gallant Indian fighter of that name halted his troops there when they came to the Black Hills on their expedition in 1874. It was in June, and the valley was luxuriant with the beauty and variety of its flowers, as many as 160 different blooms being found at the time. He, therefore, appropriately named it "Floral Valley." It was by members of the Custer expedition at that time that gold is said to have been first discovered, H. N. Ross and W. T. McKay finding small quantities of placer gold near where Custer City is now located.

Not until August 11, 1875, did the gold excitement become sufficiently substantial to encourage the laying out of a town, at which time Tom Hooper is said to have taken the initiative. All seemed to be going well for a big mining town until the following spring when the gold stampede to Deadwood occurred, practically depopulating Custer. A year later, however, the town began to revive when many of those who went to Deadwood came back, and from that time to the present it has enjoyed a substantial, steady growth.

The people of Custer have erected a handsome monument to the memory of H. N. Ross, who was the first to discover gold in the Black Hills, near Custer on July 27, 1874. Each year Custer stages an appropriate "Gold Discovery" celebration on July 27, in commemoration of that important event.

PIONEER CITIES

HILL CITY

The search for placer gold brought Hill City into existence in February, 1876, not long after Custer City had been founded. Spring Creek seemed an inviting stream for prospectors, and many seekers for nuggets began placer operations in early spring. Thos. Harvey, John Miller and Hugh McCullough laid out the town. Just about the time the young camp began to feel assured of some permanency, the Deadwood boom started. According to Annie D. Tallent's history, by the middle of May, Hill City was "as deserted as a graveyard, only one man and a dog remained to tell the story of its desertion." But like many other mining camps it came back when prospectors began to return and were encouraged by quartz showing in that vicinity.

In 1883, the discovery of tin brought Hill City into considerable notoriety. The Harney Peak Tin Mining Company, an English corporation, finally secured a great many properties that seemed to promise glowing results. Over 1,000 mining locations were purchased and the company is said to have invested over $2,000,000 in their development. A mill was constructed near Hill City in 1892, which was modern and prepared to treat the tin ores successfully. After a run of a few months the mill closed down, extensive litigation followed, and gradually the English syndicate withdrew from the scene. Nobody ever offered a reasonable explanation for the sudden abandonment, and to this day experts declare there is tin galore all over the Hill City region.

HISTORIC DEADWOOD

Deadwood has been known the world round for over half a century. It is the smallest "metropolitan" city in the world, with paving and public and other buildings such as are seldom found in cities less than several times its size. Built in a narrow valley and several "gulches," at elevation of 4,400 feet above sea level on Main Street, with streets terraced along hill sides to a height of two hundred feet above Main Street, it is one of the most picturesque cities in the United States.

Whitewood and Deadwood Creeks converge in the center of the business section of the city. Ordinarily they are quiet, swiftly flowing streams. Draining large areas of hillsides, they at times become raging mountain torrents, the combined stream rising to a height of ten or twelve feet, sweeping everything in its path and overflowing the bulkheads into streets.

Many momentous events in the history of Deadwood have been related in other chapters. At its peak, during the mining boom days, it had a population of 7,500. With the recession of mining development which occurred all over the nation from 1900 until recently, its population decreased until 1920 when the census gave it only 2,350 inhabitants. With increase in development of mines adjacent to the city the population is now about 4,000.

The first railroad train, the F. E. & M. V. (Northwestern system) reached Deadwood on December 28, 1890. The C. B. & Q. (Burlington) arrived in January, 1891.

Mt. Moriah Cemetery, on a plateau three hundred feet above Main Street, with the graves of Wild Bill, Preacher Smith and other historic characters, is visited by many thousands every year. The White Rocks, towering seven hundred feet above the city, afford a splendid view of the surrounding country.

The monument of native rocks to President Theodore Roosevelt, on Mt. Roosevelt, five miles west of the city, is annually visited by many thousands. It was constructed in 1919 by the Society of Black Hills Pioneers, of which "Teddy" was an honorary member, and was dedicated by General Leonard Wood. From its tower can be seen the hills in three states, and the prairie stretching two hundred miles to the north.

Each year during the fore part of August, the annual "Days of '76" celebration is held for three days, with historic parades which are a wonder to thousands who come from afar every year, and are a never failing attraction to residents of the Hills and vicinity.

A major attraction in Deadwood, for residents as well as tourists, is the Adams Memorial Museum. This beautiful, finely arranged building was the gift of W. E. Adams, pioneer businessman, to the city of Deadwood and to posterity.

The investment of Mr. Adams in this enterprise was approximately $100,000. It was dedicated as a memorial to deceased members of his family and to the Pioneers of the Black Hills, and was properly named the Adams Memorial Museum.

The people of the Black Hills promptly showed appreciation

by giving or loaning valuable collections of historical objects. It was opened to the public in 1931. Annually the number of visitors increases. Last year it was estimated from the registration lists, that there were not less than 150,000.

LEAD—HOME OF THE HOMESTAKE

Lead (pronounced Leed), is known as the "mile high city" because a section of its Main Street is one mile, 5,280 feet, above sea level. It is famous as the home of the Homestake Mine, the world's greatest low grade ore gold mine. It is built on the surface with shafts which penetrate the earth a mile, with hundreds of miles of tunnels radiating in all directions from the shafts.

Lead was founded in 1877 with the opening of the Homestake lode mine, and placer mining in "Gold Run," the richest placering in the Black Hills, a gulch through which the main highway now enters Lead. The city has developed with the Homestake and other adjacent mines, most of which have been absorbed by the Homestake, employing nearly 2,500 men. The Homestake Mine is Lead.

Its greatest attraction is the stamp mills and other surface workings of the Homestake. Many thousands visit these annually, under guidance of trained high school student guides, who receive a small fee for such service. Necessarily, visitors are not permitted in the underground workings except on special occasions when parties of notable visitors are thus favored.

The "Recreation Building," erected and maintained by the Homestake Company, is the center of Lead's social activities. Various provisions for entertainment and recreation are free to residents and visitors, subject only to necessary regulations.

From Lead radiates the scenic "Ice Box Canyon" road, with its wondrously beautiful scenery and trout fishing in swiftly flowing mountain streams.

SPEARFISH

The San Francisco Mining Exchange of January, 1885, which gave a historical review of the settlement of the Black Hills, in referring to Spearfish said:

"The honor of being the first settler in 1876 seems to be divided between John Johnston and James Butcher. Soon thereafter the

Spearfish Town Company was organized, consisting of W. W., J. F. and T. K. Bradley, R. H. Evans, J. E. Smith, M. B. Gordell, John Powers, J. B. Blake, Oliver Craig, William Gray and about 40 others, with Judge Bradley president. A tract of 640 acres was located and laid out as a townsite, substantially as it exists today, with broad streets, parks, etc.; and much money (for those days at least), was expended in preliminary work, including the construction of a stockade for defense against Indians, then numerous hostile, and particularly demonstrative throughout that section, so much so that a detachment of United States troops was kept for months in the neighborhood."

RAPID CITY

On February 20, 1876, a small party of Black Hills adventurers, after two days' trip from Custer, camped in Rapid Valley at the mouth of Rapid Canyon, about three miles west of the present site of Rapid City.

According to John R. Brennan's story of Rapid City's beginning, the party explored for three days the valley of the stream of the east central part of the Black Hills, and on the fourth day held a meeting for the purpose of deciding on the location of a town site. After the meeting, Mr. Brennan, who was an active leader, and Samuel Scott, with the aid of a pocket compass and a tape line, surveyed the present site of Rapid City. A meeting was then called, the town site was christened Rapid City, and a board of trustees was elected for the purpose of administering the affairs of the town.

During the summer of 1876, the Indians started to attack the settlements located around the foothills. The government took a hand and all white persons in the Black Hills were ordered to vacate at once. Following this order, soldiers were placed along all the roads leading into the Black Hills. The government blocked all efforts of people to enter the Hills and at the same time cut off all supplies from the outside. This blockade lasted for three months and practically all communication with the outside world was stopped.

While the government was attempting to drive the pioneers out of the Black Hills, the Indians were even more busy attempting to shoot them out. By the end of the government blockade, the population of the town had dwindled from over 200 people to 19. In September a small party arrived from the Missouri River with the glad tidings that the government blockade had been raised and that freight trains with supplies would arrive in a few days. This gave courage and confidence to settlers. Later stage lines came from Sidney, Nebraska, and Pierre, Dakota, bringing substantial development. The Fremont, Elkhorn and Missouri Valley Railroad, the first to enter the Black Hills, was extended to the city from Nebraska in 1886.

HOT SPRINGS

It is recorded that early in the spring of 1877 Professor Walter P. Jenney and Colonel W. J. Thornby journeyed down the east side of the Black Hills on a reconnoitering trip having heard Indian stories of the Minnekahta and of warm waters in that locality. On arrival there the two men camped for the night on the banks of the stream.

The following morning Professor Jenney investigated the formation along the river and discovered that it was fed from warm springs. At one of the springs they found what appeared to be an Indian bathtub carved from the solid rock. The two men decided that the spot would some day be the location of a famous health resort and surveyed out two claims. Thornby started to erect a cabin and while working on the foundation, two men, John Davidson and Joe Laravie, who had been trading with the Indians on the reservations, came to take the baths for their health, having heard of them from the Indians while on the reservation. When the cabin was partly completed, Thornby and Jenney were called to Custer by business and sold their claims to Davidson and Laravie.

In 1878, Dr. A. S. Stewart, who had been receiver of the U. S. land office in Deadwood and had heard of the thermal waters and otherwise inviting features of the southern Hills, with Judge Dudley who had also been impressed with the possibilities there, moved to what is now Hot Springs. Dr. Stewart at once built a two story log cabin which was the first permanent settlement of Hot Springs.

About the same time Dr. Stewart, Judge Dudley, Dr. Jennings, and others from Deadwood organized the Hot Springs Land Company, purchased land along the valley and founded Hot Springs.

In 1888, Fred T. Evans came to Hot Springs from Sioux City, Iowa. He was wealthy and invested much in early day development of the city.

In 1890, the Fremont, Elkhorn & Missouri Valley Railroad built a branch line from Buffalo Gap and the following year the Chicago, Burlington & Quincy built a branch in from Minnekahta.

Wind Cave, excelling in many ways the famous Mammoth Cave of Kentucky, is one of the greatest of nature's wonders. It is located twelve miles north of Hot Springs on the fine highway leading to Custer State Park. The Cave, which is truly a marvel of strange geological formation, has over two thousand subterranean caverns and one hundred miles of passages already explored without finding a limit. This cave became such an attraction to tourists that the government, after careful inspection of its geological formations, reserved several sections of land containing delightful mountain scenery, under which is located the cave, to be known as Wind Cave National Park. A large area of the park has been fenced and within the enclosures are herds of buffalo, elk and antelope.

BELLE FOURCHE

Belle Fourche is at the northern point of the foothills of the Black Hills area, outside of the mineral area. It became the terminus of the first railroad to enter the Hills and was for many years the largest primary shipping point in the United States for range cattle from the big branches of northeastern Wyoming, southeastern Montana, and northwestern South Dakota.

About ten miles from Belle Fourche is the Orman Dam, the largest earthen dam in the world. It impounds waters from the Belle Fourche River, backed· up for several miles. This is used to irrigate approximately 100,000 acres known as the Belle Fourche Irrigation Project. The dam was constructed by the federal government as a reclamation project.

[250]

PIONEER CITIES

Sturgis is on the eastern edge of the northern Black Hills. It came into existence in 1877 as a trading point, and into prominence with the establishment of Fort Meade, a couple of miles east of the city. For many years, as a frontier fort, large bodies of cavalry and other troops were stationed there, including the famous "Seventh Cavalry," General Custer's command, which was so badly shattered in the battle with Indians on Little Big Horn Mountain, in 1876. For a number of years, under war department policy of concentration troops near central railroad points, only a small body of troops was at Fort Meade. In recent years there has been a large increase. Over 700 are now stationed there.

LXII

GHOST TOWNS

THERE are some ghost towns in the Black Hills whose early days entitle them to more space in history than they are now accorded. There is plenty of interesting romance regarding some of those old mining camps, and much space might be used in recounting the stories of their ups and downs.

In the vicinity of Lead, there is Central City, once the booming center and mining metropolis of the northern Hills, but now only a typical "ghost town."

Terry is another memory of better days. The mining interests of both have merged in Lead.

Crook City was one of the first towns started in the Hills. It was quickly deserted in the rush to Deadwood.

Galena was for a few years a mining camp of importance. It is now another ghost town.

Rochford is now a picture of lost hopes in mining, although, like most of the other old camps, there are two or three places interesting to tourists because of their relation to the pioneer days of the Hills.

Most of these old camps are picturesquely located with scenery that is worth while. Their present status does not mean that there are not attractive mineral possibilities surrounding some of these old camps. There have been rich prospects always and developments are still progressing with very hopeful indications in many instances.

LXIII

THE GOLD RUSH PIONEERS

MEDITATING on the present physical status of our thin, gray line of Black Hills pioneers of '76, one realizes that there are few surviving members of that one time vigorous and venturesome band of indomitable argonauts, who thus far have escaped the blade of the grim reaper. Less than a score are yet living so far as is known.

One by one the remaining feeble few are laying down the burdens of this life and are silently passing on to realms, we hope, of greener fields and brighter skies. The ranks of the little band who remain are fast thinning, and soon the Pioneers of '76 will have become a memory.

These sad reflections carry me back in vivid remembrance and serious thought to an epochal period of time long past; a time when there assembled in virgin forests a mighty host of civilian immigrants, who had been incited to action by exaggerated reports of rich discoveries of gold being made in the Black Hills region of Dakota territory. This great army of agitated humanity, apparently all of one accord, had arisen simultaneously from all sections of the country and from all walks of life.

Inspired with hope and a spirit of adventure and a determination to reach and gain footing on the ground floor in that new field of glittering opportunities, they took up the lines of march in the direction of those discoveries.

Onward they rushed, beating new trails from all directions, storming the gates and trampling to nullity all prohibitive government edicts and other impediments that stood in the way.

Apparently oblivious of all authoritative restrictions, deaf to all friendly advices, heedless of warnings of danger to trespassers on a forbidden reservation of a nation of hostile and infuriated savages, that impetuous army of unlawful occupation pressed onward.

Obviously all of the heterogeneous mass of excited stampeders had the same objective, the Black Hills of Dakota territory. To those who afterwards were brought to clear realization of the actual status of the Indian situation at the time, it appeared miraculous that the almost defenseless and wholly unprotected throngs of gold seekers were permitted to reach their destination, with so little loss of life.

The swollen stream of immigration to the Black Hills in '76 flowed through the open jaws of destruction which easily could, and no doubt would, have closed down upon them, had those infuriated savages known of their practically defenseless condition. Doubtless failure to do so was due to the fact that they were ignorant of the true situation. They probably believed that this great tide of immigration, so defiantly flowing into their country, had come adequately prepared to take care of themselves and, if not, they would be protected by military forces. In fact, while the few whites who came to the Hills the previous winter, were well equipped with firearms, of the thousands who came in '76 not to exceed ten per cent were effectively armed. Their mission to the Black Hills was to hunt for gold and not for trouble. Even if those unorganized parties of civilians had come prepared to fight their way through, what defense could they have made, strung along the road as they were, against formidable bodies of Indians armed with long range needle guns, firing from ambush?

The Reds, ignorant of the advantages in their favor, turned their attention to a pursuit of lesser risk and one more profitable than that of gathering white scalps. This was harassing the whites, stampeding horses and cattle and incidentally murdering white men when it could safely be done without endangering themselves.

In view of the fact that those roving bands of Reds were never known to attack a party of whites who were anywhere near their equal in numbers, it may well be assumed that the Indians were laboring under a mistaken belief that the great multitude of white immigrants in the Black Hills were amply prepared to defend themselves against any attack that might be made.

There can be no doubt that the people of the Black Hills, especially the farmers and those of the outside towns, were in imminent danger of an onslaught by Indians all through the summer of '76; nor were they freed from perils of the red menace until September 8, when General Crook and his weary army of two thousand soldiers, after a forced march of two hundred and fifty miles through stress and storm with hunger near starvation point, overtook, fought and scattered a large band of thoroughly equipped Indians, one hundred miles north of the Black Hills.

Flushed with success in the annihilation of General Custer's little army at the Little Big Horn, that contingent of Sitting Bull's legions had started southward in the direction of the Black Hills. Undoubtedly it was the avowed intention of this formidable body of infuriated Reds to overrun this section, with possibility of making the onslaught a crowning success by a series of massacres with a total far greater than the unfortunate little army of General Custer at Little Big Horn.

In summarizing the events of that epochal period of 1876, it appears that on the whole the people of the Black Hills were highly favored by fortune, and that we all had much in common to be thankful for. While it is true that there were half a hundred or more lives lost in the Black Hills in struggles with the Reds, a goodly number of them were due to the recklessness of the victims themselves.

In speaking of the sanguinary struggles between the white invaders and Indian defenders of the Black Hills, it is not the purpose of this writer to minimize, or in any degree underestimate, the brutal and inhuman atrocities perpetrated upon the whites by their red-skinned adversaries. There were two sides to those bitter struggles for supremacy. Impartial consideration discloses that there were facts strongly favoring the Indian side of the controversy. The whites were unlawful intruders and therefore the aggressors. Although they forced themselves upon the Indian reservation, against the protests of the rightful owners, they did so with no intention of engaging in warfare with them. It was their intention, as was shown by later developments, to take whatever could be found on the reservation of sufficient value to warrant appropriation.

In these sanguinary struggles between the whites and the Reds, but little difference was shown in their tactics and methods of warfare. Aside from the murder of three women by Indians, the methods of human butchery employed by the contesting parties were equally abhorrent. The Indians scalped their victims when not too hotly pressed, and carried away the scalps; the whites retaliated by decapitating their victims and bringing their gruesome trophies into Deadwood, parading the streets with them, soliciting and obtaining recompense for their noble, or ignoble, deeds, according to the view one may take of such inhuman practices.

LXIV

DEADWOOD DESTROYED BY FIRE

On the 26th of September, 1879, Deadwood suffered its first great set-back, a disastrous fire which destroyed the entire business section of the city. The property loss was estimated at two million dollars. Coming in the early morning hours, when nearly all were in deep repose, it gained a start which took it beyond control.

The incipient blaze which led to this destructive conflagration originated in the Star Bakery on the corner of Deadwood and Sherman streets by the upsetting of a kerosene lamp, either by the proprietor or an employee.

The first warning of danger heard by the people was the reports of several pistol shots. These familiar sounds in those stirring times were not unusual occurrences and little attention was paid to them. Probably they suggested to others as they did to the writer, a farewell salute to the sleeping town by a squad of drunken and hilarious cowboys.

Closely following the pistol shots came a cry of Fire! Fire! Fire! It was quickly heralded over the city. These tidings aroused and brought the people to the streets and a grand rush was made toward the flaming section. It required but a moment's view of the appalling scene to convince every spectator that he was too deeply interested in the outcome to tarry long. Most of them hurried back to their homes or quarters, and hastily donned their wearing apparel. Then they gathered up as much of their most valued belongings as they were able to carry up the long and rickety flights of stairways which led up to Williams Street on the hillside. Here about three thousand shivering people were congregated for several hours watching in mute despair while the flaming tongues of the relentless fire licked up all of their worldly possessions.

[257]

The bakery building in which the fire originated, like nearly all other buildings in the city, was constructed of pitch pine lumber which, when thoroughly seasoned, is highly combustible and when ignited presents stubborn resistance against all effort to extinguish. Strong south winds were blowing over the fire area, scattering fire brands over the main parts of the city. The heat became so intense as to fire from one building to another on the opposite side of the street; it even forced its way against the wind up Sherman Street, burning every building on both sides to Pine Street. One building containing ammunition and other explosives had also a large amount of blasting powder in storage. This, when it ignited, belched forth a stunning report which fairly quaked the hillsides surrounding the city. An estimable lady dressmaker, three hundred feet distant from the building, had her eardrum burst, and she was deaf ever after.

The fire swept away everything of a combustible nature north of Deadwood Street from Hebrew Hill on the east to Williams Street on the west, clearing up the entire business section of the city down to a vacant space between the second and first wards. Here its force was spent.

During the four hours the flames were destroying the business section, the scene was indescribably horrifying, with the roaring of the flames, the continuous booming of every variety of explosives, of which it seemed every building held a supply, the falling and crashing of timbers, the flashing skywards of flames of ignited oils and spirituous liquors, and occasional earth shocks from exploded blasting powder. The most ear splitting was in the two story brick hardware store of R. C. Lake on Main Street where a considerable amount of dynamite was in storage. This explosion sent the entire metal roof hundreds of feet into the air and the detonation which followed seemed to not only quake the hillsides but shook the firmament above, echoing the din from many kinds of deafening noises, creating the impression that a host of bedlamites had been turned loose.

This tremendous calamity at least left the stricken townspeople one thing to be thankful for, opportunity to escape with their lives. Not a single human life was sacrificed in that holocaust.

The city soon arose again from the ashes. Even before the smoking ruins were deemed safely approachable, there could be

[258]

seen many of the owners, garbed in flannel shirts, and miners' overalls, engaged in untangling the network of wires and steel rods and clearing away the debris around the sides of their lots, preparatory to excavating for stone foundations to take the place of wooden blocks which theretofore had served the purpose for the hastily constructed buildings of the first years of their occupation. This preliminary work was immediately taken up by the owners of practically every ash lot in the burnt district, with a building boom for a new and better, more substantial and up-to-date city, than was the first Deadwood.

LXV

CONFLICT BETWEEN MINERAL LOCATIONS AND TOWN LOTS

WHEN Pat Constantine sold claims Nos. 24 and 25 below Discovery to Bob Cooper, he increased the troubles of the surface locators on the claims. Cooper apparently regarded each and every person who held a town lot on his claim to be a deadly enemy. Many of the surface claimants, realizing that they had a bad man to deal with, prepared to meet him on his own terms, whatever they might be.

Although Bob made many cracks when he was drunk, but little attention was paid to him. Nothing more than a few threats was heard until after the disastrous fire of '79, when most of the surface holders lost their buildings. Among them was John Ammerman. Before the ashes were cooled Bob Cooper hastened to a saw mill and brought loads of heavy lumber and piled it on Ammerman's lot. This wholly unexpected advantage taken by Bob forced John into action.

That night he removed all of the lumber to the opposite side of Williams Street. When Cooper came on the ground he was rabid and put in the day in carrying the lumber back on the lot, threatening vengeance on the next person who touched it, swearing that if it were moved again it would be by "lightning force." It would be guarded at night, he said.

Ammerman called on some of his friends, who were also having trouble with Bob, to stand guard over him and his assistants while they dragged the heavy timbers back across the street. Hank Beaman, Mast Girard, Jim Russell and this writer volunteered to see him through. A fully armed group went on the ground at dark, prepared for the onslaught, expecting Bob to come shooting. We

[260]

noted that he had been "tanking up" for the occasion, and we all knew that when Bob was drunk he was reckless. Jim Russell was the only one of our four who drank to excess, if at all. He was not addicted to heavy drinking, but was well fired up and seemed to be eager for the fray. He was very much disappointed in not getting into action with his big .44 Smith & Wesson revolver, which he kept swinging in all directions.

The lumber was again removed across the street where it remained. Cooper failed to put in his appearance on the ground. It was learned that Jack Smith, a particular friend of Bob's, learning what was on the tapis, kept his friend going from one saloon to another until the work was finished. Girard went home and the rest of us went down to Lee Street where we gave Russell the slip while he was in a saloon, as he was becoming dangerous. I believed that, had we met Bob, Jim would have shot him down without cause.

Ammerman went into Pat Casey's saloon while Beaman and I kept watch on the outside. It so happened that Cooper was there ordering a drink at the time. He was ignorant of what had taken place on Williams Street, and though he was furious at Ammerman, he invited him to come up to the bar and drink with him. John accepted the invitation but just as he was filling his glass Bob said, "John Ammerman is a ——!"

The insult had hardly left his lips when something struck him between the eyes and the blood ran over his face, blinding him. However, he made his way to the door and stood in it with his back to the street swinging his ivory handle revolver in all directions, calling on Ammerman to come on and come "a running." Pat Casey had quickly pushed John through a back door. Beaman and I stood close by expecting Bob to get sight of John and begin shooting, but before he could wipe the blood from his eyes John was out of sight.

That was a wild night, but through the timely intervention of Jack Smith a bloody encounter was averted. During the night Hank Beaman procured a yoke of oxen and a "stone boat," which is made of two heavy timbers fashioned like a sled, on which he dragged across the bridge from Seiver Street a small house which he placed on his then vacant ash lot.

The following morning, after Cooper had gotten his eyes cleared so that he could see his way, he came down the street pretty well sobered up. When he saw Hank standing in the doorway of his little house looking out at him, he became rabid again and ordered Hank off the lot; but before he could get his gun in action he was facing a double barrelled shot gun and heard Hank say, "Come another step and you are a dead man." At that time Louis Shoenfield, a friend of Bob's, was pulling him back and saved his life.

From that time forward Cooper apparently gave up bluffing and decided to await receiving patents to the mineral lots, and take legal action to dispossess all surface claimants who refused to meet his extortionate prices. In the legal conflict between placer locations and surface rights, the mineral locators won out. Cooper eventually succeeded in mulcting many thousands of dollars from the helpless owners of surface property, who had been led to make the improvements through the promises and assurances of the miners who wanted the town built up for their benefit and protection. Cooper, however, was not long in dissipating his ill gotten gains, and soon filled a drunkard's grave.

LXVI

DEADWOOD SWEPT BY FLOOD

SCARCELY had the citizens of Deadwood recouped their losses
and reestablished their business relations with the outside world,
lost in the disastrous conflagration of 1879, when they were again
unexpectedly summoned to witness a second calamitous visitation,
which admitted of no interception by any human agency. Although
this second infliction, ruinous as it proved to be, was not comparable
to the first in material losses, it was much more deplorable, inasmuch as its pathway for many miles was strewn with evidence of
death and destruction.

The winter of 1882-1883 was exceptionally cold with much
snow which blanketed the large areas of water sheds lying above
the sources of all streams in the northern Hills. This vast body of
snow, ranging in depth from five to ten feet and held intact
throughout the winter, was a menacing condition but inspired no
apprehension, even if thought of by the masses of people in the
gulches below. Cold weather continued that spring until the second
week in May, when it moderated and became extremely warm for
that season of the year. The spring rains came and for several days
and nights it rained almost incessantly, gradually increasing the
usual flow of water in the spring seasons. However, a radical change
in the situation developed on the 17th when it was noticed that
the waters in the creek had risen above their banks and were
inundating the lower levels. This steady increase continued until
late in the afternoon, when it seemed that every water gate in the
upper regions had been simultaneously thrown open, releasing tremendous bodies of water which came surging down the gulches
sweeping every obstacle before it.

Timely alarm had been heralded and the excitement became

intense. Many succeeded in moving their live stock and much of their valuables and portable household effects to higher grounds. Much more could have been saved had they foreseen the enormity of the disaster.

Deadwood Creek appeared to get the start, as upper Main Street was the first to become inundated. The raging stream, after having swept up all the stock sheds and other movable property and debris in Central City and along down the gulch, took everything loose on upper Main Street.

Frank C. Ayres, owner of a livery stable, who had the finest stock of vehicles in the city, had taken his horses to higher ground and was offered assistance in moving his carriages to a place of safety. This he declined as he thought they were safe. However, they went swirling down the gulch to be crushed to splinters.

Night came on. People generally expressed belief that the worst was over. The roaring of the waters and the clanking and grating of boulders continued the entire night. Morning came with no abatement of the raging torrent, and the fact that its destructive force had been materially augmented in Whitewood gulch was plainly evident. A man named George Chandler, part owner in the Deadwood-Lead toll road, had but a short time previous to this returned from a trip to Indiana, bringing his young wife, and they had immediately begun house-keeping in an apartment to which the toll gate was attached. He was warned of the danger of remaining in the house by H. A. McDonald who built it, as it stood on posts against the creek bank. He failed to heed the warning and remained in the house with his wife and a man named Gus Holthusen, who was in his employ, until six o'clock the next morning. McDonald's fourteen year old boy was looking in at an open window when suddenly something struck the main post. Mrs. Chandler shouted, "George, we are gone." Instantly the house plunged into the raging torrent and its inmates were lost to sight.

With increasing volume and velocity this irresistible force of nature continued its torrential course down Whitewood Creek, obliterating all the movable material left from the ravages of the previous night.

At the head of Charles Street the main creek channel overflowing, sent an auxiliary, of horse swimming depth, down the street.

[264]

This with tremendous force diverged to the east side, inundating that entire section, and flooding the houses to near floating point.

From the right angle junction of Sherman and Charles streets this secondary stream coursed down Sherman Street, tearing up the pavement and gouging holes five to ten feet deep. Turning to the north side it raced down to a junction with the main stream in the second ward. It was in this ward, center of the city, that the greatest confusion prevailed. Separated by waters 200 feet wide, the people on both sides were isolated. Although within a stone's throw of each other, waters drowned all voices. After many futile attempts to effect intercourse it was finally, though not permanently accomplished. A strong rope was drawn across the stream and snubbed at each end. This proved insufficient to hold the two story, $10,000 Methodist Church. This structure was followed by the public school building of about the same size and value. These were preceded and followed by many other frame buildings. Several buildings which were directly in the path of the main current were blown up with dynamite to relieve the congestion which at times threatened nearby Main Street.

Many buildings had been erected close to the creek banks, with a few directly over the stream. All bridges were swept away, the long, heavy wrought iron beams were twisted out of shape and carried down stream. The loss of many thousands of dollars worth of property, other than houses, was serious to contemplate. Thousands of unused mining timbers, saw logs, lumber, cord wood, tree tops with rubbish of every kind resembled a huge river drive.

The body of Mr. Chandler was found buried beneath a gravel bed in the fourth ward. One hand left uncovered was discovered by a little boy. Mrs. Chandler's body was found in a drift of lumber and other debris in the first ward. That of Gus Holthusen was found in a drift lower down the creek. Another life was lost the same day, four miles down the creek. A young man named Noble, together with two others, was walking along the creek bank, when a tree fell toward the bank, striking Mr. Noble and breaking his neck.

In addition to these fatalities a property loss of $200,000 was entailed by the ravages of this destructive flood.

LXVII

THE STONEVILLE BATTLE

DURING the winter of 1883-84 there was operating in the country north and west of the Black Hills, a gang of horse and cattle thieves. It was composed of a man named Campbell, Alex Grady, Charles Brown (known as Broncho Charlie), Jesse Pruden, George Axelbee, and others. This group was known as the "Axelbee Gang" and warrants for their arrest were placed in the hands of Al Raymond, deputy United States marshal for the Territory of Dakota.

One of the gang, Jesse Pruden, was arrested in Miles City, Montana, by Jack Johnson, sheriff there, who notified Raymond of the capture. Joe Ryan, a deputy, was sent after the prisoner.

After Ryan had left Miles City with his prisoner, Fred Willard, another deputy United States marshal living at Spearfish, was advised that Axelbee and his gang were waiting at Box Elder mountain, about eighty miles north of Spearfish, for the purpose of intercepting Ryan and releasing Pruden.

Upon receipt of this information Fred Willard called his brother, Capt. A. M. Willard, in Deadwood, also a deputy marshal, advising that a posse be dispatched to prevent Ryan and his prisoner from falling into the hands of the Axelbee gang.

Captain Willard decided to await further information, but Fred decided to start out. He, with Jack O'Harra and Billy Thatcher, started immediately for Stoneville, the supposed meeting point. Captain Willard then decided to follow Fred and, if possible, overtake him. These men traveled by team, all night with the mercury hovering around 25 degrees below zero.

Captain Willard and his companions arrived at Stoneville about noon. There they found Fred and his men in a house owned by a man named Stone.

[266]

This house was about 250 yards from the one saloon where practically all elements of society made their headquarters and where the major part of the business of the town was transacted.

Soon after the arrival of Captain Willard, the Axelbee gang, who were at the saloon, mounted their horses to make their escape.

Fred Willard called out to them to surrender and he and his posse fired on the gang. They returned the fire. Axelbee and two of his gang were desperately wounded, also a young man named Tuthill, who, before that day, had never been seen with the gang.

Axelbee, before leaving the field of battle, badly wounded, turned his Winchester on a camp of cowboys, located about 100 yards from the saloon, killing two estimable young men who had taken no part in the fight, but who had in some way incurred his enmity. Their names were Cunningham and Harris.

One member of the cowboy party then started shooting into the Willard posse, all of whom would probably have escaped injury but for the unaccountable interference of a man, who was a stranger to all in both parties. This man, who was at the cabin with the cowboys at the time of the battle, walked into the cabin, picked up a Winchester, stepped to the door, took deliberate aim at the Willard party and fired. Jack O'Harra fell, mortally wounded. He then took another shot at Captain Willard. The bullet passed through the captain's clothes and grazed his skin.

Firing soon ceased and the injured were cared for. The battle resulted in the breaking up of the Axelbee gang, with the loss of six lives, four of whom were innocent of any crime or violation of civil laws.

Young Tuthill, who escaped with a shattered arm, was captured the next day and taken to Spearfish where he was put in custody. He was placed in an improvised hospital and kept there for over a week while his shattered arm gradually failed to heal. Mortification set in. While he was in a dying condition he was taken from the hospital in the early morning in his underclothing, when the mercury stood at 30 degrees below zero, carried to a tree near the creek, and hanged.

Harry Tuthill was never accused of any crime. He had been found in bad company. His lynching is one of the blots on the fair name of Spearfish. The mob engaged in this affair was seen as it emerged from Bill Gay's saloon. Of the eight self-appointed dispensers of justice, three at least later qualified as real gunmen, each of whom killed his man.

Later information disclosed that the unknown cowboy who so mysteriously commenced shooting into the Willard party during the fight, was none other than "Billy the Kid," mentioned elsewhere in this volume as a companion of Jack Geisler. The governor of Arizona had put a price on his head. He later returned to that state where he was recognized and shot down by a sheriff. He was cold blooded and merciless, and killed just for the pleasure.

LXVIII

SUMMARY OF EARLY-DAY FATALITIES

In recording the numerous fatalities attendant upon the precipitous rush to the Black Hills, details are necessarily omitted here. Many are given in previous chapters.

The majority of the fatalities which occurred in the towns and mining districts of the Black Hills originated in disputes over the question of priority rights, at a time when there existed no statutory law in the Hills, nor any code of principles other than those of the great majority, which were ignored by a small, but insistent minority.

The paramount question of priority rights over which arose nearly all disputes, was by no means confined wholly to such legitimate business affairs as the adjustment of mining and city lot location disputes. They were frequently brought to a climax in the disreputable joints in the various Black Hills towns. Main Street of Deadwood was recognized as the Mother Lode of those despicable institutions, which were not only tolerated, but were also fostered, if not liberally patronized, by some of the ruling officials of the new city.

It was on the second floors of many saloons and gambling houses, as well as in the more congested, filthy dives farther down the street in the "Bad Lands district," that many incautious men were lured and easily entrapped through well planned devices of enticement, aided by a glass or two of mixed drinks, proffered seemingly with the best of motives by oily tongued spotters and cappers, assisted by a bevy of female inmates of those dens of vice. Once through the doors the fate of their unwary victim was settled so far as his personal assets were concerned, as the easy work of fleecing was the regular order of business.

[269]

The wiser of such deluded men would, after awakening to realization of their condition, quietly take their departure. Others, with less discretion, would, on finding their pockets empty, become obstreperous, enter into a noisy tirade and inaugurate a rough house. Then the proprietor would step from behind the screens where he had been waiting for the lion's share of the loot, and with fixed brass knuckles, or revolver used as a bludgeon, would quickly quiet the row by pounding the helpless sucker into a state of insensibility. The bloody victim was pushed or thrown down the stairway to a back lot, and turned over to the night watch as an intruder to be locked up for the night.

Notwithstanding the many occurrences of such description, and the brutalities which occurred in Deadwood in its early days, comparatively few fatalities were reported as resulting therefrom. It is probable that many deaths not reported, and the suicide of many inmates of brothels, materially increased the reported following fatalities:

1876—"Stuttering" Brown killed on Cheyenne stage route by "Persimmons Bill," a highwayman.

1876—The Metz party, consisting of Mr. and Mrs. Metz, the teamster, and a colored woman named Rachel Briggs, at Red Canyon, killed by Indians.

1876—Johnnie Harrison, Edwin Sadler, N. H. Gardner, Texas Jack, killed by Indians on Pierre Road near Pino Springs. Bodies stripped.

1876—James Hogan killed by Indians on Pierre Road eighteen miles east of Rapid City.

1876—A Mr. Herman killed by Indians two miles east of Rapid City. Found and buried by white men.

1876—Captain Dodge killed by Indians near Rapid City. Buried in Rapid City.

1876—"Curley," stage driver on Cheyenne stage route, killed by "Persimmons Bill" and his Indian accomplices.

1876—Jack Hinch murdered at Gayville by Carty and McCarty. One held him while the other knifed him.

1876—"Wild Bill" Hickok killed in Saloon No. 10, Deadwood, by Jack McCall, August 2. Buried in South Deadwood. Later interred in Mt. Moriah Cemetery.

SUMMARY OF EARLY-DAY FATALITIES

1876—Rev. Henry Weston Smith killed on August 20 by unknown party, generally charged to Indians, Centennial Prairie, four miles west of Crook City. Buried in Deadwood.

1876—Charles Mason killed on August 20 east of Crook City, by Indians. Said to have been buried alongside grave of Preacher Smith.

1876—Isaac Brown and Charles Holland killed by an Indian near Spring Creek, east of Spearfish, and buried at Deadwood.

1876—Mexican killed in Crook City by a white man and his body dragged out and burned in a brush pile.

1876—Shannon killed in Crook City by Tom Moore in rifle duel. Buried at Crook City.

1876—Unknown man killed by Indians in Centennial Valley. Buried on spot by white man.

1876—Teddy McGarrah killed by Indians in Centennial Valley. Found and buried by white man.

1876—Charles Nolin, volunteer mail carrier, killed near Sturgis early in August.

1876—George Miller, member of large Montana party, killed by Indians west of Bear Lodge mountains.

1876—Ward Brothers and Collins train fired into by Indians four miles north of Belle Fourche. William Ward and one other killed.

1876—Six men from Iowa, names not known, killed by Indians on White River.

1876—Ed Shaunnessey killed in Bella Union Theatre by Dick Brown. Buried in South Deadwood.

1876—John Farrell killed in brothel over saloon by Ed Cook, manager of a stage line. Nothing done about it.

1876—John D. Hunter killed by Indians near Red Canyon. Also a man named Coyer killed same day.

1877—A man named Gangis shot and scalped by Indians in southern Hills.

1877—Four men killed by Indians near Custer City logging camp. Buried by George A. Clark and others.

1877—Four haymakers, one a foster brother of Tom Hoop, killed south of Custer and buried in Custer. Kay Keifer made the coffins.

1877—Henry Herring and Charles Nelson killed by Indians at Cleghorn Springs near Rapid City.

1877—Murder of Wagner family by Indians, northeast of Crook City. Three persons.

1877—Jimmy Irons, lookout for haymakers, killed in valley near St. Onge, 12 miles north of Deadwood, by Indians.

1877—Murder of Capt. Dotson, stock herder on False Bottom. Large herd stolen by Indians.

1877—Killing of Cephas Tuttle by Keets' mine operators, Central City.

1877—Murder of Jewish citizen, shot while working on his mining claim, by one of four men employed by Homestake.

1877—John Bryant and William Adams, both killed in pistol duel in Central City over priority rights.

1877—Ben Davis and George Keating hanged by vigilantes near Spearfish for cattle stealing.

1877—Doc. Allen and "Red" Curry, horse thieves, and boy named Mansfield, hanged by mob near Rapid City.

1877—J. W. Patterson and Thomas Pendleton killed by Indians near Rapid City.

1877—G. W. Jones and John Esquart killed by Indians at Limestone Springs, near Rapid City.

1877—Johnnie Slaughter, stage driver, killed by road agent above Pluma, four miles south of Deadwood. Buried at Cheyenne, Wyoming.

1877—Murder of man (name forgotten) by Bill Hunt near Deadwood. Hunt sent to pen for twenty-one years.

1877—Murder of Charles Lee by William Bell at White Rocks. Robbery. Bell sent to pen.

1877—John Deffenbach killed by Indians west of Sundance. Stock was stolen.

1877—Two men (names forgotten) killed by Indians up the creek above Rapid City. Buried by Hugh McNey.

1877—Brodovich (Slavonian) murdered by Sam May in quarrel over a town lot in Deadwood. Witnessed by J. S. McClintock.

1877—Bob Costello was shot and killed by Kid Myers near Custer while attempting to rob the boy's father of $16,000 of gold dust.

SUMMARY OF EARLY-DAY FATALITIES

1877—"One-eyed Ed" hanged by cowboys in southern Hills for murdering a man named Porter.

1877—Dick Burnett hanged at Red Canyon for shooting with intent to kill Fuller Lambert, and also for stealing horses.

1877—Wilson, Abernethy, and another man killed by Indians east of Sundance.

1877—Henry Lundt died of wounds in his head caused by shot fired by Tom Smith, intended for Con Stapleton.

1878—McTeague killed by Ben Wadsworth in dispute over a mining claim.

1878—Murder of Hoffman by Ed Durham in Deadwood. Durham sent to pen for 14 years.

1878—Murder of miner by another miner who had been highly educated for priesthood. Names forgotten.

1878—Coburn killed by Woolsey in Woolsey Saloon in Deadwood, lower Main Street.

1878—Russell killed by Bradly Ford at Sturgis. Ford sent to pen for 14 years.

1878—Merritt killed at Sturgis by George Hebee. Result of trial forgotten.

1878—Charles Forbes murdered by Bill Gay, whose money ($10,000) saved him from justice until his next murder, when he was hanged.

1878—Mrs. Neville was shot and killed in a pistol duel with Johnnie Rogers, who was shot through the body three hours later.

1878—Con Donahue, known as "Lame Johnnie," hanged in Custer County for robbing the mails and horse stealing.

1878—Archie McLaughlin and Mansfield, road agents, were taken from a stage coach and hanged by vigilantes.

1878—The treasure coach (Old Ironsides) was held up at Canyon Springs station forty miles south of Deadwood by a gang of highwaymen under leadership of Carey, including his pals, Frank McBride, Doug Goodale, Al Speer, Big Nose George and another known as "Red Cloud." Stage was fired on when it arrived at the station and Hugh Campbell, a passenger, killed. Gale Hill was shot through the body but survived. Al Speer and Big Nose George, bandits, killed and McBride desperately wounded.

[273]

1878—John Hickland killed by Tim Dority, also known as Tim Coleman, a slugger, by a fist cuff on the neck in Lead City saloon.

1879—William Thurlow, a young man, stabbed to death by another young man over game of cards in Centennial Valley.

1879—Flaver killed by Hogan at Sturgis, the result of trial forgotten.

1879—Dr. Lynch killed at Sturgis by soldier named Hallon. Hallon hanged by vigilantes for murder.

1879—"Curley," an accused mail robber, with no evidence of his guilt, was killed by Lewellyn and Boone May.

1879—A young man (name forgotten) was arrested in Galena and killed by deputy sheriff who was in charge of him.

1879—Kitty LeRoy killed in a bawdy house over a saloon in Deadwood by Dave Curley, who also killed himself.

1880—Jack Gorman murdered in cold blood by Billy Thatcher, gunman, at Galena.

1884—Stoneville battle on Little Missouri. The dead were Jack O'Harra, officer; Cunningham and Harris, bystanders; Campbell and Broncho Charley, cattle rustlers; and Harry Tuthill, who was with the gang when the fight started.

1888—John Galvin shot and killed by Farnum, postmaster at Central City.

1890—Don Dority, saloon keeper, shot by Pat Casey, also a saloon keeper.

1890—Pat Casey committed suicide in Smoke House, corner Main and Lee streets, Deadwood.

1890—Ed Shannon, proprietor of the Shannon Hotel in Central City, shot and killed by Judge Giddings, despoiler of his home, who then shot and killed his wife and himself, and also a highly respected miner who was an innocent bystander.

1890—Judge Henry L. Clark killed in Deadwood by Thomas Rolling. Clark was known as "Deacon Clark."

1895—Roy Soule killed at Sturgis by Fred Willard. Justifiable homicide.

While this list is incomplete, it gives a fair survey of the violent deaths in the Black Hills and vicinity during the early days.

THE SOCIETY OF BLACK HILLS PIONEERS

JOHN A. GASTON, a pioneer of '76, engaged in brokerage business, was one of the city's most public spirited citizens. In December, 1888, he stated to this writer that he had conceived a plan for
organizing the Black Hills Pioneer Society, of those who came in
1876, or earlier, for the purpose of preserving their names and
history for posterity. The following day he had the preliminary
papers ready and L. F. Whitbeck, a newspaper man, and this
writer were the first to sign as members. Others signed promptly,
among them J. Harry Flynn, city editor of the *Deadwood Times*,
who took the papers to the *Times* office.

Mr. Gaston published a call for a meeting to organize on
January 8, 1889. Discussions arose which caused Mr. Gaston to
drop out of leadership and destroy the membership papers which
had been signed. However, new papers were prepared, in which
Mr. Gaston joined, and the organization meeting was held at the
court house on January 8th.

Captain Tom H. Russell, a member of the Gordon party in
1874, presided at the meeting and was elected first president of the
Society of Black Hills Pioneers. Other officials were elected and
rules of procedure adopted.

When the society was organized in 1889, membership was limited to those who came to the hills prior to January 1, 1877. In
1908, this was amended to make children of members, living or
deceased, eligible to membership. In 1921, this was again amended
to include wives and widows of pioneers. In 1932, another amend-
ment made eligible to membership all who arrived prior to the
date of the big fire, September 26, 1879.

Since organization annual meetings have been held, usually in

Deadwood during the winter months, with picnic gatherings in summer in various parts of the Hills. Among the accomplishments under auspices of the Society were:

The monument to Rev. Henry Weston Smith on the Deadwood-Spearfish highway in 1914.

The monument to Theodore Roosevelt on Mt. Roosevelt in 1919.

The gold discovery monument at Custer on July 27, 1921.

The monument to Annie D. Tallent on French Creek near Custer in 1924.

The rebuilding of the Gordon Stockade near Custer in 1925.

The presidents of the Society of Black Hills Pioneers have been:

1889-1890—Thomas H. Russell
1890-1892—Seth Bullock
1892-1894—A. Z. R. Dawson
1894-1896—James W. Allen
1896-1898—John Gray
1898-1899—P. A. Gushurst
1899-1900—George V. Ayres
1900-1904—James Conzette
1904-1906—J. W. McDonald
1906-1908—John A. Blatt
1908-1910—Jacob Goldberg
1910-1913—Kirk G. Phillips
1914-1916—George V. Ayres
1917-1920—Sol Star
1921-1922—Capt. C. V. Gardner
1922-1923—George V. Ayres
1924-1933—P. A. Gushurst
1934-1937—James Brown
1938-   —Albert M. Anderson

The secretaries of the Society have been:

1889-1890—L. F. Whitbeck
1890-1897—J. Harry Flynn
1897-1900—Paul Rewman
1900-1903—H. P. Lorey
1903-1915—Julius Deetken

1915-1929—Paul Rewman
1930-1937—Carl Kubler
1938-   —A. Marie Lawler

The treasurers of the Society have been:
1889-1890—John R. Brennan
1890-1892—John A. Gaston
1892-1905—D. M. Gillette
1905-1909—Kirk G. Phillips
1910-1913—George V. Ayres
1914-1934—Charles Zoellner
1934-   —Edna Ford

The total enrollment from 1876 up to 1908, was about 560. In 1891 there were about 300 members in good standing. Over 100 of these were known to have been dead in 1908. The 1908 list of members in good standing was as follows:

Allen, J. W.	Conzette, James	Gurley, J. F.
Ayres, Geo. V.	Cody, Wm. F.	Gentges, Paul
Alber, Mart	Deetken, Julius	Hanley, W. F.
Baer, Ben	Ellis, Dave	Halley, James
Berger, Fritz	Ervin, Green	Hage, August
Brennan, John R.	Faust, Emil	Hughes, R. B.
Beals, Geo. W.	Fassold, Jack	Hulin, Hilan
Burt, H. P.	Franklin, Harris	Heffron, Michael
Burnham, Al.	Frank, Henry	Holmes, Albe
Bullock, Seth	Floorman, Charles	Hosier, Geo.
Brodie, Jas.	Franklin, N. E.	Harrison, James
Bailey, J. W.	Geis, Stephen	Isaacs, John W.
Blatt, John A.	Grantz, Otto P. Th.	Johnson, Geo. M.
Bendeleben, L. A.	Gray, John	Jennings, R. D.
Burri, John	Grimshaw, R. E.	James, Robert
Barrett, Andrew	Gushurst, P. A.	Karrels, Theo.
Bloom, Sol	Goldberg, Jacob	Klopp, Matt
Brasch, Henry	Goldberg, Joseph	Kuykendall, W. L.
Brown, Octavia	Goldberg, Samuel	Lawler, James
Brown, James E.	Godfrey, Christ	Lachapelle, L.
Burch, Chas. P.	Goldbloom, D.	Lamb, Nathaniel
Borsch, Fred	Gossage, J. B.	Lenk, J. J.

Leppla, Henry
Ladd, G. W.
LaMontague, O. R.
Moll, Samuel
Mallory, C. L.
Manning, John
Mix, R. P.
May, Ernest
McDonald, J. W.
McVean, John
McShane, A. G.
Merrick, A. W.
Oliver, Samuel
Onstat, Andrew
Oberg, Gus
Phillips, K. G.
Purnell, O. F.
Pfrunder, Chas.
Power, Dan

Peterson, John N.
Packard, G. W.
Rewman, Paul
Rosenkranz, Henry
Rehl, John B.
Roosevelt, Theo.
Rhodes, Tom F.
Russell, Percy
Sawyer, Fred B.
Smith, F. B.
Smith, F. X.
Smith, Cleo C.
Star, Solomon
Short, David
Schmidt, A. F.
Shoudy, Jacob
Schubert, Jacob
Stacy, Chas.
Sasse, William

Schlageter, Andrew
Stannus, John
Shoun, V. P.
Schwarzwald, Sam
Simpson, A. H.
Thompson, T. W.
Tippie, A. C.
Tuller, J. H.
Teer, J. H.
Tower, Gilbert
Valentine, L. W.
Wingfield, John
Waldschmidt, Robt.
Wolcott, F. C.
Wilson, James
Williams, J. B.
Zoellner, Chas.

LXX

SURVIVING PIONEERS OF '76

AFTER careful research only nineteen persons have been found living of those who came to the Black Hills prior to January 1, 1877, the original requirement for admission to the Society of Black Hills Pioneers. While it is probable that there are others who have been away from the Hills so long that they have lost connections, or who came as children with parents now deceased, there are not many such. The names, ages and addresses of the nineteen survivors are:

Mrs. Harry S. Wright, age 93, Fruitdale, S. D.
John S. McClintock, age 92, Deadwood, S. D.
Henry A. Albien, age 92, Custer, S. D.
Mrs. Anna E. Williams, age 87, Miles City, Montana.
James E. Brown, age 86, Deadwood, S. D.
Chris Holley, age 86, Hill City, S. D.
Daniel J. Toomey, age 86, San Diego, California.
James E. Larson, age 86, Fruitdale, S. D.
Peter A. Gushurst, age 85, Denver, Colo.
Mrs. John Welling, age 82, Deadwood, S. D.
Peter La Flamme, age 80, Sundance, Wyo.
James T. Street, age 79, Deadwood, S. D.
William Brasch, age 76, Denver, Colo.
Mrs. Ina (Street) Verley, age 72, Rapid City, S. D.
Mrs. Belle (Allen) Parker, age 70, Deadwood, S. D.
Charles H. Robinson, age 69, Deadwood, S. D.
Nasby S. Street, age 68, Chicago, Ill.
Wm. H. Whealan, Lackawanna, N. Y.
Oliver P. Rose, Belle Fourche, S. D.

LXXI

BIOGRAPHICAL SKETCHES

(Compiled by the Editor of this Volume)

THIS is not a history of the Black Hills, nor even of Deadwood. Such a pretentious task would require several large volumes and many years. It must be left to abler and younger writers. This is a record of the important events during early days in the Hills, and of the pioneers who became members of, or were eligible to membership in, the Society of Black Hills Pioneers, with a few exceptions of prominent citizens who came a little too late to be eligible to membership.

Comparatively few of the many thousands who came in early days remained and attained any considerable degree of prominence. Necessarily, the following brief biographies will be largely limited to those who did. Included are not only pioneers who became members of the Society of Black Hills Pioneers, but also some who did not.

ANNIE D. TALLENT

Mrs. Annie D. Tallent was born in New York State in 1827. Her life was uneventful until she reached the age of 47, in 1874. Then she and her husband and young son Robert joined the "Gordon Party" of gold seekers, the first to reach the Black Hills, which left Sioux City on October 9th, 1874. She was the only woman in the party. They reached the Hills on December 9th at the southern edge, and on December 23d reached a point near Custer where they built the "Gordon stockade," for protection from the Indians. Mrs. Tallent was the first white woman to enter the Black Hills.

After the party was deported by military authorities in April,

1875, the Tallents remained in Cheyenne, Wyoming, until opportunity was presented to return to the Hills in the spring of 1876.

For many years thereafter she taught school and held the position of county superintendent of schools at Rapid City. The latter years of her life were given to preparation of her history of the Black Hills, making her home in Sturgis. Her death occurred there in 1901, at the age of 74. Her body was sent to Elgin, Illinois, for interment.

HORATIO N. ROSS

Horatio N. Ross was a member of the General Custer Military Expedition through the Black Hills in 1874, and is generally credited with being the first to discover gold in the creek bed near Custer, on July 27th or a few days thereafter.

Little is known of his early history. He was a practical miner and in 1875 he returned to Custer and made it his home until his death, May 17, 1904. A monument to his memory and commemorating the discovery of gold, was erected in Custer. Various dates have been given by several writers, of the unveiling of this monument. The question was referred to a well-informed citizen of Custer, who definitely fixed the date as July 27, 1921.

HENRY WESTON SMITH

The Rev. Henry Weston Smith has a notable place in the history of the Black Hills as its pioneer martyred preacher. He was born on January 10, 1827, at Ellington, Connecticut. At the age of 23 he became a licensed "exhorter" in the Methodist Church, and later was ordained as a minister.

In 1847 he was married in Connecticut to Ruth Yeomans. She lived one year thereafter.

In 1857 he was married in Connecticut to Lydia A. Joslin. She and three children survived his tragic death in the Black Hills in 1876.

In 1861, he enlisted for service in the Civil War, in a Massachusetts regiment, participating in a number of engagements.

In 1867, he was admitted to practice of medicine. In 1876, the family moved to Louisville, Kentucky. Prior to this he had resumed his ministerial work.

In 1876, he came to the Black Hills via Cheyenne. He preached his first sermon in the Hills at Custer on May 7th, 1876. Two weeks later he came to Deadwood with a freight caravan owned by Captain C. V. Gardner.

In Deadwood he performed manual labor on week days and held religious services on the street on Sunday.

On Sunday, August 20, 1876, after holding morning service in Deadwood, he left to walk the forest trail to Crook City, about nine miles from Deadwood. At a point about midway, in the foot-hills, he was shot and killed. The crime has been generally charged to Indians, but this has been disputed by some well-informed pioneers.

His body was not mutilated. It was found where he fell by a man on horseback riding by, en route to Crook City. A party went out from Crook City to get the body and brought it to Deadwood. Funeral services were held by laymen, there being no other minister in Deadwood.

Interment was made in Mt. Moriah Cemetery, and a lifesize statue of red sandstone was erected over the grave in 1891. In 1914, a monument was erected and dedicated to his memory on the Deadwood-Spearfish highway, about two miles from the scene of his death. Here, starting in 1924, memorial services have been held annually under auspices of the Methodist churches in this vicinity.

A more extended story of his life and death is given elsewhere in this volume.

JAMES BUTLER HICKOK

James Butler ("Wild Bill") Hickok was born in Illinois in 1837. He "went west" in 1855. During a checkered career, for twenty years, in Missouri as a spy and sharp-shooter during the Civil War, and in Kansas and Nebraska as a scout in Indian Wars, and as a peace officer, he attained prominent place in the history of the frontier as the world's greatest gunman of all times. It is well established that he killed at least 75 and probably 100 or more men during his stormy life.

He came to Deadwood from Cheyenne, Wyoming, about the middle of June, 1876. His only known occupation then was gambling. On August 2, 1876, while playing poker with a party of friends in a saloon in Deadwood, he was shot through the head by an assassin, Jack McCall, who had approached him from the rear without attracting attention.

His body was first interred in a grave on a slope in the south part of Deadwood, now known as Ingleside. In 1879, the casket was removed and reinterred in the permanent Mt. Moriah Cemetery. Here his grave, surmounted by a lifesize statue, is annually visited by thousands of curious tourists and hero worshipers.

An extended account of his career and death in Deadwood is given elsewhere in this volume.

MRS. MARTHA BURK

Martha Cannary, better known as "Calamity Jane," says in "her own story" that she came to the Black Hills as a scout with General Custer's troops in 1874, and with General Crook's troops in 1875. There appears to be no official or other corroboration of this claim, which was controverted by many pioneers who knew her in Deadwood in 1876.

Her first appearance in Deadwood was in June, 1876, arriving in a party with "Wild Bill" Hickok, "Colorado Charlie" Utter, Steve Utter and "Kitty" Arnold. After the killing of "Wild Bill," she left Deadwood, but remained in the vicinity of the Hills for several years, serving for a time as a bullwhacker on freight trains between Pierre and the Hills.

Thereafter she roamed the West as had been her practice. After an absence of many years she returned to Deadwood in 1895, accompanied by her husband, Clinton Burk, whom she had married in Texas in 1887, and a girl, claimed as their daughter.

The husband left after misappropriating money he handled for others. The child was separated from Mrs. Burk and placed in a Sisters' School at Sturgis and her identity and whereabouts thereafter concealed.

Mrs. Burk's death occurred at Terry, a mining camp eight miles from Deadwood, on August 1, 1903. At her request her body was buried alongside that of "Wild Bill" in Mt. Moriah Cemetery, Deadwood.

PIONEER DAYS IN THE BLACK HILLS

W. E. ADAMS

Foremost among pioneer residents of Deadwood was W. E. Adams. He was born in Bertrand, Michigan, in 1854. He came to Deadwood early in 1877, and in conjunction with his brother, James H., established a wholesale and retail grocery business. By careful management and honorable dealing, the business gradually expanded. After a number of years his brother withdrew from the business and W. E. Adams became sole owner. The retail business was abandoned and large buildings were erected for the continually expanding wholesale business. Branch houses were established in Rapid City and Belle Fourche.

In 1906, his fellow citizens, desirous of having the benefit of such ability, elected him mayor, and he served four terms, eight years. His first notable achievement was taking the city "out of the mud" by construction of the splendid brick pavement in the business section. He was elected mayor again in 1920, serving two terms. He gave freely to the city of his valuable time and managed its business affairs as carefully as he did his own. He was a member of St. John's Episcopal Church, and its financial mainstay during many years when churches had a hard time to exist in Deadwood. His crowning act was the gift of the $100,000 Adams Memorial Museum to the people of Deadwood and their posterity.

His death occurred June 16th, 1934, at the age of 80. He will long be remembered as Deadwood's foremost citizen and greatest benefactor for many years.

GEORGE V. AYRES

George V. Ayres was born in Pennsylvania in 1852. The family moved westward and were residing at Beatrice, Nebraska, at the time of the rush for the Black Hills. Mr. Ayres joined this, arriving at Custer, then the scene of greatest activity, on March 25, 1876. Two months later he joined in the rush for the new placer mines at Deadwood. After remaining there until the fore part of July, he returned to Custer to remain about a year. Returning then to Deadwood, he made it his permanent home.

He obtained employment in Richard C. Lake's hardware store, later becoming a partner. He eventually became sole owner of the

[284]

most extensive hardware business in the Black Hills, which he built up with a reputation for sterling integrity, with the assistance of his sons Vincent, Albro, and Lloyd, all of whom are yet living.

He was prominent for many years in Masonic circles, being a thirty-third degree member of the Scottish Rite. He gave efficient public service as a county commissioner and a member of the legislature. After serving as president of the First National Bank of Deadwood, he was made chairman of the Board of Directors of the First National Bank of Lead, with which the First National of Deadwood was merged.

Mrs. Ayres died on May 17, 1937. Two daughters are yet living, Mrs. Ben Lowe (Alice), of Deadwood, and Mrs. Frances Brezee, of San Francisco.

Mr. Ayres died on May 29, 1939, as this volume goes on press. He passed away quietly during the night. His funeral, one of the largest ever held in Deadwood, was attended by many notable Masons from all over this state.

CAPTAIN SETH BULLOCK

Captain Seth Bullock was born in Canada in 1847. In young manhood he went to Montana Territory, seeking gold. He came from Montana to the Black Hills, arriving in Deadwood on July 31, 1876. He was accompanied by Sol Star, with whom he was associated in the hardware business for many years.

When Lawrence County was organized in 1877, the territorial governor appointed Bullock its first sheriff. In that capacity he became widely known.

When young Theodore Roosevelt, who was then engaged in ranching on the Little Missouri River in the northwestern part of Dakota Territory, visited Deadwood in 1884, he met Bullock. Speaking of this meeting, Roosevelt in his autobiography says:

"Later Seth Bullock became, and has ever since remained, one of my staunchest and most valued friends. When, after close of my term, I went to Africa, on getting back to Europe, I cabled Seth to bring over Mrs. Bullock and meet me in London, which he did; by that time I felt that I just had to meet my own people, who spoke my neighborhood dialect."

At an early date, Bullock established an extensive ranch on

Redwater, near Belle Fourche. He was the first to introduce alfalfa into the Black Hills.

During the Spanish-American War in 1898, Bullock organized and became captain of a company of "Rough Riders," which made a notable record in the war. When Roosevelt was inaugurated for his second term, in 1905, many of the "Rough Riders," headed by Captain Bullock, went to Washington to participate in the inaugural parade.

President Roosevelt appointed Captain Bullock the first supervisor of the newly established Black Hills National Forest. Later he appointed him United States Marshal for South Dakota, and he served in that capacity for two terms.

Captain Bullock was largely instrumental in having the Society of Black Hills Pioneers erect the first monument to Theodore Roosevelt, who died on January 6, 1919, on Mt. Roosevelt, five miles from Deadwood. This was dedicated on July 4, 1919, by General Leonard Wood, with appropriate ceremonies.

Captain Bullock died on September 24, 1919. Mt. Moriah Cemetery, Deadwood, is not in sight of the Roosevelt Monument. Captain Bullock, before his death, purchased a plot of ground higher up than the cemetery, that his burial place might be in sight of the monument on Mt. Roosevelt. Here interment was made, the rock bound grave being surmounted by a tall cross, in sight of Mt. Roosevelt.

His widow died in Deadwood in April, 1939, and was buried beside her husband. Three children are alive: Stanley Bullock, Albuquerque, New Mexico; Mrs. Chambers Kellar, Lead; Mrs. Madge Mackall, New York City.

THEODORE ROOSEVELT

President Theodore Roosevelt was one of the few honorary members of the Society of Black Hills Pioneers. During the years 1883 to 1886, he resided much of the time during the spring, summer, and fall months on ranches he purchased near Medora, on the Little Missouri, west of Bismarck, for the benefit of his health. "Riding the range" in cattle round-ups took him to the range country between the Black Hills and Medora, giving him acquaintance with residents of the Hills and vicinity.

Among other duties, he served at times as a deputy sheriff. In this capacity he captured a horse thief called "Crazy Steve," who was wanted in the Black Hills. Subsequently, he went to Deadwood, probably in 1884, met Seth Bullock, and they became lifelong friends. As a result of this visit and acquaintance with Deadwood Pioneers, he was made an honorary member of the Society of Black Hills Pioneers.

It was largely through the efforts of Captain Bullock that "Sheep Mountain," an elevation of 5,600 feet, five miles west of Deadwood, was changed to "Mt. Theodore Roosevelt," and a monument to Roosevelt erected thereon by the Society of Black Hills Pioneers. It was the first monument dedicated to Theodore Roosevelt.

C. V. GARDNER

Captain C. V. Gardner was born in Ohio in 1836. He attended Cornell College in Iowa, and later graduated from the Cincinnati Law School. He went to Colorado to practice in his profession. In 1862, he entered the Union Army and served during the war. After the war he went to Iowa, where he held many important positions, and engaged in the real estate business.

Early in 1876 he joined in the rush to the Black Hills gold fields, bringing in the first large shipment of freight by ox teams, coming from Cheyenne, Wyoming. He built the first frame building in Deadwood, and, with others, brought to the Hills the first quartz mill and the first flour mill. He engaged in the newspaper business for a brief period, then in mercantile business for many years. He was active in public affairs, a gentleman of the old school, highly esteemed by all who knew him.

It was due chiefly to his efforts that a fine granite monument was erected in Golden Valley, on French Creek, by the Pioneers, in honor of Annie D. Tallent, the first white woman to enter the Black Hills.

His latter years were spent in the old soldiers' home at Hot Springs, South Dakota. He was active and able to be about and visit old time friends throughout the Hills until shortly before his death, which occurred at Hot Springs on December 5, 1930, in his ninety-fifth year. A daughter, Mrs. John (Maude) Hoover, resides in Belle Fourche, S. D.

PIONEER DAYS IN THE BLACK HILLS

JACOB GOLDBERG

Jacob Goldberg was born in Germany in 1851. He came to America at the age of 18, going to the mining city of Helena, Montana. Here he engaged in mercantile business, but lost his possessions in a big fire which destroyed much of the city. Then came news of gold discovery in the Black Hills. He joined a company of about 140, under leadership of Captain Hardwick. They drove through to Deadwood with a caravan of sixty wagons, arriving in August, 1876.

Mr. Goldberg shortly after arrival purchased of P. A. Gushurst the first grocery store in Deadwood, known as the "Big Horn" grocery. He continued in active management of the business until a few years before his death. His name became a synonym for integrity and square dealing, and he built up an extensive business on the same lot on which he originally started. His sons, Sam and Joe, were associated in this business for many years. Failing health of his wife necessitated removal to California in 1934. He returned annually to the Hills to visit, finally disposing of his business and making California his permanent home. His wife died there in 1936 and his death occurred there in 1937 at the age of 86. Surviving children are two sons; Sam and Joe, who reside at San Antonio, Texas; and a daughter, Mrs. M. A. Rosenthal (Julia), of Los Angeles.

P. A. GUSHURST

Peter A. Gushurst was born in New York State in 1853. At the age of sixteen he went to Omaha, Nebraska, and was in employ of the Union Pacific Railway for five years. He came to Deadwood in March 1876, via Cheyenne, reaching Custer on May 24th. Shortly thereafter he went to Deadwood and established a grocery business in a tent on the site of the "Big Horn" grocery. He erected a frame building on this lot and a few months later sold the business to Jacob Goldberg. He then moved to Lead and engaged in the grocery business for half a century. He was also active for many years in civic, financial and mining affairs. He and Mrs. Gushurst were the first couple married in Lead. He yet lives, in excellent health, at the age of eighty-six. His home is now in Denver. Mrs. Gushurst is still living, also four children, all born in Lead, Albert S., of Lead; Fred W., of Denver; Dr. Edward G., of Minneapolis; and Mrs. L. D. (Clara) Mulligan, of Denver.

CHARLES AND JONAS ZOELLNER

Charles Zoellner was born in Germany in 1849. He came to the United States in 1866. He lived in Tennessee, Louisiana, Arkansas, and Texas for a number of years. In 1874, he went to Denver, Colorado, then to Cheyenne, Wyoming. In 1876, he joined the gold rush to the Black Hills, arriving in Custer in February. In March he went to Deadwood, where he kept a general merchandise store in a tent for several months. Later in the year he sold his business and returned to Custer to engage in prospecting.

Jonas Zoellner was born in Breslau, Germany, in 1851; came to the United States in 1871, engaging in business at Memphis, Tennessee. He came to the Black Hills in 1877 to join his brother.

In the spring of 1877, they established a general store at Central, two miles from Deadwood. Branch stores were established at Spearfish, D. T., Sundance, Wyoming, and Deadwood, D. T., the latter being established in 1899. The firm of Zoellner brothers became well known throughout the Black Hills. They ultimately concentrated their Black Hills business in the Deadwood store, of which Charles became sole owner, Jonas leaving Deadwood in 1912 to take over their mercantile business in Scotts Bluff, Nebraska, with several branch stores. He retired from business in 1937, going to Los Angeles. A son, Charles, took over the mercantile business. His death occurred on Dec. 12, 1938, at the age of 87.

Charles Zoellner was for many years active in affairs of the Society of Black Hills Pioneers, being its treasurer for over thirty years. His death occurred in Deadwood in 1934, at the age of 85.

THOMAS RUSSELL

Captain Tom Russell was born in Pittsburgh, Pennsylvania, on January 9, 1836. He came West at an early day and had much experience on the frontier. He was one of the organizers of the "Gordon Expedition," the first to reach the Black Hills on December 8, 1874. He was a member of this party, and was expelled by the military in 1875.

Subsequently he returned to Custer, coming later to Deadwood. He engaged in business and mining. He held the office of Register of Deeds of Lawrence County. He was active in organizing the Society of Black Hills Pioneers in 1889, and was its first president.

His death occurred in 1899. His wife died in 1915. Three children survive: G. P. (Percy) Russell and Miss Mercedes, who have continued to reside in Deadwood, and Mrs. Ben Sentman, who resides in California. The death of Miss Kathryn, second daughter, occurred in Deadwood on September 24, 1938. All of the children were born in Sioux City, and came to Deadwood with their mother in 1878.

A. M. WILLARD

Captain A. M. Willard was born in Wisconsin in 1847. In 1864, he enlisted in the Wisconsin Volunteers and served to the end of the Civil War.

Thereafter, for a period of nine years, he worked as a sailor on the Great Lakes, and obtained a Master's License.

He then went west, reaching Cheyenne, Wyoming, in 1875. In 1876 he joined a party going to the Black Hills, arriving in July.

A few months later he built a cabin in Deadwood and made it his home. He spent considerable time in prospecting, and served as a deputy under the first sheriff, Seth Bullock, and as a deputy United States marshal. Later he moved to Custer and was elected sheriff of that county.

Some years later he homesteaded in the Slim Buttes country north of Belle Fourche. Here he acquired large holdings of land and live stock, being associated with his son, Boone Willard.

With age advancing upon him, he moved to Belle Fourche to reside and gave the closing years of his life to preparing, in association with Jesse Brown, a history of early days entitled "Black Hills Trails." His death occurred in 1921 at the age of seventy-four. Boone Willard yet lives, residing on the ranch near Zeona, S. D.

JESSE BROWN

Jesse Brown was born in Tennessee in 1844. In 1848, the family moved to Missouri, and resided there until the outbreak of the Civil War in 1861.

He then left home and went to Iowa, thence to Nebraska, where he became a driver in freight caravans. After several years' experience he became an assistant wagon master. In this work he had considerable experience with hostile Indians, over an area extending from Nebraska into Colorado, Wyoming and Montana.

In 1876, he joined in the gold rush to the Black Hills, and became one of the guards for the "Treasure Coach" which carried out the gold from the Hills. In this capacity he had a number of adventures and narrow escapes.

When this method of transporting the gold was abandoned, Mr. Brown went to Meade county to reside. He served as sheriff for four terms, and as county commissioner. He engaged in business in Sturgis, and in collaboration with Captain A. M. Willard prepared a history of early days, "Black Hills Trails." His death occurred in 1932.

SCOTT DAVIS

Scott Davis was born in Ohio in 1851. The family moved to Nebraska in 1858. At the age of fifteen Scott left home to make his own way in the world.

For a number of years he was employed in freighting across the plains and in working on railroads in Texas. He was among the first to join in the gold rush to the Black Hills, arriving in 1876, and engaged in freighting supplies into the Hills. He became express messenger for the Northwestern Stage, Express and Transportation Company, and for many years he was a guard on the "Treasure Coach" from Deadwood to Cheyenne. During this period he had a number of adventures. After civilization came to the Hills he left and became a stock detective for the Union Pacific railroad. Subsequent events in his life are not available.

JOHN R. BRENNAN

Born in Kilkenny, Ireland, May 22, 1841, and was reared in New York City. Came with his parents to Wisconsin in 1851. In October, 1875, came to Palmer Gulch in central part of Black Hills. Helped to locate and establish Rapid City on February 24, 1876. Was one of the eight men who laid out Rapid City. Was first postmaster at Rapid City, serving until 1884.

He was active in developing Rapid City. In 1878, he built the American House and in 1886 the Harney Hotel which he sold in 1901. He was the first city superintendent of schools and an official of the First National Bank.

He was a trustee of the State School of Mines at Rapid City. In 1900, he was appointed United States Indian Agent in charge of the Pine Ridge Reservation. His death took place on Nov. 4, 1919. His widow, Jennie L. Brennan, yet lives, residing in Rapid City.

JOSEPH B. AND ALICE R. GOSSAGE

Joseph B. Gossage was born near Ottumwa, Iowa, in 1852. Early in life he learned the printer's business. In 1873, he became publisher of *Sidney (Nebr.) Telegraph*. He came to Rapid City in May, 1876. In January, 1878, he established the *Rapid City Weekly Journal* which later became a daily paper. He continued as its publisher and editor until two years before his death, which occurred in 1927.

Actively associated with Mr. Gossage during the greater part of this period, was his wife, Alice R. Gossage, who became one of the most notable newspaper women of the West. Her maiden name was Alice R. Bower. She was born in Wisconsin in 1861. Her marriage to Joseph Gossage took place at Vermillion, South Dakota, in 1882. Her death occurred at Rapid City in 1929. Throughout her entire life she was active in many movements for social welfare of the community.

R. B. HUGHES

Richard B. Hughes was born in Pennsylvania in 1856. In 1860 the family moved to Maryland, thence to Illinois in 1864, thence to Nebraska in 1867.

As a youth Mr. Hughes learned the printer's trade. In May, 1876, he came with a party to the Black Hills. The following four years he was engaged in prospecting and in work on the Deadwood newspapers.

Late in 1880 he became editor of the *Rapid City Journal*, then a weekly paper. Later it became a daily paper, and he continued as editor until 1889.

He was active in civic affairs, holding several important city and county positions, and was elected a member of the first state legislature in 1889. In 1894, he received federal appointment as Surveyor General for the district of South Dakota, holding the position for four years, with office at Huron.

Returning to the Black Hills he resided in Spearfish. He became interested in various mining enterprises and the Black Hills Traction Co. In 1912 the family moved to Rapid City where he engaged in banking and real estate business. His death occurred in 1930. His wife and two sons survive, residing in Rapid City.

W. H. BONHAM

W. H. Bonham was born in Illinois in 1847. In 1873, he went to Denver, and for three years worked there as a printer and paperhanger. From Denver he went to Cheyenne, thence to Deadwood, arriving in July, 1877. He became an employee of the *Pioneer*, a daily newspaper, which he purchased in 1883. In 1897, he purchased the *Daily Times* and merged the two papers as the *Pioneer-Times*. He continued as publisher and editor until 1927, residing during latter years in California, turning management of the paper over to his nephews, the Morford brothers. His death occurred in California in 1927, at the age of 80.

JOHN A. GASTON

Was born in Butler County, Ohio. Arrived at Custer on April 9, 1876. Came to Deadwood in June, 1876. Had mining interests and dealt in stocks, bonds, and real estate. Also engaged in mercantile business, handling firearms, and other merchandise, being a member of the firm of Gaston and Shankland.

He was active in organizing the Society of Black Hills Pioneers in 1889 and was its first treasurer. No record is available of his early and latter history.

SOL STAR

Was born in Bavaria, Germany, on December 20, 1840. He came to the United States in 1850, residing in Ohio. He went to

Montana at an early date, engaging in business in Helena. He came to Deadwood with Seth Bullock, arriving on July 31, 1876. They were associated many years in hardware, furniture and other lines of business in Deadwood, Spearfish, Sturgis and Custer. He was also associated with Bullock and Harris Franklin in the Deadwood Flouring Mill Company, and was general manager of the mill built in 1880. He also engaged in livestock business in Belle Fourche Valley. He took active interest in political affairs. He was appointed postmaster in 1878 and served until 1881. Became a member of the city council in 1883, and mayor of the city in 1884, serving ten years. He was again elected mayor in 1896, serving four years.

In 1898 he was elected clerk of courts for Lawrence County and continued to hold that office until his death on October 10, 1917.

PAUL REWMAN

Born in London, England, on August 1, 1857. Came to the Black Hills on July 28, 1876. In 1878, he organized the Deadwood Telephone Company, the first line between Deadwood and Lead. This was later extended to Spearfish, Rapid City, Custer and Sturgis. In 1894 it was sold to the Nebraska Telephone Company.

He also organized the Black Hills Power and Light Company. This was sold about 1906 to the Consolidated Power and Light Company.

In later years he operated the Black Hills Transfer Company and engaged extensively in the coal business. This he sold in 1929 and moved to Washington, D. C. His death occurred in Hutchinson, Kansas, in April, 1936.

He was for many years the secretary of the Association of Black Hills Pioneers.

His widow, Mrs. Mabel Rewman, yet lives, residing at Pierre, S. D., where she holds an official position in the state government.

HARRIS AND NATHAN FRANKLIN

Harris Franklin was born in Prussian Poland, March 15, 1849. He came to the United States in 1867. He was married to Anna Stiner, at Burlington, Ia., on January 1, 1870.

He came to Deadwood on March 18, 1876. He first engaged in wholesale liquor business. Later he became associated with others in early day banking. He engaged extensively in mining enterprises, and in cattle raising on the range country north of the Hills. In 1905 he went to Chicago, then to New York, engaging in investment and financial affairs. His death took place in New York, in 1923. Mrs. Franklin died in Deadwood on January 10, 1902.

Nathan Franklin, his son, was born in Burlington, Ia., on Dec. 15, 1870. He was married Sept. 14, 1893, to Ada F. Keller, at Deadwood. After death of his father he took over management of their mining and banking interests, and was for many years president of the First National Bank. He served two terms as mayor of Deadwood, 1914 to 1918.

On August 13, 1919, he went to New York to reside, engaging in the investment business. He is yet alive. His daughter, Mrs. Mildred Traitel, resides in New York City.

M. R. RUSSELL

Michael R. Russell was born in Ireland in 1847. The family came to America in 1859, going first to Canada. In 1863 they came to the United States and settled in Kansas. "Mike" entered employ of the Missouri Pacific Railroad. He then became intimately acquainted with William Cody (Buffalo Bill), and they went on hunting trips together. After he came to Deadwood early in March, 1877, Buffalo Bill visited him here.

Mr. Russell engaged in business and was active in mining enterprises for many years. He possessed, and on special occasions put on display, one of the finest collections of gold nuggets in the Black Hills. He was for many years active in public affairs and had a large circle of friends among western frontiersmen. He died in 1930 at the age of eighty-three.

Two sons survive: John R. of Hollywood, Calif., and James of Deadwood. They came to Deadwood with their mother in 1879, to join their father.

H. O. ANDERSON

Was an early day resident of Wisconsin, where he was married at Neenah, in 1867. In 1871, he came to Yankton, South Dakota.

He arrived in the Black Hills in 1876 and established a planing mill at Gayville in 1877.

He moved to Sturgis in 1884, and continued to reside there until his death, August 23, 1927. He was for many years engaged extensively in the hardware and furniture business, and in undertaking. In this his son, Albert M. Anderson, was associated and yet resides in Sturgis.

SAM MCMASTER

Was born in Boardmills, County Down, Ireland, in June, 1840. Came to the United States at the age of 14. He went to California where he engaged in placer mining. Later he went to Australia and South America. He returned to the United States and arrived in the Black Hills in 1877. He was sent here by Haggin, Tevis and Hearst, California capitalists, who formed the company which purchased the Homestake Mine that year. He was the first superintendent of the Homestake, serving until his death in California in December, 1884.

JAMES E. LARSON

Was born on August 3, 1852, at Strenstop, Denmark. He came to the United States in 1871, and located at Utica, N. Y. He came to the Black Hills on April 1, 1876, locating first at Rapid City.

In 1878, he located on a ranch near Fruitdale, S. D., about 25 miles from Deadwood, and resided thereon until a few years ago, then turning it over to his son, and retired to live in Fruitdale. He was married in 1885. He is yet living, as are his wife and his son James.

JOHN S. MCCLINTOCK

Was born in the southwestern part of Missouri, on January 15, 1847. In 1867, he went to western Montana, prospecting and mining in that section for several years. In 1872, he returned to Missouri. Early in 1876 he came to Deadwood, and has resided there continuously, engaging in mining and various business enterprises. He is yet alive at the age of 92. A more extended biography is given in the preface to this volume, of which he is the author.

[296]

BIOGRAPHICAL SKETCHES

GUSTAVE OBERG

Was born in Eskelsternia, Sweden, on January 5, 1844. He came to the United States early in life and arrived in Deadwood in July, 1876. Later he moved to Central City.

He was an employee of the Homestake Mining Company for 45 years, holding responsible positions in the mining department. He was active until shortly before his death. This occurred at Central City, July 18, 1937, at the age of 93. A surviving daughter, Mrs. A. P. Holway, resides in Lead; another daughter, Mrs. J. A. Tedrow, in Chadron, Nebr.; and a son, Gustave, in Omaha, Nebr.

GALEN E. HILL

Little is on record of his early life. He was in Cheyenne in 1873, engaged in freighting. He came to the Black Hills at an early date and became one of the shotgun guards of "Old Ironsides," the treasure coach to Cheyenne. He was wounded in a fight with road agents who held up the coach in September, 1878, at Canyon Springs. He recovered from his wounds. No record is available of his subsequent history.

JUDGE GIDEON C. MOODY

Was born in Cortland, New York, in 1832. Began study of law at Syracuse, New York. Was admitted to practice in Indiana in 1852. In 1861 was a member of the Indiana legislature. He served three years in the Civil War as captain of infantry and was promoted to colonel.

In 1864, he came to Yankton, Dakota Territory. He was three times elected a member of the territorial legislature, serving twice as speaker of the house. In 1878, he became a member of the territorial supreme court. In 1879, he came to Deadwood as the second Judge of the United States Court in the Hills. In 1883, he resigned.

Thereafter for many years he was chief attorney for the Homestake Mining Company. In 1889, he was elected one of the first United States senators for South Dakota, serving one short term.

His death occurred in Los Angeles, California, March 17, 1904.

PIONEER DAYS IN THE BLACK HILLS

RICHARD W. CLARK

Was born in Waterford, Ireland, in 1850. Came to the Black Hills in April, 1876, with a party from Bismarck. Located at Crook City. Was a member of the party which went out from Crook City to Centennial Valley to get the body of the murdered pioneer preacher, Henry Weston Smith.

When Crook City was abandoned he moved to Whitewood. Later he moved to Lead, where he was in employ of the Northwestern Railroad for many years as a freight handler. In his latter years he impersonated "Deadwood Dick," a fictitious "road agent" of 1876, in the annual "Days of 76" celebration. His grave is located near Pine Crest Park, with the "Deadwood Dick" fiction perpetuated by thus marking his tombstone.

JAMES LAWLER

Was born in Ireland in 1845. At an early day he came to Yankton, Dakota Territory, coming from there to Deadwood. He arrived in the Black Hills in March, 1876. Was a millwright and contractor. Also had mining interests.

His death occurred in Deadwood on Dec. 22, 1914. His widow is yet living in Deadwood, also a son, G. B. Lawler, for many years county highway engineer.

Two daughters are yet living: Miss Marie Lawler, Clerk of Courts for Lawrence County for many years; and Mrs. Dorothy Curnow, wife of Judge Walter Curnow, at Lead.

KIRK G. PHILLIPS

Was born in Wisconsin, November 25, 1851. At an early age he went to Montana and engaged in mining. Came to the Black Hills, April 20, 1876. Had mining interests and built up an extensive drug store business in Deadwood, which he operated for many years.

He took active part in political affairs, serving as mayor of Deadwood for four years, three terms as County Treasurer, and two terms as State Treasurer.

He was married in 1897. His widow yet lives and resides in Denver.

[298]

BIOGRAPHICAL SKETCHES

JOHN WOLZMUTH

Was born in Oneida City, New York, on December 27, 1850. He came to the Black Hills in July, 1876, freighting for the firm of Evans, Wolzmuth and Hornick. In 1880, he located at Spearfish, fourteen miles from Deadwood.

In 1890, he engaged in the hardware business in Spearfish, associated with William Valentine. He was married in 1881. He was for many years active in the business life of Spearfish.

He was mayor of Spearfish for several terms, and was one of the first board of county commissioners for Lawrence County. His death occurred on December 25, 1924.

His widow survives, residing in Spearfish; also a son, Elmore, of Spearfish, and a daughter, Mrs. Frank (Vella) Martin, of San Diego, Calif.

JUDGE DIGHTON CORSON

Was born at Somerset, Maine, October 21, 1827. Was admitted to the bar at Milwaukee in 1853. Was district attorney there for two years. He moved to Virginia City, Nevada, where he served as U. S. District Attorney for five years.

Came to Deadwood in July, 1877, and was at once recognized as a prominent member of the bar. Was married in 1882, in Massachusetts, to Mrs. Elizabeth Hoffman. In 1889, he was elected a member of the first Supreme Court of the state of South Dakota, and repeatedly reelected, serving until his death, May 7, 1915.

JULIUS DEETKEN

Was born near Heidelberg, Germany, October 27, 1844. He was son of a Lutheran clergyman. Came to the United States in 1857.

He arrived in the Black Hills on May 1, 1876, locating first at Custer. Later the same month he came to Deadwood. He established, shortly after arrival, the first exclusive drug store in the Hills, and became associated in that business with E. C. Bent. When this partnership was dissolved, after many years, he became sole owner of the extensive business. He was one of the organizers of the First National Bank and for many years was active in the city's business affairs.

He was married in 1890. After his death on April 19, 1915, his widow and daughter moved to California. His widow died several years ago as a result of being run over by an automobile in San Francisco. His daughter, Mrs. Martha Casebolt, died in California in December, 1938. His son Albert died a number of years ago, leaving no surviving member of the family.

FRED BORSCH

Fred Borsch was born in Sioux City, Iowa, in 1865. He arrived in the Black Hills in June, 1876, with the family.

He was employed by the Homestake Mining Company for many years. Subsequently he made his home in Galena, a few miles from Deadwood, and developed mining interests. Later he operated a ranch and established a summer resort there. His death occurred on June 5, 1933.

The family home is yet at Galena. Surviving relatives are his widow and two sons, Fred G. and Chester, who reside at Galena.

JAMES W. ALLEN, WIFE AND DAUGHTER

James W. Allen was born in Pennsylvania in 1841. He went to the West in 1864, and was in various sections. He first came to the Black Hills as a gold seeker in the vicinity of Custer, on July 7, 1875. He was among the "sooners" expelled by military authorities. He returned, arriving in Deadwood on December 28, 1875.

He then engaged in freighting into the Hills and was owner of the horses which brought in the first stage. He carried out the first gold from Deadwood and vicinity. One of his drivers, Johnny Slaughter, was killed while thus engaged. Later he operated a livery stable at Central City.

He brought his wife and an adopted daughter in by stage, arriving on March 9, 1876. Mrs. Allen died in December, 1930. The daughter, Mrs. Gilbert Parker, five years old at the time of arrival, is yet living in Deadwood.

HENRY AND CHARLES H. ROBINSON

Henry Robinson was born in Pennsylvania in 1841. In 1863 he went to Fort Benton, Montana Territory. He came to the Black

Hills from Cheyenne, Wyoming, March 21, 1876. In early days he engaged in the grocery business in Deadwood, the firm being Robinson and Ross.

His death occurred in Seattle in 1913. His eight year old son Charles H. Robinson, who was born in Clarksburg, West Virginia, in 1868, came with him to Deadwood, and is yet living here. He has been superintendent of Mt. Moriah Cemetery for forty years.

ELLIS T. PIERCE

Was born in Pennsylvania in 1846. Served on the Union side in the Civil War, with Missouri Mounted Infantry. Came to the Black Hills on March 16, 1876, and located on French Creek. Later he was in Deadwood for a short period and in Rapid City where he was a barber in 1878. Later he located in Hot Springs and made his home there for many years.

He has written an account of his experiences on the frontier. In this he states that he acted as undertaker in preparing the body of "Wild Bill" Hickok for burial. He was generally known as "Doc" Pierce, though he was not a physician.

His death occurred at Hot Springs on August 13, 1926.

COLONEL WILLIAM H. PARKER

Was born May 5, 1847, at Portsmouth, New Hampshire. Enlisted in the Union Army in New Hampshire Volunteer Infantry, as a musician at the age of 14 for a period of three years, but was discharged a few months later because of youthful inability. He again enlisted about a year later, to serve three years, and served to the end of the war, being brevetted first lieutenant of volunteers in March, 1865. He again enlisted in the army April 29, 1865, as a second lieutenant in Ohio Volunteer Infantry, and was honorably discharged with his company, at Fort Kearney, Nebraska, in 1866.

He entered the law department of Columbia University in Washington, D. C., and graduated in 1868, and was admitted to the bar. In 1874, he was appointed collector of internal revenue for Colorado Territory by President Grant. Resigned in 1876 to become assistant United States Attorney for Colorado, and became United States attorney.

[301]

He came to Deadwood in July, 1877, and was soon recognized as an able member of the bar, and continued practice until death. Was a member of the State Constitutional Convention in 1885. In 1890, he was elected member of the South Dakota legislature.

In 1902, he was elected states attorney for Lawrence County and reelected in 1904. He made a notable record in enforcing law against gambling and liquor interests.

He was elected a member of Congress from South Dakota in 1906. His death occurred in Deadwood on June 26, 1908, before completion of his term.

He was married in 1867 to Clara E. Thomas in Washington, D. C. Surviving children are: Francis J. and William, of Deadwood.

JOHN W. ("CAPTAIN JACK") CRAWFORD

John Wallace Crawford, famous "poet-scout" of the West, was born in Ireland. The family moved to New York City. At the age of fifteen he enlisted in a Pennsylvania regiment in the Civil War. He was wounded severely, but returned to service shortly before close of the war, and was again wounded.

After the war he came west and became an army scout. He was among the founders of Custer and was in Deadwood and other Black Hills cities in their early days. During the Indian campaign of 1876 he was chief of scouts for General Crook's forces. He became an intimate associate of "Buffalo Bill," "Wild Bill" and other scouts and frontiersmen. He wrote many characteristic poems of western life and became widely known as the "poet scout of the plains." His death occurred in Brooklyn, N. Y., February 28, 1917.

H. O. ALEXANDER

Was born at Urbana, Illinois, September 19, 1860. Came to the Black Hills in 1879. Was clerk in a store in Central City and bookkeeper in a bank in Deadwood. Was for many years a well known traveling salesman, representing a wholesale firm until 1914. He then engaged in the mercantile business at Nisland and Belle Fourche.

In 1884, he was married to Gertrude Hayes of Urbana, Ill. His death occurred in 1936. Surviving members of his family are, his

widow, in Belle Fourche, South Dakota, and children: Mrs. Gene-
vieve A. Morris, Los Angeles, California; Dr. O. O. Alexander,
Terre Haute, Indiana; Mrs. Kathryn A. Quarnberg, Rapid City,
South Dakota; Miss Frances Alexander, Gary, South Dakota; and
Mrs. Dorothy Williams, Bozeman, Montana.

JOHN A. TREBER

Was born in Germany, March 2, 1853. Came to the United
States in 1874. Came to Deadwood on June 11, 1877, and engaged
in the wholesale liquor business in the firm of Hermann and Treber.
Was active in business and community affairs for many years. Was
member of the city council for 24 years. Was a member of the
state legislature in 1910.

On June 11, 1878, he was married to Herminia Pasche. His
death occurred on October 8, 1936. Surviving members of his family are three sons, William L. and Albert P. of Deadwood, and
John A. of Denver.

SAM SCHWARZWALD

Was born in Germany, in 1839. In early days he went to Montana Territory. He came from Helena to Deadwood, arriving
August 19, 1876. Shortly thereafter he engaged in the furniture
business, under the firm name of Stone and Schwarzwald. Later
he became sole owner.

He continued in this business, building up one of the largest
mercantile establishments in Deadwood, until his death which occurred in Deadwood on March 20, 1917. His widow survives and
is living in Deadwood.

D. A. MCPHERSON

Was born near Montreal, Canada, in 1841. Arrived in the Black
Hills in 1877. Shortly after arrival he engaged in the banking business in the Exchange Bank, Miller and McPherson. For over two
years he served as agent for mail and express lines. He became
cashier of the First National Bank when it was organized in 1878,

and absorbed other banking interests. He served in that capacity for many years until his death, which took place on August 4, 1920.

A son, Kenneth, residing in Detroit, Mich., and a daughter, Mrs. Edith Stirrett, of Denver, are yet living. They left Deadwood many years ago.

C. F. DE MOUTH

Was born in Boonton, New Jersey, in 1845. Was engaged in the hardware business in Chicago from 1872 to 1876. He came to Deadwood in the spring of 1876. He established the first department store in Deadwood, known as "The Ark," dealing in furniture, glassware, crockery and other lines. His death occurred in Deadwood in 1921. His widow Perla DeMouth, continued to reside in Deadwood until her death in 1937. A surviving daughter is Mrs. H. K. Hartley, of Deadwood.

JOHN WRINGROSE

Was born in England in 1837. Came to the United States in 1873. Arrived in Deadwood in 1877. Engaged in the livery business. Became member of the firm of Browning & Wringrose, which operated an extensive grocery business.

Death occurred in California on March 6, 1904. Mrs. Carl Dawson, a daughter, now resides at Trojan, near Deadwood. Another daughter, Mrs. J. E. Ford, lives in Deadwood. Another daughter, Mrs. Emily Wardman, lives in California. Mrs. Wringrose died in Deadwood on October 3, 1937, at the age of 91.

JOSEPH KUBLER

Was born in Alsace, France, on August 3, 1854. Came to the United States in 1870. Became a printer. He arrived at Custer in the Black Hills on April 4, 1876. He was one of the first employees of the *Pioneer*, in Deadwood. Later he returned to Custer and in 1880 established the *Custer Chronicle* which he published for half a century. His death occurred on October 12, 1929. Three sons and two daughters survive: Joseph W. and William L. of Custer; Carl H. of Deadwood; Eva E. (Mrs. Joseph Baker) of Belle Fourche, South Dakota; and Louise, of California.

BIOGRAPHICAL SKETCHES

MR. AND MRS. GEORGE A. CLARK

George A. Clark was born in Newcastle, Pennsylvania, in 1849. Prior to coming to the Black Hills he resided in Iowa. He came to the Hills on May 4, 1876. In the fall he returned to Cheyenne to get his bride. They arrived at Custer on November 2, 1876, with a wagon train comprising 500 men. It took 16 days to make the trip.

Mr. Clark brought in a load of groceries and supplies to use in the locksmith business. Later they resided in Keystone, Hermosa, and Rapid City. He was engaged extensively in mercantile business, being associated with Tom Sweeney in Rapid City. He also had mining interests in the Keystone district.

Mr. Clark's death occurred on July 28, 1925. Mrs. Clark married John Welling, and they came to Deadwood to reside. She is yet living, having passed her 83rd birthday on November 1, 1938, making her home with her daughter, Mrs. W. H. Graham (Grace Greenwood Clark), in Deadwood.

MICHAEL HEFFRON

Was born in Ireland in 1846. He came to the United States at the age of thirteen. He went west at an early age and prospected in Utah, California, Colorado, and Montana. He came to Deadwood from Montana, driving an ox team, arriving on April 17, 1876. He was for many years active in developing mining interests adjacent to Deadwood. He was married in 1878. His death occurred on July 24, 1915. Mrs. Heffron died on September 18, 1920. A son, William, died on April 4, 1930.

Three sons are living. John T. is assistant United States District Attorney for the district of South Dakota, residing in Deadwood; David is state's attorney for Mellette County, South Dakota, residing at Martin; James resides in Deadwood.

CHARLES PFRUNDER

Was born in Switzerland. Arrived in Hills January 12, 1876. Worked at mining. In fall returned to Colorado. Returned to Deadwood in spring of 1877, with milk cattle, and took homestead in

Centennial Valley, ten miles from Deadwood, and operated a milk supply ranch in early days. Resided on his ranch until his death on July 13, 1918, at the age of 87. His son, Charles Pfrunder, born in 1888, now resides on the ranch.

JOHN P. BELDING

Was born in Binghamton, N. Y., in 1833. As a youth he went to St. Louis, where he was in railroad employ at time of the Civil War. He enlisted on the Union side in Missouri Infantry and served during the entire war, rising to the rank of captain and participating in many engagements. He had intimate acquaintance with General Grant, under whom he served.

After the war he was among the gold seekers in California, thence to Montana. Here he resided in Last Chance Gulch, now a part of Helena. In February, 1876, he came to the Black Hills, with a party under leadership of Jim Bridger, a famous scout of that period.

He made his home in Deadwood and engaged in mining. In 1880 he was wedded to Mary Della Tovey, who came to the Hills in 1877 from Nebraska. He was one of the locators of the water rights which supplied the "Foster Ditch," which subsequently entered largely into the Deadwood "Water Question."

He served as sheriff of Lawrence County, from 1880 to 1882. He was deputy United States Marshal under E. G. Kennedy and Seth Bullock.

Residence in Deadwood was continued until his death on Feb. 19, 1917, at the age of 84. He was at all times active in public affairs. His widow is yet living, in Billings, Mont., at the age of 81. Surviving children are: Mrs. J. C. (Gussie) O'Donnell, of Billings, and Mrs. Alexander (Gladys) Retzlaf, of Fairbanks, Alaska. Another daughter, Mrs. John (Jessie) Treber, died in Deadwood in 1910.

W. L. KUYKENDALL

Arrived in the Black Hills in January, 1876, and located in Deadwood. Was a practicing attorney and was selected by the citizens to preside over the miners' court which tried Jack McCall for the murder of Wild Bill Hickok. No record is obtainable of his history subsequent to leaving Deadwood, at an early day.

[306]

BIOGRAPHICAL SKETCHES

STEPHEN T. GEIS

Came to the Hills in March, 1876. In early days operated a boarding house and meat market in Deadwood. In later years he resided in Wyoming. His death took place in Deadwood on January 19, 1913, at the age of 77. Four daughters and one son survive: Mrs. Theresa Ashe, Mrs. Andrew Olson and Mrs. Kinnear now reside in Deadwood, and Mrs. E. P. Roberts at Rapid City; Stephen Geis resides at Aladdin, Wyoming. The daughters came with their mother to Deadwood in 1879. Stephen was born in Deadwood.

ASCHMER FULTON

Was born May 3, 1857, Nova Scotia, Canada. Went to Colorado in 1875. Came to the Black Hills in October, 1876. Located in Custer, later in Central City and Deadwood. Married Theresa Carr in 1887. Engaged in various lines of business and had mining interests near Deadwood. His death occurred on February 12, 1937. Three daughters, Miss Margaret Fulton, Mrs. Mable Stoner and Mrs. Arthur Welf now reside in Deadwood. A daughter, Mrs. Etta Gunn, resides in Los Angeles.

R. E. GRIMSHAW

Arrived in the Black Hills, May 24, 1876. Was engaged in the corral business in Elizabethtown (later a part of Deadwood) in 1878. Engaged in various business enterprises and was active in politics. He held several local offices and was postmaster of Deadwood for eight years. His death occurred in Deadwood on July 27, 1924, at the age of 76.

ALBERT BURNHAM

Was born in Canada in 1850. Came to Deadwood August 5, 1876. Was a contractor and builder. Built the city hall and the Adams Block. His sister became wife of W. E. Adams.

During the Alaska "Gold rush" in 1898, he went there, but returned the following year. His death occurred on June 6, 1920, at the age of 70. Mrs. Burnham died in 1935.

PIONEER DAYS IN THE BLACK HILLS

THOMAS H. WHITE

Was born in Cornwall, England. Came to the Black Hills in
1876. Made home in Deadwood. Was a civil engineer and surveyor. Was a builder and built the largest apartment house in
Deadwood, long known as the "White House." His death occurred
in 1894, at Lead, South Dakota. His widow, later Mrs. J. G.
Thomas, died in Deadwood, August 8, 1934.

A son, Herbert G. White, survives and resides in Deadwood.

OTTO P. TH. GRANTZ

Was born in Sweden, in 1849. He arrived in the Black Hills
on November 18, 1876, and engaged in prospecting and mining.
He discovered the richest gold ore deposit ever found in the Black
Hills, on the present site of Lead. He continued active in mining
enterprises until a few years before his death, which occurred in
California on March 6, 1923, at the age of 74. A surviving daughter, Mrs. Ager, resides in California.

W. J. THORNBY

Col. William J. Thornby was born in Troy, New York, April
27, 1857. He arrived in Deadwood on April 19, 1877. For a time
he was engaged in newspaper work with the *Deadwood Pioneer*.
Later he went to Custer. He was the first city judge and assessor
in Custer, and the first justice of the peace for Custer County.
In 1879, he and Prof. W. P. Jenney located the thermal springs
in the present city of Hot Springs. He was elected state senator
from Custer and Fall River counties in 1892.

In 1887, Governor Church of Dakota Territory appointed Mr.
Thornby a member of his official staff, with the rank of Colonel,
being the first man west of the Missouri River to receive this
honor.

In 1893, he was one of the judges in the mining department of
the World's Columbian Exposition in Chicago. In 1896, he graduated from the State School of Mines at Rapid City. In 1898, he
was appointed assayer in charge of the United States Assay office
in Deadwood, holding this position for many years. Thereafter

he was active in civic affairs in Deadwood, holding various positions of trust.

His death occurred in Hot Springs on July 15, 1919. Mrs. Thornby died in Deadwood in 1931. Surviving members of the family are two daughters: Mary (Mrs. Tom Hayter) of Sioux Falls, South Dakota, and Kathryn of Deadwood.

MAJOR ANDREW JACKSON SIMMONS

Born at Crown Point, New York, in 1834. Family moved to Indiana in 1836. At the age of 19, joined a caravan of 70 people, including seven women, bound for California gold fields, arriving there in October, 1853, the trip requiring six months, from Council Bluffs, Iowa.

Went to Nevada and served three terms in the territorial legislature, being speaker of the house in 1863-1864. Several years later he moved to Montana and engaged in placer mining in Alder Gulch. Was appointed Special Indian Agent by President Grant, to deal with the Indians in obtaining right of way for the Northern Pacific Railroad, with title "Major." Made trip to Indian reservations, negotiated with Sitting Bull and other chiefs, and took a party of them to Washington in 1872. Right of way was obtained, and Major Simmons was appointed Indian agent at Milk River Agency, Montana, in 1873. Was married in 1873 to Kate Elizabeth Coates, and shortly thereafter went to San Francisco, California, to reside. Here he engaged in mining enterprises.

In 1878, he came to Deadwood, and became interested in several mining projects. In 1882, he purchased a homestead tract of 160 acres adjoining the original townsite of Rapid City, and moved there. Here he served as alderman and mayor. Participated actively in efforts to get School of Mines established in Rapid City. Act creating this was passed by territorial legislature in 1885, and school was located on a five acre tract donated by Major Simmons and William Steele. He became president of the first board of trustees of the school.

Major Simmons gave land to the Fremont, Elkhorn and Missouri Valley Railroad for depot site and yards, and erected a number of business buildings on his land, including the two-story brick Park Hotel. The first train arrived there on July 5, 1886.

This location was half a mile from the business section of Rapid City at that time. The city failed to make anticipated growth and a number of years later the railroad moved its station to the business section.

In 1897, he returned to Deadwood to reside and engaged in mining enterprises. Later he moved to Denver. Mrs. Simmons died in Deadwood in 1905. Major Simmons died in Denver in 1920. Both are buried in Mt. Moriah Cemetery. Their only son, Jesse, born in Deadwood in 1880, survives and resides in Denver.

HENRY C. CLARK

Was born off Cape Hatteras in August, 1837. Came to the Black Hills in 1877. Was auctioneer and commission merchant in Deadwood. His family arrived in 1878. His death occurred in Deadwood in 1882.

Two sons and a daughter are yet living in the Black Hills. Horace S. Clark, of Lead, is the largest real estate owner in both Lead and Deadwood. Damon Clark, of Lead, was for many years a mill superintendent for the Homestake Mine, and served continuously for 18 years as member of the South Dakota legislature. Mrs. John T. Ayer resides at Sturgis. All came with their mother to Deadwood in 1878.

JOB LAWRENSON

Born in Ontario, Canada, in April, 1846. Came to the United States in 1870, and located in Helena, Montana, where he engaged in mining. He came to Deadwood in April, 1876, and shortly thereafter purchased the historic "Montana Corral," which he operated until shortly before his death, which occurred in 1903.

Surviving members of his family are his widow and his daughter, Evelyn, who reside in Portland, Oregon, the daughter being a teacher in the public schools. A sister, Miss Catherine Lawrenson, who came to Deadwood in January, 1883, is yet residing here.

CHARLES AND WILLIAM SASSE

Charles arrived in Deadwood in 1876. Established one of the first butcher shops in Deadwood. Had mining and cattle ranch interests. Died on October 23, 1918.

His son, William Sasse, said to be the first white boy born in Deadwood, who became associated with his father in the meat market business, is yet operating the same market.

WILLIAM AND HENRY BRASCH

William and Henry Brasch were twins. They were born in 1862. Henry B. arrived in the Black Hills, April 29, 1876, William on August 10, 1876. These well known brothers were for many years actively engaged in mining in the Roubaix District in Lawrence County. Henry was for several years on the Deadwood police force. His death occurred at Sturgis, S. D., Oct. 22, 1933, at the age of 71. He was buried in Mt. Moriah cemetery. His widow survived, and resides in Deadwood. William is yet living and resides in Denver, at the age of 77.

MR. AND MRS. HILAN HULIN

Mr. Hulin arrived in the Hills in November, 1875. He had mining interests and operated a stage line. Later he engaged extensively in cattle raising in the range country, north of the Hills. Mrs. Hulin arrived in 1876.

Mr. Hulin's death occurred on May 11, 1919, and Mrs. Hulin's on October 19, 1907. The only surviving child is Mrs. Ruth Todd, of Lead.

WILLIAM E. CAREY

Was born in Maine in 1826. Attended Yale Law School for two years. Went to Galena, Illinois, in 1856, and was admitted to the bar. Was a member of the Illinois Constitutional Convention, 1869-1870. Member Illinois Legislature, 1870-1872. Was appointed United States district attorney for Utah, and went to Salt Lake City. Served four years. Came to Deadwood on May 1, 1877, and engaged in practice of law. Subsequent history not available.

DANIEL J. TOOMEY

Was born in Brooklyn, N. Y., in 1850. At an early age went to Chicago. After the great fire in 1871, he went west and engaged in buffalo hunting to supply meat for the Union Pacific Railway employees located at Sidney, Neb.

He arrived at Custer in the Black Hills on March 27, 1876, and in Spearfish Valley on May 1. Here he settled on a homestead which became very valuable, and was operated by him for many years.

In 1898, he joined in the gold rush to Alaska. In 1900, he returned to his farm, and engaged in the flour, feed and milling business at Spearfish. This was extended to Sundance and Beulah, Wyoming, by the Toomey Milling Co., which included his sons. Later, mills were built at Newcastle, Wyo., and Crawford, Neb.

In 1922, Mr. Toomey retired from active business life and moved to San Diego, Calif., where he yet lives, turning the business management over to his sons. Living children are Mrs. Oscar (Ella) Anderson, of Saco, Montana, and Eugene H. of Spearfish. Allen Toomey, another son, who was prominent in business and political life, died in 1936; Ralph, another son, was killed during the World War in France. Mrs. Toomey is yet living and resides in San Diego.

C. F. AND T. W. THOMPSON

Charles F. Thompson and Thomas W. Thompson, father and son, arrived in Deadwood in July, 1876. The father engaged in mining and operated a toll gate on the Galena Road. He was an early day treasurer of Lawrence County. He was born December 2, 1828, in Susquehanna County, Pennsylvania. His death occurred on March 31, 1892.

Thomas W. Thompson operated a flour mill at Whitewood for many years. Born in Monticello, Wisconsin, January 3, 1858. His death occurred on May 11, 1910, in Omaha. A son, Charles F., now lives in Whitewood. A daughter, Mrs. Fred Gramlich, was for many years a resident of Deadwood. Mr. Gramlich became owner of the stores of the Zipp Shoe Co. in Deadwood and Rapid City. He was for many years active in the civic and commercial life of Deadwood prior to moving to Rapid City. Later they resided on their ranch near Whitewood. Mr. Gramlich's death occurred early in 1939.

BIOGRAPHICAL SKETCHES

MR. AND MRS. HARRY S. WRIGHT

Harry S. Wright was born in Boston, Massachusetts, in 1842. He came to the Black Hills in January, 1876, and located at Custer where he became postmaster.

Mrs. Harry S. Wright (Anna Vallery) was born in Ohio, on January 10, 1846. Before coming to the Black Hills she operated a boarding house at North Platte, Nebraska. She came to the Hills from Cheyenne, Wyoming, in August, 1876, and operated a boarding house in Custer. In February, 1877, she was married to Mr. Wright, one of her boarders. Subsequently they moved to Lead, and built the Globe Hotel in 1878, which they operated until they moved to Fruitdale, South Dakota, in 1885.

Mr. Wright died in 1910. Mrs. Wright, who was known to many by the soubriquet, "Gentle Annie," made her home in Nisland, S. D., being a sister of P. P. Vallery, a prominent rancher in that vicinity. She is yet living, and on January 10, 1939, celebrated her 93rd birthday, in good health, the oldest living pioneer of 1876.

Their only son and daughter died several years ago.

CHARLES C. BOHL

Was born in Jefferson City, Missouri, December 25, 1847. He arrived in Deadwood in December, 1875. Was engaged in mercantile business in early days. Later located on a ranch on Redwater Creek. In later years was an employee of the electric plant at Pluma. His death occurred on June 4, 1928. His widow, Mrs. Minnie Bohl, and a daughter, Mrs. Florence Boland, survive and reside in Deadwood; also a stepson, John Bohl, who resides in El Monte, Calif.

R. C. LAKE

R. C. Lake came to Deadwood in 1876 and engaged in the hardware business. In 1879, he engaged in the banking business with several associates at Rapid City. In 1882, he sold the Deadwood business to Ismon and Ayres. One of these partners, George V. Ayres, subsequently became sole owner of the business, who developed it into the largest establishment selling hardware and mining supplies in the Black Hills, still doing business.

He left Deadwood in 1887 and went to Rapid City. Subsequently he went east and further record is not available.

JOHN W. MCDONALD

Was born in Canada in 1848, on Cape Breton Island. Came to the United States in 1868. Arrived in the Hills on April 23, 1876. Soon after arrival he engaged in the hardware, tinware and miners' supplies business at Central City. He was for many years prominent in the business life of that city. He was at one time president of the Society of Black Hills Pioneers. His death occurred on May 15, 1917, at Cosmopolis, Washington.

HENRY FRAWLEY

Was born in Washington County, New York, in 1850. Graduated from the state university at Madison, Wisconsin, in 1874. Was admitted to the bar in 1876.

Came to the Hills in 1877, as a practicing attorney. He was for many years a prominent member of the Deadwood bar. He purchased a number of ranches in Centennial Valley, six to eight miles from Deadwood, consolidating and improving them into one of the largest ranches in the Black Hills. This was farmed extensively by members of his family for many years.

His death took place in Lincoln, Nebraska, January 24, 1927. Surviving members of the family are his widow and son Henry, who reside on the ranch near Deadwood, and a daughter, Honore, residing in New York.

FRED ZIPP

Was born on August 8, 1838. He arrived in the Black Hills in 1877. Shortly thereafter he established a mercantile business, which was continued for over half a century, with a branch at Rapid City, becoming one of the most widely known business enterprises in the Black Hills. He also had extensive mining interests.

His death occurred on December 20, 1904. A son, Robert Zipp, is yet living and resides in Lead, South Dakota.

BIOGRAPHICAL SKETCHES

MR. AND MRS. JOSEPH KING

Joseph King was born in Ontario County, New York, in 1840. He served on the Union side during the Civil War. He arrived in Deadwood on April, 1876. He had mining interests and operated the Cosmopolitan Hotel.

Mrs. Joseph King (Miss Mary W. Wilson) was born in New York state in 1853. Prior to coming to the Black Hills, she resided at Rochester, New York, where she was wedded to Joseph King on February 24, 1876.

She arrived in Deadwood on June 20, 1877. She is yet alive at the age of 86, having resided continuously in Deadwood. Mr. King died in 1901.

THE FISHEL BROTHERS

Max Fishel was born in Austria and came to the United States in 1863. Came to Deadwood in 1876, and engaged in the stationery and notions business. His death occurred in Deadwood on September 6, 1907, with no surviving relatives in the United States except his brothers Adolph and Louis.

Adolph Fishel was born in Austria, July 9, 1857. He came to the United States in 1873 and to Deadwood in 1879. For a number of years he was in the employ of Strass, Cohen & Co., clothing merchants.

Louis Fishel was born in Austria on July 11, 1859. He came to the United States and Deadwood in 1883, and entered employ of the same firm with his brother Adolph.

In 1892, Adolph and Louis started a business of their own in stationery, fancy goods and notions in Deadwood. This they continued to operate with branch stores at Sturgis and Rapid City, until they retired from business in 1934.

Adolph is yet alive at the age of 82. He was married to Tala Friedlander of Toledo, Ohio. She is yet living. They reside in Deadwood. The only child Hazel (Mrs. Emil Willoth), resides in Deadwood.

Louis Fishel was never married. He yet lives in Deadwood, at the age of 80.

PIONEER DAYS IN THE BLACK HILLS

GEORGE AND ED WYNN

George E. Wynn was born in Maine in 1825. He came to Deadwood in 1877 and was engaged in livestock selling. Later he engaged in the transfer business for many years. His death occurred on November 9, 1918, at the age of 94.

Ed Wynn, son of George Wynn, was born in Maine in 1852. In May, 1879, he came to the Black Hills and associated with his father in business. For many years he operated a hack line and transfer business. He is yet alive at the age of 87, and resides in Deadwood.

Surviving children of Ed Wynn are three daughters, Mrs. Ted (Lucretia) Cole, of Oklahoma City; Mrs. Phoebe Sullivan, of California, and Mrs. Harold (Margaret) Turner of Deadwood.

Mrs. Bertha Talbott, a daughter of George Wynn, is yet living in Deadwood. George Leman, a son of Mrs. Talbott, by a prior marriage, born in Deadwood in 1877, is living and resides in Deadwood.

DR. ALEXANDER S. STEWART

Was born in Indiana in 1839. Moved to Iowa in 1850. Educated at Mt. Pleasant (Iowa) State University, and Eclectic Medical College, Cincinnati, Ohio. Moved to Nebraska and began practice of medicine; was a member of the state constitutional convention. Served four terms as member of state legislature. Came to Deadwood in 1877. Was register of United States land office in Deadwood from 1877-1881. Then moved to Hot Springs, where he served as postmaster for several years. His death occurred in Hot Springs on January 22, 1911. Surviving members of his family are a son, Charles A., and a daughter, Blanche S., both of Hot Springs, South Dakota.

FRED T. EVANS

Was born in Ohio in 1835; located at Sioux City, Ia., in 1868. Arrived in the Black Hills in July, 1876, to establish and direct affairs of the Evans Transportation Co., operating in communication with the Chicago, Milwaukee, and St. Paul Railway, with boats on the Missouri River. The company first operated freight trains to the Hills from Running Water and Pierre, South Dakota.

In 1884 he employed 300 men, 2,000 oxen, 300 mules, 400 wagons. After establishing the business, Mr. Evans made headquarters at Sioux City, Iowa.

In later years he resided in Hot Springs, South Dakota, and became prominent in its business life as president of the Hot Springs Corporation which built the Evans Hotel.

His death occurred at Hot Springs on October 11, 1902.

BENJAMIN BAER

Was born in Paris, France. He came to the United States early in life. He arrived in the Black Hills in August, 1876.

He was active in the business affairs of Deadwood in early days, and was president of the First National Bank, into which other early day banks were merged. He had extensive cattle interests in the range country north of the Black Hills.

He was accompanied by his wife to Deadwood. Her maiden name was Ida Florsheim, born at St. Joseph, Missouri. Her death occurred in Deadwood in 1899. A few months thereafter the family moved to St. Paul, Minnesota, where Mr. Baer became president of the American National Bank.

His death occurred on July 27, 1921. Surviving children are: Ira B., Helen (Stamm), Jerome B., Fernand B., and Edwin B. All were born in Deadwood except the oldest, Ira B., who was born in St. Joseph, Missouri. All the sons now reside in St. Paul, and Mrs. Stamm in New York City.

JOHN F. AND JAMES T. STREET

John F. Street was born in New Jersey on May 4, 1807. He served in the Union Army under Grant and Sherman from 1861 to 1864 and was in many engagements. He arrived in the Black Hills on May 20, 1876, and brought a sawmill from Illinois up Smith Gulch on June 4th, which sawed some of the first lumber used in Deadwood. He located the Mark Twain lode in 1877. His death occurred on January 8, 1911.

James T. Street was born in De Witt County, Illinois, on February 22, 1859. In 1876 he accompanied and assisted his father in his sawmill and mining enterprises. He was in employ of the

Homestake Mining Company for over 31 years. He now resides in Sheeptail Gulch near Deadwood, and is in vigorous health at the age of 80.

Another son of John F. Street, Nasby S., came with other members of the family, in December, 1876. He is yet alive at the age of 68 and resides in Chicago, where he has been in business the past 35 years.

A daughter Ina (Mrs. F. Verley) also came with the family at that time. She is yet alive at the age of 72, and lives near Rapid City.

DOLPH EDWARDS

Was born in Utica, New York, in 1845. Came to the Hills early in 1876. Taught the first school in Lawrence County and the Black Hills, at Central City. Was principal of Deadwood school for two years.

In 1878 he was elected Superintendent of Public Instruction for the territory of Dakota and served four years.

In 1881 he established the *Lead City Tribune,* which was published for a number of years by Edwards and Pinneo brothers. No information of subsequent history is available.

MR. AND MRS. HENRY A. ALBIEN

Henry A. Albien was born in Germany in 1847. He came to the United States in 1872. He arrived in the Black Hills in 1875, but was among the "sooners" expelled by the military. He returned to Custer on February 13, 1876, helped lay out that city, and located Lot 1, Block 1.

He engaged in mining and was one of the first in Deadwood Gulch. In 1878, he established a general merchandise business on his lot in Custer, which he operated for many years. He has continued to reside in Custer County and is yet living, age 92.

Mrs. Albien was born in Germany in 1855. She accompanied her husband to the United States and to Custer on February 13, 1876. Her death occurred in Pocatello, Idaho, in 1933.

Three children survive: Henry who was for a number of years, until recently, engaged in business in Deadwood, now resides in St. Petersburg, Florida; Anna, who resides in Pocatello, Idaho; Clara (Harris) who also resides in Pocatello.

BIOGRAPHICAL SKETCHES

JOHN HUNTER

Was born in Caledon, Canada, in 1845. Came to Deadwood early in 1877, bringing a small sawmill. This was located first on Polo Creek, later moved to a point near the now deserted Crook City. After the big fire in 1879, the lumber business boomed. In 1883, the firm of Fish & Hunter was organized by combining their businesses. A small office building was erected on lower Main Street, which is yet standing, with sign painted thereon.

Other consolidations followed, and in 1887 a general merchandise business was established in a large frame building, across the street from the lumber office, subsequently occupied by the Waldschmidt Bakery.

Absorption of other businesses led to formation of the Fish & Hunter Company in 1891. In 1905 the large building on Sherman Street was erected, and a wholesale and retail business expanded, with six branch lumber yards now at Lead, Rapid City, Belle Fourche, Wasta, New Underwood, and Owanka.

He was married to Elizabeth Weaver in Minneapolis in 1870, who came with him to the Hills. Of the eight children, only two yet survive: Lillian (Mrs. F. S. Howe), who was born in Minnesota in 1871; and George Hunter, born in Deadwood in 1886, now head of the Black Hills Mercantile Co., Deadwood.

Mr. John Hunter was active in the business affairs of the city until his death on February 13, 1920. Mrs. Hunter died on December 23, 1928.

JUDGE LORING E. GAFFEY

Loring E. Gaffey was born in 1850. He came to Deadwood in 1877, and at once became a prominent member of the bar. He was a member of the senate of the territory of Dakota, from 1880 to 1889. Later he went to Pierre where he was elected circuit judge, serving in that capacity for many years.

He was married in 1878 to Fannie B. Price and in 1900 to Adelaide Warwick. His death took place on February 20, 1936. His widow resides in Pierre, S. D.

J. A. HARDING

Was born in Licking County, Ohio. Came to Deadwood in the spring of 1877. Engaged in mining and mercantile business. Later in the livery business with the firm of Jewett, Harding and Hale. He made a specialty of raising fine horses on a ranch near Postville.

In 1881 he was appointed postmaster for Deadwood. Nothing can be learned of subsequent history.

THOMAS D. MURRIN

Was born in 1864. In 1877, when twelve years old, he came to the Black Hills, residing at Central City. He entered the employ of a mercantile establishment which thereafter became the Hearst Mercantile Company of Lead, one of the largest department stores in South Dakota. He was eventually promoted to be general manager of the business and was president of the corporation for many years.

In 1907, he married Julia Corcoran. A few years ago he retired from active business life and went to Los Angeles to reside.

JACOB WERTHHEIMER

Jacob Werthheimer was born in Baden, Germany, in 1843. He came to Deadwood in the spring of 1876. In 1879, he erected and operated the Merchants Hotel, a large, three story building. Nothing can be learned of later history.

M. J. AND LOUIS WERTHHEIMER

When the Werthheimer brothers, who for many years were prominent in the mercantile field in Deadwood, arrived is not of record. It was not later than 1877, possibly earlier. They established a clothing and men's furnishing business, which became one of the most extensive in the Black Hills, and was continued under their management for over forty years. Both left Deadwood about 20 years ago. Both are dead.

GENE DECKER

Was born in Missouri. In early days he went to Montana territory and engaged in mining. Had experience in fighting Indians.

Walked to the Black Hills from Montana. Worked on a Deadwood newspaper. Became a guard on the "treasure coach." Later he engaged in the curio business in Billings, Montana. His death occurred several years ago.

EDWIN VAN CISE

Was born in Pennsylvania in 1842. Went with his parents to Mt. Pleasant, Iowa, in 1857. Admitted to practice law in 1865. Practiced there until 1871, then entered newspaper business for five years.

He came to Deadwood and opened a law office in 1877. Shortly thereafter he went to Rapid City and became county attorney for Pennington County. He returned to Deadwood in 1879 and became prominent in his profession, as a member of the firm of Van Cise, Wilson, and Martin. Subsequently he moved to Denver where he was prominent in legal circles. His death occurred on Sept. 30, 1914, in Denver. His widow's death occurred in 1938. A son, Philip S., and a daughter, Ethel, survive and reside in Denver.

W. P. JENNEY

Professor W. P. Jenney was a scientist in the employ of the federal government. In that capacity he led an exploring expedition into the Black Hills, which arrived in May, 1875, and spent several months here. Subsequently he came to the Hills to reside for a time at Hot Springs. He and Colonel Thornby discovered the thermal springs now used for a big plunge bath in that city. No record of Mr. Jenney's subsequent history is available.

L. W. STILWELL

Was born in Manilius, New York, on March 3, 1846. Went with family to Fond-du-Lac, Wisconsin. Was the oldest of eight children. Established a grocery business in Cairo, Illinois, in 1864, which he operated for 10 years.

He came to Deadwood in 1879, and was employed as bookkeeper in a bank. Established a curio business which grew to such extent that after 1890 he gave it his entire time until his death.

It became one of the most extensive collections in the west, and supplied dealers all over the world with Indian, mineral, and other western curios.

In 1873, he married Julia A. Bristol who came with him to Deadwood. Her death occurred in 1916. Mr. Stilwell died on November 24, 1932. Surviving children are: Mrs. L. C. Berry of Lead, South Dakota, and Dr. Donald Stilwell, of Detroit, Mich.

EDMUND WOLFE

Came to Hills early in 1876. Located at Crook City, ten miles from Deadwood. Was one of party which went out from Crook City to pick up the body of Preacher Smith. Became a pioneer rancher in Centennial Valley, and for many years thereafter. In latter days he went to Wisconsin to live. In 1926, he returned to Deadwood, on request of committee of citizens, to locate the spot where Preacher Smith's body was found and relate circumstances surrounding this event. Information is not available as to whether he is yet alive.

JOHN BELL

Was born at Stanley, England. Came to the United States in 1868, locating in Pittsburgh, Pa. Was married in 1873. Went to Cheyenne, Wyoming. Came from Cheyenne to Custer in April, 1876, the trip requiring 23 days.

He operated a blacksmith shop in Deadwood, one in Central City, and one in Spearfish. In 1883, he located on a ranch. In 1887, he moved to Spearfish, and was postmaster of that city for many years. His death occurred in Spearfish, April 6, 1933.

ISAAC H. CHASE

Was born at Kingston, New Hampshire, in 1843. At the age of 18 went to Minnesota. Engaged in real estate business there. Came to Deadwood in July, 1877, and established a mercantile business. As business expanded he established stores at Belle Fourche, Lead, Sturgis, Hot Springs, Newell, and Rapid City. Went to Rapid City to reside in 1897. Engaged extensively in real estate and loan business, and acquired extensive holdings of land.

[322]

His death occurred in 1919. Surviving members of his family are his widow and six children: Mrs. F. E. (Elizabeth) Steele, Sturgis; Mrs. Fred J. (Fanny C.) Knochenmuss, Rapid City; Mrs. George (Blanche C.) Williams, Rapid City; Mrs. Leslie (Ellen M.) Robinson, Tulsa, Oklahoma; Mrs. C. W. (Newell Helen) Hughes, Rapid City; Isaac H., Jr., Rapid City.

ABE JONES

Abe Jones was born in Wales in 1851. Taught school there. Came to the United States in 1872. He lived first in Kansas. Prior to settlement of the Black Hills he was located at Bismarck, Dakota Territory, arriving there in 1874. He was a contractor and built many miles of the Northern Pacific Railroad. He erected the first brick building in Bismarck. He was an extensive breeder of horses, and for several years supplied the United States government with 1,000 lots. He brought the first Percheron stallion west of the Missouri River.

He came to the Black Hills on June 18, 1876, and was located for many years on a ranch near Whitewood. He supplied United States government horses and the Homestake Mine with horses and large quantities of wood, thousands of cords at one delivery.

He died in Deadwood in 1938 at the age of 88. A daughter, Mrs. Harvey (Patti), Simons, resides in the state of Washington.

JUDGE DANIEL MCLAUGHLIN

Judge Daniel McLaughlin was born in Troy, New York, in 1831. In 1891, the family moved to Wisconsin. He was educated in Cornell College, Waukesha, Wisconsin. Studied law in offices in Wisconsin and Iowa. Admitted to the bar at Dakota City, Nebraska, in 1860. Practiced law in Nebraska, and was a member of the territorial legislature in 1861. Was married in 1861. In 1862 went to Auburn, Oregon. In 1863 he went to Idaho City, Idaho, where he was elected probate judge for three years. Went to Salt Lake City in 1866, and served as editor of the *Vidette* until 1867.

Then went to Cheyenne, Wyoming, where he practiced law until the gold rush to the Black Hills. Arrived in Deadwood in April, 1877. Here he continued in practice of law until his death about 1900.

He had two sons: William L., who practiced law with his father and was active in mining enterprises. His death occurred in Deadwood on July 28, 1911. Daniel J. died in San Francisco on May 22, 1905.

THE ICKES FAMILY

SAMUEL ICKES. Came to Deadwood by bull train, arriving in the early fall of 1876, and establishing a blacksmith shop in a little log building on what is now known as Lee Street. He continued this business for several years, and then returned to the family home in Fremont, Ohio, where he died September 26th, 1894.

JOHN C. ICKES. Arrived in Deadwood in the early fall of 1876; was interested in various mining activities and also worked in the United States postoffice during the time Sol Star was postmaster. In 1884, he moved to Hot Springs, and in October of that year was married to May Crask. A daughter, Myrtle, was born in December, 1885. In 1886, the family returned to Deadwood, and Mr. Ickes was connected with the Deadwood Flouring Mill until it was destroyed by fire. After that he engaged in various occupations until his death in November, 1913. In December, 1913, Myrtle Ickes was married to Allan Atherton Coburn, and they have two children: Ruth and Alan. The family reside in Deadwood.

FRANKLIN E. ICKES. Joined his father and older brother in Deadwood in 1877. He was employed for years in the American National Bank in Deadwood. Married Florence Jones in 1885, four sons being born to this family: Eugene E. Ickes and Sydney F. Ickes, both married and living in California; Howard R. Ickes who died in 1938; Paul A. Ickes, now living at Greyrock Park, Rye, N. Y. After the death of his wife about 1910, Mr. Ickes moved to California, where he died several years later.

WILLIAM A. ICKES. Came to Deadwood about 1879, where he joined his father and older brothers. He was employed for some time in a bank in Carbonate Camp. Later he returned to Deadwood, served as city treasurer for several years, then followed various occupations until 1904, when he purchased an insurance and real estate business in Deadwood. He conducted this business until 1920, when he moved to California where he resided until his death in November, 1932.

BIOGRAPHICAL SKETCHES

S. C. AND CHARLES G. FARGO

Sylvester C. Fargo was born in the state of New York in 1830. In 1863 he migrated to Illinois and the following spring joined a caravan from New York going to Dakota Territory. They stopped at Yankton and in 1865 he homesteaded in Clay County, near Yankton. This farm is yet the home of his son James and grandchildren.

In 1877, he came to the Hills with six wagon loads of flour, pork, butter, and other farm produce, coupled three together, each section hauled by 13 yoke of oxen. He located in Elizabethtown, now First Ward of Deadwood, and established a mercantile business.

In 1878, he took "mountain fever" and returned home, wiring his son Charles G. Fargo to come immediately to Deadwood to take charge of the business. He did so and established the mercantile firm of S. C. Fargo and Son, starting a branch store at Hot Springs, Dakota, in 1884.

S. C. Fargo came again to Deadwood in 1880, with a herd of 241 cattle, but did not remain long. After selling them he returned to Clay County where he died in 1900.

The firm's business was operated in Deadwood and Hot Springs until 1890. The Deadwood store was then sold and he moved to Hot Springs where he continued in business for many years. In 1915 he went to Twin Falls, Idaho, where he died in 1935 at the age of 78.

Surviving sons of S. C. Fargo are James on the Clay County homestead, and Will who for many years operated a grocery business in the First Ward of Deadwood. About ten years ago he moved to a ranch near Hot Springs, South Dakota, where he yet resides.

CAPTAIN A. W. MERRICK

Arrived in Custer early in 1876 with a printing outfit. He and his partner W. A. Laughlin published one issue of a paper there, then joined the stampede to Deadwood, arriving in April. They set up their printing plant and on June 8, 1876, published the first issue of the *Black Hills Pioneer*, a weekly paper. This became a daily paper a year later and is yet in existence.

PIONEER DAYS IN THE BLACK HILLS

JOSEPH E. GANDOLFO

Was born in Dubuque, Iowa. Arrived in the Black Hills in 1877. Established a restaurant business shortly after arrival and later operated a fruit and tobacco store. In later years he was a traveling salesman. His death occurred in September, 1926, in a store in Deadwood, from heart trouble.

His widow died in California in June, 1938, and her body was brought to Deadwood for interment beside Mr. Gandolfo's, in Mt. Moriah Cemetery.

Two sons, Forest and Melvin, survive, and reside in Los Angeles, California.

H. B. WARDMAN

Was born August 22, 1845; came to Deadwood in 1878. Engaged in hardware business. The firm Wardman and Ayres continued for many years after it was dissolved, and he opened his own store as H. B. Wardman Hardware Company. A son, Warren, of his first wife, lives in California. Later he married Catherine Phillips who survives him and lives in Deadwood. He died on December 30, 1926.

THOMAS SWEENEY

Was born in Booneville, New York, in 1856. He came to the Black Hills in the fall of 1877, and located in Rapid City. In 1879, he established a hardware business there which was developed into one of the largest mercantile establishments in the Black Hills, under Mr. Sweeney's supervision until his death. He was for many years active in the business life of Rapid City. His widow, now Mrs. Charles J. Buell, survives and resides in Los Angeles.

ERNEST AND HENRY MAY

Ernest May was born in Saxony, Germany, on November 8, 1847. Came to the United States in 1867. Arrived in Deadwood on December 8, 1876.

Shortly thereafter he engaged in the grocery business in Lead, in the firm of May and Johnson. This was sold to John Gilroy in

1901. In 1903, it was repurchased by Mr. May and he built up an extensive business which he operated until his death.

He was married in 1883. His death occurred on December 22, 1928. Two sons, Ernest and William, survive, and reside near Cody, Wyoming.

Henry May came to the Black Hills on September 10, 1879. He is a cousin of Ernest May, and became affiliated with him in the grocery business. He is yet living at the age of 77. His sister, Mrs. Fred Rose, came at the same time and is living in Lead.

AMOS E. AND FRANK MCLAUGHLIN

Amos was born in West Salem, Pennsylvania, in 1849. Went to California, gold digging, thence to the Hawaiian Islands, Australia, and South America. Returned with a fortune, and married Mary Jane Bush in Buff, Nebraska, in 1857. The same year went to Denver to reside, and became an extensive property owner. Enlisted in 2d Colorado Cavalry, and served throughout the war. Came to the Black Hills on January 7, 1876. Located the settlement of Maitland, six miles from Deadwood, and operated mining property there. Was first recorder of Ida Gray mining district. Died on March 23, 1905, at Spearfish, S. Dak.

Surviving members of the Amos E. McLaughlin family are a daughter, Mrs. Jos. Soutar of Deadwood, and F. E. McLaughlin of Denver, who in the early days resided in Deadwood as a member of the firm Temple and McLaughlin of Deadwood. Later moved to Denver where he was for many years prominent in legal circles.

EMIL, WILLIAM L. AND MAUDE FAUST

Emil, born in Hessen Cassel, Germany, December 11, 1838. Went in a sailing vessel to Melbourne, Hong Kong, Hawaii, San Francisco, around Cape Horn, and South America, thence to New Orleans, where he left the vessel. In February, 1861, he enlisted in Company K of the 8th Louisiana Infantry. Was discharged July, 1865. Came to Custer, Dakota, on December 24, 1875, and to Lead in 1877. On July 4, 1868, he married Minnie Statler of Pennsylvania. They had two children, W. L. Faust, druggist, who died

[327]

in Deadwood, and Maude. She and her husband were killed in an auto accident on their way home to Lead from California.

RICHARD BLACKSTONE

Was born October 16, 1843, in Connellsville, Pennsylvania. From July 20, 1861, to July, 1865, he was in Company C, 32d Ohio Voluntary Infantry. He was promoted to Captain. He was married on December 28, 1871, to Mable R. Noble. Surviving children are Alex J. of California, and Mary L., now Mrs. D. C. Regan, of Lead. He was the third superintendent of the Homestake Mining Company of Lead, following the death of T. J. Grier. He lived for many years in Central City.

JUDGE E. G. DUDLEY

Was born in Caldwell, Ohio, in 1832. Educated at Sharon College. Admitted to the practice of law in 1857. Recruited a company of Ohio Volunteer Infantry and was made Captain. Participated in many battles. Later served as police judge at Omaha. Was a member of the Nebraska legislature. Came to Deadwood in May, 1876, and engaged in mining and lumbering. Moved to Hot Springs, Dakota, in 1883, and engaged in business there. A surviving son, William B. Dudley, resides at Hot Springs.

DAVID GOLDBLOOM

Was born on May 21, 1841, in Germany. Arrived in the Hills on September 20, 1876. In early days he established a dry goods business which he operated for many years. His death occurred on November 25, 1904. Two of his daughters, Jenny Goldbloom and Mrs. Will Faust, now reside in Deadwood; another daughter, Dorothy, resides in Niagara Falls, New York. A son, Bonnie, resides in Meade County, S. Dak.

MR. AND MRS. NATHAN COLMAN

Were married in December, 1874. Mr. Colman came to Deadwood in 1877, Mrs. Colman in April of the same year. He engaged in mining and mercantile business. His death occurred in 1906. Mrs. Colman died in 1939. Surviving children are Blanche C. and Tessie C., of Deadwood, and Mrs. Maurice Neiderman of Chicago.

BYRON P. DAGUE

Came to Deadwood from Minneapolis in the spring of 1877. He was for fifteen years assistant cashier of the First National Bank. After that until his death in 1910, he operated the oldest insurance agency west of the Missouri River. He is survived by his widow, Mrs. Mary E. Dague, a son, Darrell B. Dague, both of Deadwood, two daughters, Mrs. E. L. Rickards of Chicago, Mrs. E. L. Clark of Minneapolis. He was responsible for the organization of the Scottish Rite Masonry here and one of the first to be honored with the 33d degree in South Dakota.

JOHN BAGGALEY

Came to Deadwood in 1877. He came first in the spring of 1875, only to be turned back by government soldiers. He engaged in insurance and real estate for many years. Associated with him was his son, George Baggaley. He died on December 4, 1922. Surviving children are George Baggaley of Deadwood and Mrs. Stilwell of New York.

HERMAN BISCHOFF

First came to the Black Hills in 1876, returning to Wyoming. In 1877, he returned to the Hills permanently. Resided in Deadwood until his death on May 13, 1929, at the age of 80. He gave much time and effort to development of mining interests in Spruce Gulch. Was for many years a justice of the peace. Surviving children are: Madge Bischoff and Mrs. Alice Laird, residing in California, and three sons, Ivan Bischoff of Long Beach, California, and Lester and Albert Bischoff, both of Los Angeles, California. His widow also resides in California.

FELIX POZNANSKY

Was born in Poland in 1832. Came to the United States in 1849, and to the Black Hills in 1878, where he established a dry goods store in that year. In 1879, he established a general merchandise store in Rapid City. Surviving relatives are two sons: Joe of Sturgis and A. J. of Rapid City.

CHRIS JENSEN

Chris Jensen was born in Schlesing, Denmark, in 1855. At the age of 15 he came to the United States. He resided for several years in Alabama, then went to Sioux City, Iowa. After residing there for two years he started for the Black Hills with the second Gordon party in the spring of 1875. This party was intercepted by soldiers near Ft. Randall (Dakota Territory) and compelled to turn back after their outfit and provisions had been burned by the soldiers. He came to the Hills in the spring of 1876, locating in Deadwood, where he engaged in the stage business. Later he moved to Rapid City, and in 1891 to Hot Springs in the southern Black Hills. Here he organized the People's Telephone and Telegraph Company in 1895. This is yet in existence, operating in Fall River and Custer Counties.

His death occurred on January 14, 1930, at the age of 75, and he was buried in Hot Springs. Surviving children are Leslie, who, after serving as Collector of Internal Revenue for South Dakota, was elected governor in 1936, serving two years; and Maude, who for many years was an instructor in Columbia University, New York City.

CHRIS HOLLEY

Was born at Ft. Laramie, Wyoming Territory, in 1850; his father (William) being then in charge of the Fort. The father was transferred in 1859 to Fort Thompson, Dakota Territory, and his family accompanied him. In 1861, he was transferred to Fort Hall, Idaho, where Chris attended school in Virginia City, Montana Territory, leaving there in 1868. He served as a packer in the U. S. Army in the 7th Cavalry, under General Custer.

From 1870 to 1874, he was engaged in carrying dispatches from Fort Laramie, Wyoming, to Fort Abraham Lincoln, Dakota Territory, located near the present capital of North Dakota, Bismarck. He also served under Lieut. Col. Richard T. Dodge.

In June 1875, he came with the Prof. W. P. Jenney scientific expedition to the Black Hills, and helped build the Jenney Stockade. He has continued to reside in the Black Hills since that time, most of the time at Hill City, engaged in various mining enterprises. He is yet active at the age of 89, residing at Hill City.

SOL BLOOM came to Deadwood in September, 1876. Shortly thereafter engaged in mercantile business, establishing a clothing and shoe store which became one of the most extensive in the Black Hills. This he operated until his death in Sheridan, Wyoming, and it was continued under ownership of Sam Brown, a long time employee, until 1937.

BOONE AND BILL MAY came to the Black Hills in 1876. Became early day guards on the "treasure coach" which carried gold from the Black Hills to Cheyenne, Wyoming. In that capacity they had many thrilling adventures, which they survived. They left the Hills at an early day, and no information is available as to their subsequent history.

MOSES MANUEL came to the Hills early in 1876, and on April 9 discovered and located the gold lode which was the beginning of the present world famous Homestake Mine. He and his brother developed the property and in 1877 sold it to Hearst, Tevis, and Haggin, California capitalists; they organized a company capitalized at $10,000,000 to increase and develop the property, which was subsequently increased to $25,000,000.

JACK LANGRISHE came to the Hills early in 1876, and established the first legitimate theater in Deadwood in July. He also established theaters in Central City and Lead. He was a talented comedian and author of many popular "ditties" of that day. He was enterprising and brought to the Hills some good theatrical talent of that day. No information is available as to his subsequent history.

T. D. EDWARDS was born in Rome, New York, in 1849. Came to the Hills in the spring of 1877, and established a stationery and news business in Lead. He was appointed postmaster for Lead in the early eighties. Later in life he was appointed United States consul at Juarez, Mexico, and held that position for many years, until his death a few years ago.

DR. L. F. BABCOCK was born in Pennsylvania. Graduated at Rush Medical College, Chicago, in 1864. He was one of the pioneer physicians of Deadwood, arriving prior to August, 1877. A picture taken at that time shows his sign on a small office building on Main Street, and he is listed in the 1878 directory. He built up an extensive practice which he continued until his death about 25 years ago.

GEORGE W. LADD arrived in the Black Hills in July, 1876. Had mining interests in early days. He established a mercantile business at Sturgis and was for many years prominent in the business and civic affairs of that city.

J. J. WILLIAMS came to the Black Bills on December 9, 1874, as a member of the Gordon Expedition to Custer. After being expelled by the military in the spring of 1875, he returned to the Hills and located one of the three placer claims on which the townsite of Deadwood was laid out by Brown, Williams, and Lee. Well known streets in the center of the present city were named after Williams and Lee.

ANSE C. TIPPIE arrived in Deadwood in July, 1876. Was bartender in the Nuttall and Mann Saloon when Jack McCall killed Wild Bill Hickok. Developed mining property in Bear Gulch for many years. Died on August 13, 1924.

J. J. LENK arrived in the Hills on April 3, 1876. Engaged in the meat market business in Central City at an early date, and was for many years prominent in the business life of that city. Died on March 27, 1913.

H. P. LOREY was born in Illinois in 1853. Went to Montana in 1870, where he engaged in clerking and mining. Came to the Black Hills in July, 1876. Subsequently he engaged in mercantile business in Lead. No other data available.

TOM COOPER was born in 1850. Was a scout for General Crook and Custer in the Indian troubles in 1873-1876. Came to Deadwood in 1876 as a driver on the Deadwood-Cheyenne Stage. Resided in Wyoming 42 years. Was for many years an employee of the Union Pacific Railroad, being a depot master the last fifteen years of his life. His death occurred in Wyoming in 1915.

THOMAS WHITTAKER arrived in Deadwood in 1877. In early days operated a grocery business. Subsequently became owner of considerable real estate and erected one of the early day brick blocks in Deadwood known as the "Whittaker Block," on the site of the present day Adams Memorial Museum, which was purchased and demolished by W. E. Adams to permit this construction. He lived here most of his life, moving to California about fifteen years ago, where his death occurred recently.

ISAAC BROWN arrived in the Hills in 1875. Was one of the three owners of placer claims on which they laid out the townsite of Deadwood, the others being J. J. Williams and Craven Lee. He was leader of the party which pursued Jack McCall into Shoudy's market after he killed Wild Bill Hickok, and was made sheriff ex tempore during McCall's trial.

M. E. LILLEBERG came to Crook City in 1876, and followed his trade as carpenter there and in Sturgis. He helped to build many of the buildings at Fort Meade. He died in August, 1938. There are no surviving relatives.

ALBE HOLMES was born June 13, 1848, in Belfast, Maine. He came to the Hills in 1876. Married Ellen N. Hines on April 3, 1886. He was prominent in mining, and was the manager of the Two Johns and Spearfish Mining Company. He died on August 26, 1910. Mrs. Holmes died on January 23, 1931, in Deadwood.

JOHN MANNING was born in Ireland in 1841. He went first to Montana in the early days, and came to the Black Hills from there, arriving on March 16, 1876. He was the first elected sheriff of Lawrence County in 1877. He died on September 15, 1911. A sister married Michael Heffron, a Deadwood pioneer.

JAMES W. CARNEY came to the Black Hills at an early date. Engaged in placer mining near Deadwood. Had other business interests. Was postmaster of Deadwood and held other official positions. Died on December 29, 1922. His widow is yet living in Deadwood.

WILLIAM M. BAIRD was born in Wisconsin. Arrived in Deadwood in December, 1876. Became a bookkeeper in one of the banks. Was county treasurer from 1880 to 1884. Was interested in the Black Hills Telephone Exchange. At an early date had large interests in two cattle ranches north of the Hills, running 2,750 head of cattle. No information of subsequent history is available.

JACOB SHOUDY arrived in the Hills on March 1, 1876. Shortly thereafter established a butcher shop and meat business in Deadwood. Subsequently he operated a cattle ranch in Whitewood Valley. Died on February 28, 1911.

SAM SOYSTER came to Deadwood, and was an auctioneer and commission merchant; also operated a second-hand store business. Located and operated one of the homesteads which subsequently became part of the extensive "Frawley Ranch," seven miles from Deadwood.

JACK GRAY was born in Durham, England, on February 28, 1846. Came to the United States in March, 1869. Arrived in Custer on July 14, 1876. In 1875, he married Ellen Chamberlain, a native of England, in Chicago. She died March 13, 1898. He was manager of the Wasp No. 2 Mining Company, and also director of the First National Bank of Deadwood.

NOAH NEWBANKS was born on December 25, 1841, in Seneca-ville, Ohio. Came to Custer, Dakota, in April, 1876. Operated a general store in Rapid City until 1878, when he engaged in freight-ing until 1886, from Fort Pierre to Rapid City, the end of the Elkhorn Railroad. He freighted from Rapid City to Deadwood until 1889, when he engaged in the cattle business in Custer county. On October 29, 1884, he married Mary Josephine Ander-son of Sparta, Illinois. Subsequently he engaged extensively in the cattle ranching business in Stanley county.

JOE HATTENBACH arrived in Deadwood in 1875. Engaged in mercantile business for many years. No record can be found of his death many years ago. His widow died in Sioux City in 1938. Surviving children are Monroe of Sioux City, Jay of California, and Frances of California.

CLARA D. COE was a daughter of C. A. Coe, a pioneer listed in the 1878 directory. He engaged in the real estate and insurance business, which was continued by his daughter for many years until her death. She was prominent in women's club circles. Her death occurred on October 10, 1921.

B. E. SALMON was born in England in 1840. Came to the United States in 1850. Arrived in the Black Hills in the spring of 1876. In 1877, he established a hardware business in Lead. Death occurred on October 9, 1907. A son, Harry, is living on a ranch northeast of Rapid City, South Dakota.

FRANK DENNIS came to Deadwood in May, 1876. In early days he was engaged in the sewing machine business. For many years he operated a transfer business in Deadwood. Served as a member of the city council. Died on September 20, 1918.

BIOGRAPHICAL SKETCHES

DAVID ELLIS came to the Hills in 1876. He had mining interests in Carbonate Camp. He resided in Deadwood many years.

JAMES CONZETTE came to the Hills on September 20, 1876. He resided in Deadwood many years while developing mining interests in the Galena district. His death occurred in Deadwood on January 24, 1912.

OTTO F. PURNELL arrived in the Black Hills in August, 1876. He was for many years active as a contractor and builder. Died on March 21, 1914.

HENRY ROSENCRANZ arrived in the Hills on August 10, 1876, and located at Central City. He operated a brewery there and had mining interests. He died at Central City on January 12, 1919.

CHARLES P. BURCH came to Deadwood in 1876. He was a deputy sheriff under Seth Bullock. For many years he resided on a ranch and developed mining interests near Custer Peak.

JOHN BURRI came to the Black Hills in August, 1874. He was for many years a member of General Custer's Seventh Cavalry, part of which was annihilated in the battle with Indians on Little Big Horn, Montana, in June, 1876. Mr. Burri was not in that engagement. He resided for many years in Whitewood, near Deadwood. He died on December 1, 1927.

NEAR PIONEERS

This record would be incomplete without mention of several men who, though they did not arrive in the Hills early enough to be eligible for membership in the Society of Black Hills Pioneers, came at an early date and have been prominent in civic and business affairs of the Hills for many years. Among such are:

WILLIAM A. REMER

Was born in Penn Yan, N. Y., in 1855. Came to Deadwood, Dakota Territory, in 1880. For several years was cashier of the bank of Stebbins, Fox and Co., at Sturgis, a few miles from Deadwood, which opened in 1883. Later he was in employ of the Homestake Mining Co. as paymaster and took part in capturing the men who held up the pay train in Reno Gulch in 1888. He was elected sheriff of Lawrence County in 1892, and served 4 years.

Subsequently he was for many years secretary of the Trojan Mining Co. which carried on active mining operations in the Bald Mountain country. He is yet living in Deadwood, and is in good health and active.

HON. EBEN W. MARTIN

E. W. Martin was born in Jackson County, Iowa, in 1855. He came to Deadwood in 1880 to practice law, and soon became associated with some of the most able attorneys in the city including Edwin Van Leise and John R. Wilson. Later he became senior partner in the widely known firm of Martin and Mason, which association was continued for many years. He was elected a member of Congress in 1901 and served continuously, with exception of one term, two years, until 1915. He then resumed practice of law. In 1920, he went to Hot Springs, S. D., to reside.

During his long residence in Deadwood, he was very active in church, school and other civic affairs. His death took place on May 22, 1932, at Hot Springs. In 1883 he was married at Cedar Falls, Iowa, to Jessie A. Miner, who is yet living, at Hot Springs. Surviving children are Mrs. Sherman Finger (Lois W.) of Iowa, Paul E. and Charles C. of Hot Springs, S. D., and Mrs. Stanley Allen (Jessie) of Denver.

JUDGE W. G. RICE

William G. Rice was born in Memphis, Mo., in 1858. He came to Deadwood in 1889, and engaged in practice of law. He became one of the most prominent members of the Deadwood legal fraternity, serving as city attorney, and for six years as county attorney.

In 1894 and 1896 he was elected member of the State Senate of South Dakota. In 1902 he was appointed circuit judge to fill out the unexpired term of Judge Washabaugh, and continued in that position until 1914. He then retired from the bench and resumed practice of law, in which he is yet actively engaged.

In 1885 he was married to Minerva Smoot. They have resided in Deadwood continuously since that time.